PAMELA SOVOLD

MARGARET WHERRETTE

EILISHA DERMONT

# The Market Notebook

*Madrona Publishers*        *Seattle*

Library of Congress Cataloging in Publication Data

Sovold, Pamela, 1954-
   The market notebook.

   Includes index.
   1. Pike Place Public Markets. 2. Food.
3. Cookery. I. Wherrette, Margaret, 1931-
joint author. II. Dermont, Eilisha, 1952-
joint author. III. Title.
TX346.U62S47      641.3      80-16856
ISBN 0-914842-44-7

*Drawings by Claudia Denney*

FIRST PRINTING JULY 1980
SECOND PRINTING OCTOBER 1980


Published by
Madrona Publishers, Inc.
2116 Western Avenue
Seattle, Washington 98121

# PREFACE

The Pike Place Market is a perfect reflection of the seasons. In early spring, the farmers bring in the hardy bedding plants, a sure sign of winter's end in the Northwest. Later come the red radishes, the scallions, the first thinnings of lettuce. Spring lamb is at the meat markets, and the first big harvest from the spring run of salmon is at the fish markets. The static winter displays of citrus fruit and nuts at the produce stands are brightened by the first of the Florida strawberries, and the appearance of Mexican watermelon and California asparagus means that the sun and summer are moving up the coast.

Summer and fall bring the full bounty of the local farms. The succession of peas, berries, beans, and sweet corn on the farmers' tables marks the months to the pumpkins and great squashes of autumn. Bing cherries signal summer at the produce stands, and then come the peaches and nectarines from Yakima, pears from Oregon. At the fish markets, it's the height of the salmon and fresh halibut seasons.

The Market does not hibernate in winter. This is the time of the glorious Dungeness crabs and the January run of Columbia River smelts. The farmers are here with their winter storage crops and braids of garlic and shallots. There is fresh goose and fresh turkey, lutefisk and herring for the holidays.

The Market Notebook is all about the seasons — at the produce stands, the fish markets, the farmers' tables. It is a guide to the wealth of food you will find at the Market — at its meat, cheese, dairy, and poultry counters. It is a primer on how to use the Pike Place Market and how to use it well.

## ACKNOWLEDGMENTS

During the writing of The Market Notebook, the three of us swarmed (if three can be said to swarm) all over the Market, yellow pads in hand, pens at the ready. We stood in water behind the farmers' tables and sat on crates at the back of the high stalls. We walked among the carcasses in the meat coolers and hung around the fish markets watching the fishmongers fillet fish. We asked questions and pestered and generally got in the way. Market people must be very happy that the Notebook is finally in print and we are back in the office.

We have many to thank for their patient sharing of knowledge and memories:

The farmers and high-stallers, especially Dan Manzo and Anthony Genzale, who helped us complete the produce "dictionary" and who gave us so many recipes.

The people at the fish markets and owners John Yokoyama, Sol Amon, and Gary and Jack Levy, who explained gaspergoo and skate wings, too. Especially Jack, for his stories—about fish and the old Market.

Ron Irvine, the Pike and Western wine merchant, who told us all about wine and, what's more, made it intelligible. And to Greg Finger, for his enthusiastic help and advice about wine.

Lee Spencer at Chicken Valley who, in good cheer, boned chicken breasts and cut up rabbits until we got it straight.

Nancy Douty of the Pike Place Creamery who separated egg facts from fiction as easily as yolks from whites.

Terry Finlay of the Cheese People who spent time on a busy Saturday afternoon going through his stock of cheese, flavor by flavor.

Ralph Bolson and Mary Hutsell of Pike Place Cheese who gave us enough taste tests to make six fondues and who told us more about cheese than we could ever assimilate.

The Market butchers, especially Don Kuzaro of Don and Joe's Meats and Denny Loback of Loback Meats, who made things like lamb cheeks and hog maughs respectable.

David Guren who, even though he shoots rabbits (see his recipe for rabbit stew), is OK and gave us so much support when he was director of the Merchants Association.

We thank, too, people outside the Market. People like:

Al Aries of Pacific Fruit and Produce who pondered our produce questions and answered them in one of his long newsletters.

Jan Grant, home economist with the King County Cooperative Extension Service, who made us confident that our recipes were at least safe.

The Washington State Department of Fisheries, whose brochures were especially helpful in defining what's what at the fish markets.

Because of all the help and cooperation we got in the writing of *The Market Notebook*, the three of us are still talking to each other. We thank you for that, too.

*Pamela Sovold*
*Margaret Wherrette*
*Eilisha Dermont*

# CONTENTS

*The Market Notebook*

# THE PIKE PLACE MARKET

It was Saturday, August 17, 1907, Seattle's first Market day. A chill wind was blowing off Elliott Bay, numbing the thousands of people who had been waiting at Pike Place since dawn for the farmers to appear. The weather had been no better at three that morning when H. O. Blanchard loaded his wagon with vegetables, hitched up his horse, and started on the long trip from Renton Junction to Seattle. The roads were muddy, almost impassable, and his progress was slow. When Blanchard finally came down Pike Street, a cheer went up from the crowd. The first farmer to sell at the Market was swamped, his produce sold out within the hour. Another pioneer farmer was quoted that day: "The next time I come to the public market, I'm going to get police protection, or place my wagon on stilts."

The Pike Place Market came about because of high food prices. The commission men were buying cheap from the farmers and selling dear to the consumers, and both the farmers and the public were angry. The Market was established by city ordinance as an experimental farmers' market to provide direct contact between the producer and the consumer. More and more farmers came to Pike Place, and more and more Seattle housewives bought their produce at the Market. The experiment proved a success, and the Market thrived.

By the mid-twenties, the Market stretched for blocks. There were restaurants and permanent shops, a post office and a library. Uniformed pages carried packages to the auto parks. At the main entrance on Pike, men gathered to smoke and debate the issues of the day.

The Market continued to prosper through the 1930s. Food

was plentiful and cheap, and business brisk, during the Depression.

But the war years brought radical changes to the Market. Many of the Japanese farmers were interned, and other farmers went to work in the defense plants. After the war, many of them (and many of their children) chose not to return to the farms. Life was changing. The move was to the suburbs, and the local supermarket became a more convenient place to shop than the old public market. People stayed away, and the Market buildings fell into a gentle decline.

By the late 1960s, plans were being made to demolish the Market. Through an energetic citizens' effort, an initiative to save the Market was put to the people of Seattle, and on November 2, 1971, the people responded by voting to make the Market a Historical District. It has since been listed in the National Register of Historic Places.

Today, the Market is once again a bustling, living part of Seattle. Old buildings have been faithfully restored. Old tradi-

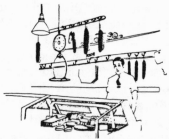

tions have been carefully maintained. The farmers still come from the farms in the rich agricultural valleys of western Washington. The merchants still do business in the old Market way—hawking their wares and cajoling their customers. New businesses have been started and are thriving. More and more craftsmen are coming to the Market, setting up on the tables alongside the farmers. The old ways live quite comfortably with the new.

The carefully restored Market sign under the old clock reads "Meet the Producer." The Pike Place Market is one of the few places where this is still possible. The Market customer buys produce from the farmer who grew it and jewelry from the craftsman who made it. And, if not dealing directly with the producer in a technical sense, the Market shopper buys meat from the butcher who cut it and fish from the fishmonger who just got back from the docks. The philosophy of 1907 is very much the philosophy of today at the Pike Place Market.

# PRODUCE

You can buy produce at the Market high stalls and at the farmers' tables. Confusion sometimes arises over which is which, and what is the difference?

A high stall is just that—a permanent stall with a display area built up from the floor. If you are at eye level with an artichoke, you are at a high stall, at least at a high stall on the east wall of the main arcade. The other produce stands in the main arcade and on the other side of Pike Place are also permanent installations, but they are built lower, and many allow the customer to wander through the displays. At the Market, the term high stall has come to mean all permanent produce stands.

The farmers' tables are the low, metal-covered tables that run along the east wall of the main arcade. They are rented by the day by local farmers.

What is the difference between the two? Only local produce is sold at the farmers' tables, and *local* means produce grown in western Washington, primarily King, Pierce, and Snohomish counties. When you buy lettuce at the tables, you are buying it from the farmer who grew it, and he probably doesn't live all that far from you.

The high stalls, on the other hand, sell fruits and vegetables from wherever the weather is warm and produce is growing and ripening. They, too, sell local produce, but the definition of *local* is here extended to include produce from east of the Cascade Mountains. The asparagus you buy at a high stall may be imported from Mexico or California, or it may be local from Yakima.

The first farmers to come to the Market were truck farmers, and the "dirt" farmers are still what most people think of as the

5

# When to Expect Local Farm Produce

| FRUIT | JAN | FEB | MAR | APR | MAY | JUNE | JULY | AUG | SEPT | OCT | NOV | DEC |
|---|---|---|---|---|---|---|---|---|---|---|---|---|
| blackberries | | | | | | | | ███ | ███ | | | |
| blueberries | | | | | | | ███ | ███ | ███ | | | |
| boysenberries | | | | | | | ███ | ███ | ███ | | | |
| currants | | | | | | ███ | ███ | | | | | |
| gooseberries | | | | | | ███ | ███ | | | | | |
| quince | | | | | | | | | ███ | | | |
| raspberries | | | | | | ███ | ███ | ███ | | | | |
| rhubarb | | | | ███ | ███ | | | | | | | |
| strawberries | | | | | | ███ | ███ | | | | | |
| **VEGETABLES** | | | | | | | | | | | | |
| basil | | | | | | | ███ | ███ | ███ | | | |
| beans | | | | | | | ███ | ███ | | | | |
| bedding plants | | | | ███ | ███ | | | | | | | |
| beets | | | | | | | ███ | ███ | ███ | ███ | ███ | |
| boktoy | | | | | | | ███ | ███ | ███ | ███ | ███ | |
| broccoli | | | | | | | ███ | ███ | ███ | | | |
| Brussels sprouts | | | | | | | | | ███ | ███ | ███ | |
| cabbage, Chinese | | | | | | | | | ███ | ███ | | |
| cabbage, green | | | | | | | ███ | ███ | ███ | ███ | ███ | |
| cabbage, red | | | | | | | ███ | ███ | ███ | ███ | ███ | |

| | JAN | FEB | MAR | APR | MAY | JUNE | JULY | AUG | SEPT | OCT | NOV | DEC |
|---|---|---|---|---|---|---|---|---|---|---|---|---|
| cabbage, Savoy | | | | | | | | | | | ■ | |
| carrots | | | | | | | ■ | ■ | ■ | ■ | | |
| cauliflower | | | ■ | ■ | | | | | | ■ | | |
| celery | | | | | | | | | ■ | | | |
| chard | | | | | | | | ■ | ■ | | | |
| chiles | | | | | | | | | ■ | | | |
| collards | | | | | | | | | | | ■ | |
| corn | | | | | | | ■ | ■ | | | | |
| cucumbers, pickling | | | | | | | | | ■ | | | |
| cucumbers, slicing | | | | | | | | | ■ | | | |
| daikon | | | | | | | | ■ | ■ | | | |
| dill | | | | | | | | ■ | ■ | | | |
| eggplant | | | | | | | | ■ | | | | |
| garlic | | | | | | | | | | | | ■ |
| gourds, ornamental | | | | | | | | | | | ■ | |
| horseradish | | | | | | | | ■ | | | | |
| kale | | | | | | | | ■ | | | ■ | |
| kohlrabi | | | | | | | | ■ | | | | ■ |
| leeks | ■ | ■ | ■ | | | | | | | | | ■ |
| lettuce, head | | | | | | ■ | | | | ■ | | |
| lettuce, leaf | | | | | | ■ | | | | ■ | | |
| melon, bitter | | | | | | | | ■ | ■ | | | |

| | JAN | FEB | MAR | APR | MAY | JUNE | JULY | AUG | SEPT | OCT | NOV | DEC |
|---|---|---|---|---|---|---|---|---|---|---|---|---|
| mint | | | | | | ● | ● | ● | ● | ● | ● | ● |
| mushrooms, wild | | | | | | | | | ● | ● | | |
| mustard greens | | | | ● | ● | ● | ● | ● | ● | ● | ● | |
| onions, green | | | ● | ● | ● | ● | ● | ● | ● | ● | ● | |
| onions, Walla Walla | | | | | | ● | ● | ● | | | | |
| parsley | | | | | | | ● | ● | ● | | | |
| peas, green | | | | | | ● | ● | | | | | |
| peas, snow | | | | | | ● | ● | | | | | |
| potatoes, Finnish | | | | | | | | | ● | ● | ● | ● |
| potatoes, German | | | | | | | | | ● | ● | ● | ● |
| potatoes, red | | | | | | | | | ● | ● | ● | ● |
| pumpkins | | | | | | | | | ● | | | |
| radishes | | | | | ● | ● | ● | ● | ● | | | |
| rutabaga | | | | | | | | | ● | ● | ● | ● |
| shallots | | | | | | | | | ● | ● | ● | ● |
| spinach | | | | ● | ● | ● | ● | ● | ● | ● | ● | ● |
| sprouts (alfalfa, bean, etc.) | ● | ● | ● | ● | ● | ● | ● | ● | ● | ● | ● | ● |
| squash, summer | | | | | | ● | ● | ● | ● | | | |
| squash, winter | | | | | | | | ● | ● | ● | ● | ● |
| tomatoes | | | | | | | | ● | ● | | | |
| turnips | | | | | | ● | ● | ● | ● | ● | ● | ● |
| watercress | | | | | | ● | ● | ● | ● | ● | | |

Market farmers. They bring in crops raised in their fields, as well as crab apples, dandelion greens, and wild blackberries picked on their land. Their produce reflects their ethnic backgrounds—bitter melon, all kinds of hot and mild peppers, squash perpetuated from seeds brought years ago from the Philippines, oriental greens, Italian parsley, and Chinese broccoli. There have also always been an egg lady and an herb lady at the tables. In recent years other kinds of farmers have come to the Market. There are young organic and hydroponic farmers now—and sprout farmers and cider makers and apiarists. The definition of *farmer* has broadened over the years.

The produce on the farmers' tables is local; the seasons are easy to distinguish. In the spring, Market regulars eagerly await the first of the bedding plants, which replace the winter storage crops of rutabagas and turnips. From then on, every week brings the surprise and pleasure of a new local crop. Bets are taken on which farmer will be first with the peas, the corn, the raspberries.

## How to Shop the High Stalls

*First, don't fiddle with the displays. The perfectly parallel rows of peas and Brussels sprouts are painstakingly constructed early each morning, and they are meant for display only. The signs on the tomatoes and avocados—Pleeza, no squeeza—are serious. You'll be reprimanded if you ignore them. Perfectly good produce is stored in boxes and bins behind the displays. If you want a ripe avocado and tomatoes for slicing tonight, ask for them.*

*The key to shopping at the Market is to remember its original (and present) philosophy of direct dealing between the consumer and the seller. Get to know the produce people. Let them know what you want, and if you don't like what you get, let them know that, too. (It is also good to tell them that the avocado was perfectly ripe and the tomatoes fine for slicing.)*

*Don't be intimidated by the free give-and-take of the Market. A great deal of shouting goes on, all of it good-natured. Talk back. But if you prefer plastic to patter, you'll probably be happier at your local supermarket.*

Local seasons don't dominate the high stalls. Long before the nectarines and peaches in Yakima are picked, the high-stallers are selling nectarines and peaches from New Zealand. Chilean grapes precede those from California by several months, and Mexican peas come in January. In midwinter you can pick a tropical salad of papaya, melon, and strawberries from a high stall or enjoy a Florida ear of corn.

When you shop the high stalls or the tables, it is important to keep seasons in mind, as difficult as that may be. The quality of a fruit or vegetable is usually best at the peak of its season. Any produce tends to be more expensive at the beginning and the end of its season, and you are certainly going to pay more for Mexican asparagus in February than for Yakima asparagus in May. The seasonal notations in the produce guide that follows are only approximate—weather, and therefore growing seasons, can be unpredictable—but they will give you some idea of when to expect your favorite fruit or vegetable.


## APPLES

*High stalls: year-round, peak September to January*

Some of the world's finest apples come from Washington. Unfortunately, most people know only the overrated Red Delicious. Americans seem to have developed a taste for Red Delicious apples, a variety with a very limited use. Sixty percent of Washington apples are Red Delicious, 30 percent are Golden Delicious, and the Winesaps, Jonathans, Gravensteins and Romes, Granny Smiths and Newton Pippins account for the remaining 10 percent.

The Washington apple harvest is an exciting time in the Yakima-Wenatchee area. If you have ever been there during harvest, you know how the air buzzes. Everyone and everything seems to be moving at once. A lot of hard work is done, a lot of satisfaction results, and it's over in just a few short weeks.

Though apples are harvested only once a year in September, they are available "fresh" year-round. Apples bound for market between September and February are kept in cold storage. The rest are put into what is called *controlled atmosphere* (CA). In CA storage rooms the oxygen level is lowered; this slows down the apples' aging. When they come to the Market six to eight months after being picked, the apples look, feel, and taste fresh. CA apples come into the Market in March and are available until the new fall harvest.

## Cider

Every Friday and Saturday, the cider man comes to the Market from Vashon Island and sets up at the farmers' tables in the North Arcade. His cider is fresh and unpasteurized. No preservatives and no sugar are added.

The island orchard has about thirty different varieties of apple trees. As many as five or six different varieties, always a blend of sweet and tart, may be used at any one time in making the cider.

The apples are picked when they are perfectly ripe; then, depending on the time of year, they are either used immediately or pulped and frozen. In summer the cider may come exclusively from frozen apples; the rest of the year, from a mix of fresh apples and the frozen pulp.

Because the cider is unpasteurized, the natural fermentation process continues, and proper storage is important. The cider must always be refrigerated. Stored at thirty-eight degrees or less, it will keep fresh for at least ten days. When the cider becomes sparkling, it is semi-dry. It is still good to drink (even better, some think) and makes an excellent baste for roast pork and ham. When the cider becomes a bit too tart to drink, it has reached the dry-hard stage. At this point it is most useful in cooking, but it can be made potable by adding fresh cider, or it can be made into vinegar. (Pour the cider into a stoneware crock, cover loosely with cheesecloth, and keep it in a cool place for about four months; you'll have a good, pungent vinegar.) The fresh cider also makes an excellent dry white wine, and the cider man can give you the recipe.

Unpasteurized cider is versatile. It can also be volatile. Don't leave it tightly capped in a warm kitchen for too long. You will have instant applejack—all over.

Granny Smith apples are on the upswing, thankfully. Their increasing popularity is understandable. Granny Smiths are very firm, crisp, tart, green apples of unbeatable quality. They crunch beautifully when you bite into them and leave a fresh, tangy taste in your mouth. Grannies are good eating, baking, and freezing apples; they store very well, not becoming mushy as many varieties do.

The crisp, tart Granny Smith apple makes an excellent garnish with curried soups. Try one diced and sprinkled over a bowl of hot (or very cold) Senegalese soup, a rich chicken soup lightly laced with curry. The contrast in textures and tastes is very good.

Another excellent eating apple is the Winesap. It, too, is crisp and tart, almost spicy. It is one of the better varieties for freezing.

The Rome Beauty is considered a baking apple. It is slightly tart and makes exceptional pies and strudels. Dried, it is sweet and flavorful.

An unusual pie variety that is good and quite tart is the Spartan. There are not many commercial Spartans. Those you do find in the Market probably come from a farmer's or a high staller's own tree.

Jonathan apples are a little more tart than the Spartans or Romes, and they cook down well to make good applesauce. Both Jonathans and the Newton Pippins are good, all-purpose apples; they stand up well in the freezer and are good eating apples.

The Gravenstein is a soft-skinned apple. It is good for eating—nice and tart—but not for keeping. Many people believe Gravensteins make better sauce than any other apple.

The only sweet apples are the Red and Golden Delicious. The Golden is more versatile than the Red and may be baked, sauced, or frozen. The Red is strictly an eating apple.

## APRICOTS

*High stalls: July*

Apricots, another eastern Washington crop, are a special treat. They are a delicate fruit, easily bruised, and should be handled carefully. When you buy apricots, avoid shriveled fruit, an indication that it was picked too early. Choose instead plump, mature fruit that is fairly firm, yet juicy. If you have underripe fruit, it will ripen quickly if unrefrigerated.

Apricots should be enjoyed fresh while they last; the season is very short. They make a healthful summer snack food because they are high in vitamin A and iron and quite low in calories (about twenty in one apricot).

# Stuffed Zucchini with Apricots

This is a lovely summer dish made with fresh apricots and a Mediterranean-influenced rice stuffing. The first local zucchini arrive in the Market in July, along with the apricots, and you should have no trouble finding the right size. The recipe comes from Carol Ludden, an excellent cook who does not write anything down. Feel free to make adjustments, even additions, to the recipe. If you do not feel flush enough to buy the pine nuts, try substituting one-fourth cup sesame seeds; you will get a different, but very crunchy, stuffing.

2 cloves garlic
1 onion, finely chopped
olive oil
1/2 cup rice
1 cup water
1/2 cup dried currants
  (or raisins)
1/2 cup pine nuts
2 tablespoons parsley,
  chopped

1/2 teaspoon cinnamon
1/4 teaspoon ground allspice
salt
pepper
pinch of fresh mint
1 pound fresh apricots,
  halved and pitted
2 medium-size zucchini,
  sliced lengthwise and
  centers removed

In a skillet, sauté garlic and onion in olive oil. Add rice, water, and currants and simmer until rice is just about done and all liquid is absorbed (add more water during cooking, if necessary). Add to the rice the pine nuts, herbs and spices.

Coat an 8-inch square baking dish with olive oil. Layer bottom of dish with half the apricots. Set zucchini halves on apricot layer and fill them with rice mixture. Cover with the remaining apricots. Sprinkle olive oil over the top and add a little water to the pan. Bake at 350° for 45 to 60 minutes or until the apricots and zucchini are tender. Check from time to time and add water, if necessary. Don't let the apricots dry out. Serves 4.

## ARTICHOKES

*High stalls: fall crop, October to December; spring crop, March to May*

American artichokes are grown almost exclusively in the mid-coastal areas of California, where they take well to the mild climate. They are native to Africa and have been cultivated for centuries by the Italians and other people of the Mediterranean.

The two times of year that artichokes are worth seeking out are spring (about April), when they are at their peak, and late fall, when the "winter-kissed" artichokes come in. (Winter-kissed

artichokes are a favorite of artichoke lovers; the frost which bronzes the leaves also enhances the flavor.)

When buying artichokes, look for firm, unspotted ones that squeak when rubbed together. A good artichoke will seem heavy for its size, but remember that size is not an indication of quality.

Artichokes are not considered a common vegetable (unless you live in Castroville, California), and many people do not know how to prepare them. Most often they are simply boiled, served one to a person, and eaten by hand. They are, however, quite versatile. In southern Europe they are stuffed, braised, deep fried, or sautéed. Often only the heart or "bottom" is used. The bottom is exactly that, the bottom of the artichoke with the leaves and choke (the fuzzy, prickly portion of the heart) removed.

When stuffing artichokes, cut off the top third of the vegetable, strip off the tough outer leaves, and cut the stem flush with the bottom. Then open the top and remove the choke with a grapefruit spoon. Work with a bowl of cold water mixed with lemon juice handy, and drop the cut artichokes into the water to prevent discoloration.

## Anchovy Sauce

Most boiled artichoke leaves are dipped in butter, lemon juice, or mayonnaise. This sauce is a good alternative.

1/2 onion, chopped
2 cloves garlic, chopped
4 anchovy fillets
generous pinch oregano

3/4 cup olive oil (you may
substitute white wine for
part of the oil if you prefer)

Combine all ingredients in a skillet and simmer 5 minutes. After placing the whole artichoke in its serving dish, dribble the sauce over it and serve immediately. Serve with French bread for sopping up the sauce; you won't want to waste it. Enough sauce for 2 artichokes.

### ASPARAGUS

High stalls: Mexican crop arrives in January
California crop arrives in March
Washington season is May and June

Dan Manzo, Market high-staller, says that when the grass in your yard begins to grow again in spring, local asparagus is just weeks away. In fact, according to Dan, if you are passing through Sunnyside, Washington, on a warm spring day, you can actually hear the asparagus growing in the fields. The arrival of local asparagus is a sure sign that spring is well entrenched in the Market.

Asking advice on buying and preparing asparagus may be a mistake. It is one of those topics on which some have very strong opinions. There are thin-stalk asparagus lovers, and there are those who prefer thick stalks. Probably those holding the strongest opinion are those who tell you the only way to cook asparagus is tied in bunches and standing straight up in a pot. This vicious rumor was probably started by someone trying to market very tall, slender pots. It is good that way, but it is not the only way. (If you must cook it this way, use your coffee pot rather than investing in an asparagus cooker that is only useful three months of the year.)

Cook asparagus in whatever you have, and don't feel guilty if you must lay it down in a sauté pan with a bit of water. Just be careful not to waterlog it (don't boil it) or overcook it (it turns emerald green when properly cooked). If you overcook it, you will get asparagus the color of canned peas.

There are three grades of asparagus; small, standard, and large. Some people insist that thin-stalk asparagus is the most tender. This is not necessarily the case, and the more mature stalks often have the better flavor. Snap off the white portion at the bottom of the stalk, and you will be left with the tender best. Peeling asparagus is not necessary, and unless you've nothing better to do on a spring day, don't bother.

When buying asparagus, choose firm, straight stalks with tightly closed tips. Limp, flat stalks are usually tough. Use your asparagus as soon as possible; it does not keep long.

## AVOCADOS

*High stalls: year-round*

The avocado is a fruit, even though we use it most often as a vegetable, and is native to tropical America. Most all of our avocados are grown in California, but one variety comes from Florida.

Without a doubt, the best of the avocados is the Black Haas, the small, dark, almost black variety with the thick, pebbly skin. Black Haases are from California and have a long season. They are in the Market from spring until just before Christmas. Actually, they are available all winter but sell at such outrageous prices that most merchants don't bother to carry them. They have a smooth, creamy, yellowish green flesh and a nutty flavor that is unbeatable.

Probably the number-two avocado is the Fuerte, also from California. It, and the other major California varieties, the Bacons and Zutanos, are available through the winter months. They are smooth-skinned varieties. Their major problem is that they must be picked so very green for shipping that by the time they are ripe, quality and flavor loss is high.

The major avocado variety from Florida is simply labeled Florida or Florida Jumbo. These are large, light-green fruits with thin, smooth skins. They are the least desirable of avocados; the flesh is hard and tasteless and lacks the creamy texture of the Black Haas.

When buying avocados, look for uniform color, and avoid those with cracked or bruised skin and sunken spots. If you intend to use an avocado immediately, you want a slightly soft one that yields to pressure. For later use, choose a firm avocado and keep it at room temperature until it ripens.

Cut avocado discolors rapidly. To prevent this, rub the exposed areas with lemon juice. If you are storing half an avocado, leave the pit in place. It will help prevent discoloration.

## BANANAS

*High stalls: year-round*

Bananas are the biggest selling item in the produce market. Everybody eats bananas, probably because of their high caloric and carbohydrate content. Bananas, if you were wondering, come to us from Central America and sometimes Ecuador. Bananas are delicious in bread.

## BASIL

*Farmers: July and August*

Basil is a favorite herb of many cooks, and the Market is one of the few places where it can be purchased fresh. It is a tidy little bush with bright, green leaves and an incredibly strong fragrance. Sold by the bunch on the farmers' tables, basil is the base of some great dishes, like pesto, and the perfection of many others, like fresh tomato soup, a treat at the height of local tomato season in August. You may dry basil for later use, or, if you are planning to make pesto anyway, you will get a better product if you make it with fresh basil and freeze the pesto.

---

# Pesto

This is the Desimone family pesto recipe, shared by Rose Desimone Maselli. (The Desimones owned much of the Market until the City of Seattle purchased it from them in the early 1970s.)

*1 large bunch fresh basil*　　　*pasta, cooked al dente,*
*1/4 cup good olive oil*　　　　　*tossed with butter*
*2-3 cloves garlic*　　　　　　　*parsley*

*freshly grated Parmesan and*
  *Romano cheese, mixed*
  *half and half*

In food processor blend basil, olive oil and garlic until they form a thick liquid. Add enough of the cheese mixture to make a thick sauce. Serve over hot pasta. Garnish with more grated cheese and fresh parsley. Serves 2. Note: If you want to freeze pesto, freeze only the basil and olive oil mixture. Add garlic and cheese to the thawed product.

---

## BEANS

*Farmers: July to September*
*High stalls: year-round, peak summer*
*some Mexican in winter*

Green beans have been around a long time. The Egyptians cultivated them, and they have been cultivated in the Americas since prehistoric times. But the varieties we know today were developed only in the last fifty years. Popular locally grown varieties are Kentucky Wonder and Blue Lake, both "stringless" beans that grow both as pole and bush beans.

The farmers bring less well-known beans to the Market in summer, too. Horticultural beans—the large, red-striped beans—are sold under the name Romano, although they are not the true Romanos. Also available is the broad bean, or Fava—a large, flattened green bean, with both edible seed and pod.

Beans should be picked when they are young; as they get old, the seeds inside the pod become large and tough. In the Market, choose beans that are crisp, tender, and without scars. They should snap easily to reveal a moist, bright green interior with small seeds. They should have a pliable, velvety skin.

Beans should be rinsed with cold water, the ends snapped, and strings pulled. Young beans need very little cooking. Be careful not to overcook them, because this will destroy their high vitamin C and A content.

---

# Scalloped Green Beans

This recipe comes from Jo Anne Laskowski, high-staller at Manzo Brothers produce stand.

2 large white onions, coarsely
   chopped
1 cup celery, coarsely chopped
1 green pepper, coarsely chopped
1/2 bunch parsley, finely
   chopped
2 or 3 tablespoons butter

6 or 7 cloves garlic, diced
1/2 teaspoon each, basil,
   rosemary, and thyme
1 pound green beans, snapped
   to desired length
salt and freshly ground pepper

Mix onions, celery, pepper, parsley. Melt butter in skillet. Sauté garlic until soft; then remove and toss in with vegetable mixture. Add basil, rosemary, and thyme to butter. Butter baking dish. Place in it alternating layers of beans and vegetable mixture, starting and ending with beans. Sprinkle each layer with salt and pepper. Pour melted butter and herbs over all. Bake, covered, at 350° for 1-1/4 hours or until tender. Serves 4.

---

## BEETS

*Farmers: late June to October*
*storage crop November through March*
*High stalls: year-round*

Beets are completely edible plants, and both the leafy tops and bulbous root are nutritious and good. Young beets come to the Market early—tender greens with small, one-inch beets attached. These are best cooked whole, beet and green together. It is surprising how many people don't know that beet greens are good. They are, in fact, one of the most flavorful of all greens. The Greeks grew beets only for these tops, ignoring the fleshy root that we cultivate.

As beet roots get larger, they also get tougher; so select small beets, two to three inches across. Cook them whole with the crown still in place. This will help preserve the color and keep beets from "bleeding." When they are tender, cut off the crowns and peel and slice the beets for serving. Beets and beet greens are very inexpensive, and they are good diet food, low in calories, high in vitamin content.

Beets are served cold as often as hot. Sliced cooked beets are excellent in salads, in sour cream, or pickled. Be careful when mixing beets with other ingredients. If left to stand, they will transfer their color to everything they touch.

# Pickled Beets

1 cup vinegar
1 cup water
1/2 cup sugar
1/2 teaspoon salt

1/4 teaspoon pepper
3 cups cooked beets, peeled and
    thinly sliced
1/4 teaspoon celery seed

Combine vinegar, water, sugar, salt, and pepper in a saucepan and bring to a boil; cool. Place the beets in a glass bowl and sprinkle with celery seed. Cover with vinegar brine. Cover bowl and refrigerate overnight before serving. Serves 4.

---

## BELGIAN ENDIVE

*High stalls: October to March*

This small vegetable is used most often in salads. It is imported exclusively from Belgium and is in best supply in the winter months. Belgian endives are cylindrical with pointed ends, about six inches long, and have white leaves with greenish tips. The leaves should be crisp, tightly packed and show no signs of browning when you buy it. Belgian endive has virtually no nutritional value, but if you are on a diet and need filler, it has virtually no calories either. It has a slightly bitter taste which adds an interesting twist to salads. Many people enjoy it chopped and sautéed in butter.

## BITTER MELON

*Farmers: August and September*

A favorite of many of the Market's Filipino farmers is bitter melon, a green gourd that is about six inches long and has a very wrinkled skin. It looks something like a severely shriveled cumcumber. On first tasting, you are sure to agree that it is appropriately named. It is *very* tangy. Parboiling for a few minutes before cooking gets rid of some of the bitterness, but it will still be pungent.

Bitter melon should not be peeled. After washing, slice, cube, or halve it (depending on how you plan to cook it) and remove the few seeds. It can be stuffed with seasoned ground pork and baked, and it can be stir-fried with pork, shrimp, or other vegetables. It can also be added to chicken soup for a few minutes, then removed and discarded. (Do not stir, Market farmer Frances Primero has warned, or the bitter flavor will be released.) Frances also makes bitter melon pickles in a sweet-and-sour brine that will knock your socks off.

## BLACKBERRIES

*Farmers: mid-July through August*

Not widely cultivated, blackberries are still considered one of the wild berries to be picked along the roadside (unfortunately, the county sprays these). Market farmers bring blackberries picked on their land in late July and August when the berries are at their peak. Choose blackberries that are fully ripe but are still firm and that have not stained the bottoms of their cartons. If you must wash them, do it lightly in a colander so that they will not get soaked.

## BLUEBERRIES

*Farmers: mid-July to mid-September*
*High stalls: same*

The local blueberry season begins as strawberries start to fade. Blueberries are a time-consuming, labor-intensive crop, and they are not cheap even at the peak of their season. If you can afford them, they are a great snack food, high in vitamins A and C and low in calories.

Blueberries keep fresh much longer than other berries, a full week in the refrigerator, longer if they are very fresh when purchased. The fresh berries are delicious baked in muffins and pancakes and on cereal. Blueberries also freeze well for use later and, because of their tough skin, once thawed they are firmer and juicier than other frozen berries.

## BOKTOY

*Farmers: June to November*
*High stalls: year-round*

Boktoy is a mustard plant that is in the Market throughout the year. There are two kinds of mustards as far as shoppers are concerned, white stemmed and green stemmed. One white-stemmed variety is usually called boktoy—usually, because the name placed on a mustard depends largely on who is growing it and what his ethnic background is. Boktoy may be labeled gaitoy, pakchoy, or any of a number of similarly spelled names.

All of the mustards have yellow flowers and a similar appearance and taste. They are loosely bunched greens that join at the base like a Napa cabbage. The leaves are dark green and have a sharper flavor than other greens. When young, the bunch is completely edible, and the crisp stalk and tender leaf are excellent steamed or sautéed in butter and seasoned simply with salt, pepper, and a touch of lemon. Boktoy is also good stir-fried with other vegetables and meat and, if not overcooked, has a fresh crunchy consistency that makes a welcome addition to these dishes.

## BROCCOLI

*Farmers: July to September*
*High stalls: year-round, best October to April*

One of the most well-known cabbage family members, broccoli is a popular green vegetable, native to the Mediterranean. Like most green vegetables, broccoli is high in vitamins and low in calories. Shipped in from warmer places, it is available most of the year, but the local season is midsummer to fall.

In addition to standard broccoli, you will find an oriental variety on some of the farmers' tables. It looks like broccoli but is packed in looser heads and has lovely yellow flowers.

When buying standard broccoli, look for closely packed heads that have a good green color, no yellow flowers, no fading color. It is always somewhat irritating to pay for the long, useless stems of the broccoli, but there is no way around it, so it makes sense to find a way to use them. First, peel them. They are good raw in salads and may also be cooked. If you are going to cook both stems and flowers, cut the stems in quarters lengthwise or put the stems on a few minutes before the flowers; they will take longer cooking to be tender.

## BRUSSELS SPROUTS

*Farmers: September to November*
*High stalls: November to February*

Brussels sprouts are not a widely used vegetable and, consequently, they are not available as often as beans and broccoli. They are another member of the large cabbage family. Brussels sprouts grow in clumps surrounded by leaves. The sprouts are best when small, about one inch in diameter.

Very few Market farmers sell Brussels sprouts, though it is possible to grow them locally as a fall crop. Most high stalls carry them through the winter months. When buying Brussels sprouts, look for small, firm heads with no yellowing or brown spots. Trim the bottoms and cut a cross in each before cooking so the sprouts will cook faster. Don't overcook Brussels sprouts; they are really horrid when overcooked. Brussels sprouts combine well with carrots; their colors and textures blend pleasantly. If you are going to try this, parboil the carrots first because they take longer to cook. Then toss the vegetables together in a little chicken stock and steam until just tender.

## CABBAGE

*Farmers: July through November*
*High stalls: year-round*

*"Wife, quick, some cabbage boil of virtues, that I may rid me of this seedy feeling."*
                                        *Eubuleus*

The ancients considered cabbage a miracle drug, one to cure any ailment. Cato went so far as to suggest that Rome expel all her physicians because the city had so many cabbages, it needed no doctors. Cabbage is very good for you, high in vitamins and low in calories, but most of us do not hold it in such high regard today.

The cabbage family is a large one and includes cauliflower, broccoli, kohlrabi, Brussels sprouts, and kale. But cabbage generally means the globular, compact-headed, white, red, Savoy, or Danish cabbages, and Napa, or Chinese cabbage.

Savoy cabbage is the variety with the loose head and crinkly leaves. It has a mild, almost delicate, cabbage flavor and is wonderful simply steamed or sautéed with lots of butter, salt, pepper, and a bit of nutmeg.

Red cabbage is the best "pickler." It is also used fresh in salads for both its color and its flavorful "bite."

The white domestic cabbage is the most common variety. It is really a pale green color and comes in a tightly packed head. The most solid cabbage is the Danish, sometimes called the hard-headed cabbage. This is a very large cabbage, a late maturer used for sauerkraut, and is picked after the first frost.

Napa cabbage, often called Chinese, looks like a bleached-out head of romaine. It has large, broad leaves and a white heart.

When choosing cabbage, look for solid heads that are heavy for their size and are not discolored. Cabbage has the formidable advantage of being cheap most of the year and consequently is worth getting to know and use. One family can take only so much corned beef and cabbage, though, so try some variation. It is good with sausages, stuffed, or simply steamed and served as a vegetable. It is certainly worthy of more attention than most of us give it.

---

## Golabki

These stuffed cabbage rolls are a Polish tradition.

2 quarts water
1 head cabbage
1-1/2 cups partially cooked white rice
2 pounds lean ground round
1 onion, chopped and sautéed in butter until transparent

1 egg
salt and pepper to taste
2 cups tomato sauce, mixed with 1 teaspoon oil and 1 teaspoon water

Bring water to a boil in a large stockpot. Turn heat to simmer. Submerge cabbage and heat until the outer leaves are slightly soft. Cut the leaves away, one by one, as they become parboiled. (Use a large fork and a sharp knife to anchor and cut the cabbage.) Set the leaves aside. Mix rice, meat, and onion. Add the egg and salt and pepper. Mix. Take a cooled cabbage leaf, put in a tablespoon or so of the rice mixture, and fold the leaf over it, securing it into a small packet. Repeat until all the mixture is used. Arrange these in a baking dish. Pour over tomato sauce and bake at 350° for 90 minutes. Serves 4 to 6 and keeps well.

---

### CARROTS

*Farmers: July to October, stored carrots through February*
*High stalls: year-round*

One of the bright spots on the farmers' tables in winter is always a large heap of carrots. There is something cheerful about carrots—the bright orange color, the green fluffy tops—and their presence in even the darkest of months is appreciated. Of course, the dead of winter is not the best time of year for carrots, most of which are pulled out of the ground after the first frost and stored. The sweet baby carrots come in the late summer and early fall, and they are, without doubt, the best carrots you will ever taste. They are small, four to five inches at best, and very tender. They must be cooked only a very few minutes until tender and served immediately.

Carrots store better than most any other vegetable and, because of this, are available year-round. In fact, nutritionally, carrots improve with age. It has been found that carotene, the vitamin A precursor carrots are known for, increases in a twenty-week storage period. It was for this reason carrots were such an important vegetable to early Americans, who could keep them all winter in root cellars.

When buying carrots look for bright color and, if it's summer or early fall, fresh, unwilted tops. The tops are cut off carrots that are stored. Stay away from discolored stems; they are a sign of overmature carrots that may be slightly bitter. Large carrots are not necessarily overmature. The good carrot taste you enjoy comes from the bright yellowish orange core where the sugar is stored. So don't be afraid of fat carrots; they can be sweet and good. As with corn, carrots should not be cooked with salt, but a little sugar in the water enhances their natural sweetness.

---

## Carrot Soup

This recipe comes from Phil Walkden and Theresa Saludo, both former members of the Soup 'n Salad collective here in the Market and active members of the Market community. Made in the early fall with sweet baby carrots, this soup is an excellent first course. It is very rich, sweet, incredibly carroty.

2 medium-size onions, sliced
2 tablespoons butter
1 pound carrots
1 to 2 cups milk

salt, pepper, ground nutmeg
to taste
raw cream

Sauté onions in butter until they become translucent. Steam carrots until tender. In blender, purée carrots and onions together in the water from steaming (should be about 1/2 cup). The purée will be very thick. Thin with milk to desired consistency. Season with salt, pepper, and a pinch of nutmeg. Just before serving, add a dollop of rich cream to each bowl. Serves 4.

---

## CAULIFLOWER

*Farmers: summer crop, July to October*
*spring crop, March through April*
*High stalls: year-round*

Mark Twain called cauliflower a "cabbage with a college educa-tion," the aristocrat of cultivated cabbage. It is certainly the most delicate of the cabbage family.

Cauliflower is not easy to grow. It requires a moist, cool envi-ronment. If the weather is too hot, cauliflower won't head up, and so its best growing areas are proving to be Long Island and the Pacific Coast.

Cauliflower grows well in the Puget Sound region, but it is a labor-intensive crop. Consumers insist on white heads, and these are achieved by a process called blanching. To blanch, the farmer must carefully tie the cauliflower plant's long, narrow, green leaves around the head to shield it from the sun.

There are basically two kinds of cauliflower: white and purple (which turns green when cooked). The winter cauliflower (usu-ally Saint Valentine) is actually a broccoli, but it looks just like a cauliflower, and most people cannot tell the difference. The Saint Valentines are planted around Labor Day and are on the farmers' tables about March.

The size of a head of cauliflower has nothing to do with its quality. Look for compact heads with their curds packed closely together. The curd is an aggregate of stems and flowers clustered into a solid mass. When a cauliflower is overmature, its buds will begin to flower and separate from the stems. Avoid bruised and speckled cauliflower, often an indication of aphids.

Use cauliflower soon after purchasing. Old cauliflower ac-quires a bitter taste. Look at the leaves at the base of the head; they should be fresh and green. If they are yellowed and old, so is the cauliflower.

Cauliflower, like all white vegetables, should be cooked with a lid on the pot to help retain its whiteness (a pinch of sugar or a piece of lemon peel will also help).

Green grapes complement cauliflower. Cook cauliflower until just tender, drain it, and coat with butter. Just before serving, add seedless green grapes and toss so the butter coats them, too.

## CELERY

*Farmers: September and October, very scarce*
*High stalls: year-round*

Anyone who has been on a diet knows about celery—fifteen calories in one full cup, 94 percent water, and very little else.

There is never a bad time of year for celery. It is always available. It is cheap. It is entirely edible, and it is versatile.

Celery is a large commercial crop in America but is not grown by many small farmers. It is difficult to grow well and takes a long time to mature. It is grown in cool, mild climates and makes a good winter crop in the south, where the summer weather that is good for citrus is too warm for celery. A small amount of local celery comes to the Market, but it seems that we see less of it each year.

Most celery is green Pascal celery. The golden variety is rarely available. Celery hearts, stalks, and leaves are all eaten. The hearts, which are white, crisp, and tender are best eaten raw. The leaves are an excellent addition to the soup pot; so are the stalks.

When buying celery look for crisp stalks with fresh leaves, of medium size. The very thin, dark green stalks tend to be bitter and stringy. Celery will keep in the refrigerator up to two weeks. Do not separate the stalks from the root. If celery begins to get limp, stand the stalks up in the refrigerator in a pitcher of cold water with a dash of salt for an hour or so to crispen, then use immediately.

---

## Celery Victor

1 bunch young celery or hearts of
   celery, tops trimmed
3 cups chicken broth

2/3 cup olive oil
1/3 cup vinegar
salt and pepper to taste

Trim end and top of celery but leave in one, secure piece. Place in pan, cover and cook gently in a rich chicken broth (broth should reach half-way up the celery) until just tender. Let cool in broth and then drain. (The celery may be cut lengthwise in two or left whole.) Put in a shallow, oval dish, and pour vinaigrette sauce over the celery. Turn several times. Marinate 2-3 hours at room temperature. Serve with anchovies, black olives, and pimento strips.

___

## CELERY ROOT (CELERIAC)

*High stalls: September to April, irregularly*

Celeriac is a variety of celery grown for its root. It looks like a knobby potato, with a rough, brown skin and white flesh and has a firm, almost crisp texture, excellent sliced raw for salads. It has a more concentrated celery flavor than celery stalks and makes a good addition to soups and stews. Celery root should be peeled. It will darken quickly after peeling, so work near a bowl of water and lemon juice in which to drop the peeled pieces.

When purchasing celeriac, pick out the smallest roots, ones firm and clean. If the root is beginning to deteriorate, you will notice a soft spot on the top side. Don't buy it.

Celeriac is a good vegetable with which to experiment. It is not widely used or available, but in winter when the choice of fresh vegetables is slim, celeriac is a delightful change.

___

## Marinated Celery Root

1 celery root
1 tablespoon vinegar
3 tablespoons olive oil

salt and pepper to taste
pinch of sugar
1 teaspoon Dijon mustard

Boil celery root until just tender. (It's easier to peel and clean after it has been cooked.) Slice, and marinate in a vinaigrette made of the remaining ingredients. Serve at room temperature. Serves 2.

___

## CHARD

*Farmers: July to September*

Swiss chard, when young, tender, and fresh, is a superb green. It is a leaf beet that has been known for centuries and grows wild in the Mediterranean. It almost grows wild here, as any gardener knows, and because it is so easy to grow, it is often available. Chard grows like other greens, but instead of harvesting by pulling the plant from the ground, it may be cut an inch from the ground; new leaves will replace the old in a matter of weeks.

Chard has large, glossy leaves, heavier and firmer than beet or spinach greens. This makes chard easier to clean because dirt and sand do not accumulate between the leaves. The entire leaf, stem included, is edible, and it is cooked like spinach.

Chard is cheap and, like all greens, it is very nutritious, an excellent source of vitamin A, calcium, and ascorbic acid. It is also low in calories unless, of course, you serve it heaped with butter. Delicious.

## CHERRIES

*High stalls: June to August*

Cherries rarely make it home with some people. They are so easy to eat out of the bag. If you have not enjoyed this, you are truly missing something. Once you get them home, they are washed, and a proper receptacle is found for the pits and stems. This takes the fun out of cherries, though, fortunately, not the flavor. Cherries are a great summer snack food, high in vitamins, low in calories, guaranteed to "clean you out." They also provide youngsters with a wonderful opportunity to have cherry-pit fights, a rather disgusting, but thoroughly enjoyable, pastime.

The Yakima cherry season begins in June with the ripening of the Bings, those dark maroon—almost black—sweet cherries preferred by most consumers. The Bings are followed in July by the Lamberts and Royal Annes.

Lamberts are much like Bings, only a bit lighter in color— usually a deep red. The flavor is interchangeable. The Lambert extends the cherry season into August.

Royal Anne cherries are the most flavorful sweet cherries available. They are also the most perishable; they ship poorly, but since they are grown only a three-hour truck ride from here, the Market gets a good supply. They are large cherries with a light golden color and a crimson red blush. When you see them, buy them, and eat them; they will not keep well. They turn brown at the stem and become mushy soon after they are picked. The only way to serve them is in a large bowl, fresh. The season is very short, and if you miss this treat, you will have to wait another year.

## CHESTNUTS

*High stalls: November to January*

Most fresh chestnuts arrive in the Market for the holiday season in November and are gone by January. They are all imported from Europe, usually from Italy, where they have been a staple, not a holiday treat, for centuries.

The price of imported chestnuts is high, but they are worth it for a few special dishes during the holiday.

When you buy your chestnuts choose plump, glossy mahogany brown shells that seem heavy for their size. Avoid nuts that appear shriveled or cracked.

Chestnuts do not keep as well as other whole nuts, perhaps a week on the shelf. Before use, the hard shells and inner peel must be removed, a tedious chore. Here are some hints to get you moving and a fine recipe for soup that makes a good first course or a light supper. Chestnut soup is quite sweet and should be served with a sherry.

---

## *Chestnut Soup*

4 cups chestnuts
1/3 cup butter
2 quarts chicken bouillon

2 cups heavy cream
1 teaspoon sugar
pepper and salt

Cut a cross in the flat side of each nut. Place the nuts in boiling water and simmer for 15 minutes. Cool and shell. With a sharp knife, remove the brown skins.

Heat butter in a three-quart saucepan. Sauté nuts in it for just a minute, stirring constantly to keep them from burning. Add the bouillon. Bring to a boil, cover, reduce heat, and simmer until chestnuts are tender, about 20 minutes.

Strain the mixture, and return the bouillon to the pot. Purée the chestnuts in a blender. Add the nut mixture to the bouillon and bring to a boil. Stir in the cream, sugar, and pepper and salt to taste. Reheat and serve. This makes 8 to 10 servings.

---

## CHILES

*Farmers: September*
*High stalls: some year-round, peak in variety,*
*quality, quantity in fall*

Chiles, in this case all peppers other than the Sweet Bells, are very good for you. They are high in vitamins and if used in concentration will clear up your sinus congestion. And they are lovely to look at. During the fall in the Market you will find boxes of lovely yellow, green, and red peppers ranging from the mild Anaheims to the hot Serrano and Jalapeño.

There are dozens of kinds of chiles, and some have many names, depending on who grew them. Most red chiles are sold dried, most green chiles are sold fresh—but this is not a hard and fast rule.

The chiles that come to the Market may come from one of three places: local farmers, eastern Washington, or California. They may or may not have names attached to them, but that matters little. What is important to know is whether the chile is mild, hot, or hottest.

The large yellow or green Anaheim peppers are mild. They can be used raw in salads if you wish. Another relatively mild pepper is the yellow wax pepper, a quite small one. You see it often on antipasto trays. The Serrano is the hottest of the fresh chiles, about an inch and a half long and green like the Jalapeño.

Most all the red peppers are very hot. The most common is the Ancho, a wrinkled, reddish brown chile that is not as hot as many of the Mexican red chiles. The Cascabel is sometimes brought in from eastern Washington. It is lovely to look at, resembling a small cherry tomato. It is hot.

Whatever chile you buy, make sure it is plump, with a clear, glossy skin. Avoid blemished, shriveling peppers. Fresh chiles will keep in your refrigerator for about a week. Chiles may also be dried or pickled for later use.

## COLLARD GREENS

*Farmers: July to November*
*High stalls: year-round*

Another of the greens abundant on the farmers' tables from mid-summer to late frost is the collard. (The word comes from the Anglo-Saxon "colewort," meaning cabbage plant.) Collard is well known in the southern part of our country; most locals have never tried it. It is a great crop for local farmers and gardeners because it has a long season and practically takes care of itself. It is a hardy plant that can be kept well into our mild winter. Some connoisseurs of the collard will only eat it after the first frost, claiming that the taste improves.

Choose collard greens as you do spinach or chard—crisp, fresh-looking leaves that are unblemished, with no signs of yellowing. You may prepare collard as you do spinach, but keep in mind that this green requires a longer cooking time to become tender.

Collard is traditionally cooked with bacon or salt pork. It has a more assertive flavor than spinach and holds its own against the strong flavors of the pork fats. Try browning a few strips of salt pork and then adding chopped collard. Stir the greens in the fat a minute or so until they turn a brilliant green; then add about half a cup of chicken stock and simmer until the collard is tender. Don't cover the pan. Greens keep their color better if cooked without a lid. Season liberally.

## CORN

*Farmers: mid-July through September*
*High stalls: January through October*

Corn, which used to be a seasonal vegetable, is fast becoming a year-round vegetable. Each year Florida corn seems to hit the Market a little earlier—as early as January, if you can believe it. But local corn is worth waiting for. Corn flavor deteriorates very rapidly so, ideally, corn should be eaten just hours from the field.

Corn is actually an American grass, not a vegetable. Fossils date corn as far back as 3000 B.C. and, as television ads surely have informed you by now, maize (the proper name for corn) was widely cultivated by American Indians.

There are six types of corn. Until hybrid corn was developed, most of the corn grown in the corn belt was dent corn; each kernel had a dent, or dimple, in its top. The Northeast grew flint corn, with hard, smooth kernels, and the Indians grew mostly soft flour corn, with white kernels. Popcorn has very hard starch in its kernels that expands explosively when heated. There is popcorn that has grains individually enclosed in small leaves, and the sixth type is sweet corn.

Sweet corn was almost unknown until it was found grown by a group of Indians in western New York late in the eighteenth century. The seeds were carried "back east" and by 1828 sweet corn was in the seed catalogs. By 1900 there were sixty-three varieties and today, with many hybrids, there are over two hundred varieties.

Sweet corn differs from the other types in its ability to produce and retain sugar. When sweet-corn kernels are young and small, they are filled with a clear, watery juice. As the kernels mature, the juice becomes milky and the corn is ripe. If the corn is not picked, the juice quickly passes on to the dough stage. The sugar that makes the corn sweet turns to starch and the corn becomes tough and tasteless. After the corn is picked, the sugars quickly turn to starches. This is the reason corn should be eaten quickly after harvesting.

Eastern Washington sweet corn comes to the Market about July. Before that all fresh corn in the high stalls comes from Florida and California. Market farmer Mike Mendez is usually the first to bring local corn. It appears sparsely in July and reaches its peak in mid-August.

When choosing corn, look for fresh-looking, green husks, moist enough to fit snugly on the cob. The kernels should be milky, not dry, and either young or well-developed depending on taste. Watch out for mushy, brown kernels at the tips of ears. If you plan to eat your corn on the cob, you must eat it immediately. Leave the husks on the corn until you are ready to use it.

If you have some corn that is getting old you can either get ambitious and bake corn pudding or try serving it this way— very high in calories, but delicious:

Cut corn from the cob and, using the dull side of your knife, scrape the cob to remove the milk. Put the kernels and milk in a saucepan on low heat with a disgusting amount of butter. If you can't (or know you won't) watch the pot carefully, use a double boiler. Season with salt and pepper. Cook just briefly.

## CRANBERRIES

*High stalls: early November through December*

Cranberries have been a part of our Thanksgiving tradition for so long that we rarely think of them any other time of year. A pity, as these delightful red berries deserve more attention. They are a perfect accompaniment to almost any fowl any time of year.

Cranberries are grown in bogs—low wetlands—usually around large bays. The ground is spongy and the soil acidic. There are not many natural bogs now that are fit for cranberry cultivation. Most cranberries are grown on the East Coast, around Maryland, and right here in Washington, near Willapa Bay.

Cranberries come to the Market but once a year and sell out in a very short time. They arrive in time to be put up as preserves for Thanksgiving and are gone by Christmas.

Most of the cranberry crop is canned, but there is always a supply of fresh, packaged cranberries for those who like to put up their own sauces.

## CUCUMBERS, PICKLING

*Farmers: late July to September*

The Pike Place Market is one of a very few places you can buy pickling cucumbers in Seattle, and in August and September the farmers' tables are overflowing with them. Anyone who puts up pickles can tell you that the cucumber is the most crucial ingredient.

Pickling cucumbers sold in the Market are divided by size; the smaller ones usually are the most expensive. Check them carefully when you buy and avoid shriveled ends, an indication of bitter flavor. Watch also for soft cucumbers and those that have begun to turn yellow; they are overmature and will not make good pickles. Choose firm, well-shaped cukes with a good green color.

Cucumbers are best in the middle of the season, and they are also least expensive then. Prices drop as August progresses and there are more cucumbers in the Market. By mid-September the season is dwindling and you will begin to pay more for less-than-prime cucumbers. Do your pickling (this is true for any preserving) at the peak of the season, when availability and quality are best and prices lowest.

Pickling cucumbers deteriorate very rapidly. Ideally, they should be picked in the early morning hours, bought at the Market by eight or nine o'clock, and put into the brine at home by noon. Whatever you do, don't buy cucumbers and then leave them in the trunk of your car on a warm day.

## CUCUMBERS, SLICING

*Farmers: August and September*
*High stalls: year-round*

Slicing cucumbers are one of the most pleasant of the salad vegetables on a warm day. You know the saying "cool as a cucumber." It is based on fact. On a warm day the internal temperature of a cucumber will be as much as twenty degrees cooler than the air. And you can taste the coolness. A platter of sliced cucumbers, tomatoes, and Walla Walla sweet onions is a refreshing accompaniment to any summer meal.

There are two kinds of slicing cucumbers, the standard cucumber and the English. English cucumbers are the fine, straight variety with small seeds. They are hybrids, grown in

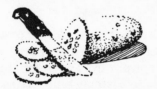

greenhouses, where the vines are trained on trellises so that the fruit grows hanging straight down. A Market hydroponic farmer brings English cucumbers from his greenhouse, but most of the cukes brought by farmers are the common variety.

When buying slicing cucumbers choose firm, green ones. Avoid those that are yellowing, a sign of overmaturity and probably large seeds. Some cucumbers, not the local ones but those brought in from other areas, are waxed. This is done to preserve them longer. There is nothing wrong with a waxed cucumber, but it must be peeled. If you plan to eat the skin, be sure to purchase an unwaxed cucumber.

Cucumbers are good sliced, salted (to draw out the water), and refrigerated. Drain and serve layered and sprinkled with dill. Or marinate the slices in white wine vinegar diluted with water, sugar to your taste, and lots of dill.

# Cold Cucumber Soup

3 large cucumbers
3 slices onion
2 cups chicken stock
dill
2 egg yolks

2 tablespoons butter
2 tablespoons flour
1 to 1-1/2 cups milk or
    half-and-half
radishes

Sauté cucumber and onion slices in butter for about 10 minutes. Sprinkle with flour and stir with a wooden spoon. Add stock and dill and cook until cucumbers are mushy. Purée in blender or food processor. Beat egg yolks into a bit of the hot purée and then stir into remaining purée. Add milk or cream. Refrigerate. Serve ice-cold with thinly sliced radishes on top. Serves 4.

---

## CURRANTS

*Farmers: June*

Very few currants come to the Market now, and those that do are red currants. They have a rather short season, so if you fancy red currant jelly keep your eyes open for their arrival. They are small, firm berries, like small blueberries, but they grow in clusters like grapes. Currants are sold in pint and half-pint boxes. Look for firm, bright berries that look moist rather than dry or shriveled.

## DAIKON

*Farmers: July to November, stored to March*
*High stalls: year-round, irregularly*

This large, white radish is usually in abundant supply in the summer and early fall on the farmer's tables. An oriental radish, the daikon is mildly pungent and is excellent raw. It is shaped like a fat carrot and is usually five or six inches long, but it can be well over a foot long and three or four inches in diameter.

# Frances Primero's Daikon Pickles

Daikon is not served as a cooked vegetable, but it is commonly pickled or served grated as a side dish. This recipe comes from Market farmer Frances Primero.

1 large daikon radish
1 gallon salt-water brine (1 cup
   kosher salt diluted in 1 gallon
   water)

1 cup water
3 cups white cider vinegar
2 cups sugar

Peel and slice daikon. Place in a ceramic or glass crock and soak 4 to 5 days in the salt-water brine, being sure that brine *completely covers* daikon. Combine in a saucepan the water, vinegar, and sugar. Bring to a boil; remove from the heat and cool. Place drained daikon in a glass bowl and cover with vinegar mixture. Refrigerate 3 days before serving. These pickles will keep several weeks in the refrigerator. Makes about 3 pints.

---

## DILL

*Farmers: July through September*

Large buckets of fresh dill indicate pickling season in the Market, but fresh dill is far more versatile than the pickling cucumber it comes to market with. Dill is said to stimulate the brain, fire the will, and overcome the depressing effects of fatigue and stale air.

Dill grows very tall, two to three feet, in a very short time. If you buy fresh dill, you are getting two things: dill seed and dill weed, the feathery leaves of the plant. The seed is stronger than the weed and is best used to season bread or pickles. The weed can be used to flavor many dishes. To enhance salmon, try laying bunches of dill weed on your barbecue coals as you are cooking. It may also, of course, be crushed and put directly onto your fish or added to a mayonnaise or cream-based sauce to be served alongside. Dill is also good with new potatoes and green beans.

## EGGPLANT

*Farmers: August and September*
*High stalls: July through March*

Eggplant is a beautiful vegetable, underused by most of us. Several varieties appear in the Market. The large commercial variety is available most often, but in August and September, local farmers bring us a selection of Japanese eggplants, the small, pear-shaped oriental varieties.

Eggplant is very perishable and should be chosen carefully and used immediately. Its shiny, deeply purple skin should be unbroken and show no rough, spongy spots, signs of decay. Buy the smaller eggplant, ones that feel heavy for their size.

The eggplant is supposed to have originated in India, where it still grows wild, but it is used most in the Mediterranean area, the best source of ideas for preparing it.

Eggplant is a watery vegetable, and some people say that it must be salted and drained before use. Just as many claim this is nonsense, so take your choice. The large plants may have tough skin and should be peeled, but you will not find this necessary with the small oriental varieties.

Ratatouille is a classic dish with many variations. If you are not familiar with eggplant, this is a good way to introduce yourself to it. Ratatouille is perfect with lamb.

---

## *Ratatouille*

2 large eggplants
2 zucchini
2 medium onions, sliced
1/4 to 1/3 cup olive oil
2 sweet red peppers, thinly
   sliced
2 cloves garlic, chopped

2 or 3 large tomatoes, skinned
   and chopped
1/2 teaspoon coriander seeds,
   crushed
basil
salt and pepper

Cut unpeeled eggplants and zucchini into 1/2-inch slices, sprinkle with salt, and put into a colander with a weighted plate on top for about an hour. Drain, pat dry, and cube. Sauté onions in olive oil (do not brown). Add eggplant, zucchini, peppers, and garlic. Cover and cook gently for about 40 minutes. Add tomatoes and coriander seeds. Cook for another 30 to 40 minutes or until all the vegetables are very soft. Stir in basil and salt and pepper to taste. Serve at room temperature (taste improves by the next day). Serves 4.

## Eggplant Relish

This recipe for eggplant relish comes from Marjan Willemsen, chef at Rex's Market Delicatessen. She suggests it be served with crackers or a coarse dark bread.

| | |
|---|---|
| 1 eggplant, diced | 1/2 cup tomato sauce |
| 1 onion, diced | 1 teaspoon salt |
| 2 cloves garlic, minced | 1 teaspoon pepper |
| 1 green pepper, diced | 1 teaspoon marjoram |
| 1 tablespoon olive oil | 1 teaspoon basil |

Sauté eggplant, onion, garlic, and green pepper in olive oil; add the remaining ingredients. Cook the mixture down in a heavy casserole for about an hour. Drain off excess liquid before refrigerating. Makes 2 cups.

---

### ENDIVE/ESCAROLE

*Farmers: summer, occasionally*
*High stalls: year-round, peak summer*

These two plants are not the same but are often confused. In fact, it is not entirely uncommon to see endive sold with the name escarole on it. No wonder the confusion.

The plants are closely related. They, along with Belgian endive, are members of the chicory family. Endive is a curly-leafed green that grows in a loose head like butter or red leaf lettuce. It has a slightly bitter flavor that combines well with other salad greens. The leaves are narrow with white centers. Escarole is a broad-leaf version of endive. It also is slightly bitter in taste, and its leaves are crisp, with the same white stems and curly ends.

You will find one or the other on the shelf, but rarely both at the same time, another reason it is easy to confuse them.

### FENNEL

*High stalls: October to April*

Fennel is considered an herb, but it is a member of a vegetable family, that of carrots. It has a bulbous root that may be cooked like a vegetable, but its leaves and stalks are used most often as a dried herb. Fennel has long been popular with cooks in southern France and Italy. In these countries, dried fennel stalks are put on the fire while grilling fish, or they are used to stuff it when it is being broiled. Fresh fennel is becoming increasingly popular in Seattle and so is turning up in the Market more often. It used to be that only dried fennel was available.

Fennel has an aniseed flavor which is quite strong when it is raw but which fades somewhat when the fennel has been cooked. Raw fennel root combined with red radishes and seasoned with oil and lemon makes a nice salad. To serve the root as a cooked vegetable, boil it in salted water; drain, chop, or slice it, then toss with butter, lemon and salt and pepper.

Fennel, in combination with garlic, is used a great deal to season pork. Try substituting it in recipes that call for rosemary.

### FIGS

*High stalls: black figs, April*
*green figs, September and October*
*dry figs, year-round*

There are two fresh fig crops brought to the Market. The spring crop of purplish black figs comes from California and is usually high in quality. These figs are excellent sliced and served with cream, but they are very rich.

The green figs you see in the fall are local and come from trees in someone's backyard, often that of your produce man. These figs are quite fragile and have an interesting combination of great richness and a delicate flavor. Their wonderful aftertaste lingers long after they are gone. A perfect dessert fruit with a ripe Brie.

### GARLIC

*Farmers: August through December*
*High stalls: year-round*

Garlic is surely nature's best gift to man, at least in the kitchen. Garlic has been cultivated by mankind for thousands of years, and not only for its culinary uses. At one time or another, garlic has been said to cure just about every disease and ward off every evil spirit that ever was. No other plant is and has been so highly revered as the garlic. And it is well deserving.

Some people put garlic in everything. It is incredibly versatile, and there are few nonsweet dishes in which a place for it cannot be found. Garlic is one of the lily family, whose other members include the leek, onion, shallot, and chive, also widely used in cookery.

Garlic grows underground in bulbs, each made up of many small cloves. It is sold by the bulb or in the long braids that look delightful hanging in the kitchen (and serve the additional purpose of warding off evil or unfriendly spirits). A word of caution about garlic braids. They are lovely, but garlic does not keep forever. If your braid has more garlic on it than you will use in a month or so, expect it to spoil. It will continue to look nice hanging, but the garlic will not be useable. For cooking, it really is best to buy garlic fresh in small quantities. Buy bulbs that feel heavy and are clean and dry.

The amount and strength of flavor garlic imparts to food depends on how it is used. Whole, unpeeled garlic is used in huge quantities in some classic dishes, but its taste is not unbearable; none of its volatile oils are released. On the other hand, garlic peeled and mashed is incredibly strong. A lot of commercially raised garlic is processed into flakes (tasteless), salt (useless as garlic) and powder (foul stuff). It is a convenience but a poor one. Fresh garlic is always available, is quite cheap, and the processed products do not compare at all to the fresh in flavor.

---

## Garlic and Anchovy Pasta

3 cloves garlic, chopped finely
1/4 cup olive oil
1 tablespoon butter
1/2 to 3/4 of a 2-ounce can
   anchovies, mashed

celery seeds
1/2 pound rotini pasta, cooked
1/4 cup Parmesan, grated
parsley

In a large frying pan, sauté garlic in olive oil and butter until garlic is slightly crisp. Add mashed anchovies, plus a few whole ones if you like, and mix. Add a sprinkling of celery seeds and the pasta, tossing lightly. Remove to a serving dish, toss with Parmesan, and top with chopped parsley. Serves 2.

---

## GINGER ROOT

*High stalls: year-round*

This knobby little root is irreplaceable in most oriental cuisines and is, consequently, always available in the Market. There is no substitute for fresh ginger. It is bought by the piece, a whole root or a part of one.

It usually is not necessary to peel ginger because it is removed from most dishes before they get to the table. Ginger should be bought in the smallest possible quantities. It will keep best in the refrigerator in a tightly closed glass jar with a tablespoon or two of sherry.

## GOOSEBERRIES

*Farmers: June*

These funny berries are not widely used or grown, but they do come to the Market every June with at least one berry farmer. Sized and shaped like blueberries, gooseberries have a thin, transparent skin that shows off their green flesh (some varieties turn a purple red when ripe).

Gooseberries grow in lovely clusters. They are tart berries, not eaten raw, but good in preserves, sauces, and desserts.

## GRAPES

*Farmers: Concords, fall, limited*
*High stalls: June to December*

Most all of our grapes come from California, and the Thompson seedless are by far the best sellers. They are not the best grapes. Unfortunately, the really exceptional grapes are riddled with seeds.

One really superb grape is the Ribier, a large, black-skinned grape. Ribiers arrive in August and continue into November. Arriving a bit later in the season is the Calmeria grape. It is a lightish green grape with white flesh, a cut above the Thompson seedless in quality, but with seeds. The Calmerias and Ribiers are both excellent served with Kasseri cheese.

The first grapes to arrive in summer are the Thompsons and Tokays. The Tokay is a pleasant, purplish red grape of medium size. Both the Tokays and Thompsons end their season in October, slightly overlapping the arrival of the Red Emporers. These are the only winter variety grape at the Market. They are good in October and November. Grapes kept in cold storage are available in fair amounts until March. They are usually far less than exceptional.

## GRAPEFRUIT

*High stalls: year-round, peak winter*

A big, juicy Indian River grapefruit is one of winter's treats at the fruit market. Grapefruit comes to us from California, Texas, Arizona, and Florida. The Indian River, Florida, grapefruit is by far the best quality, and it peaks between January and March.

Grapefruit from somewhere is available year-round, but supplies are short in summer and what does arrive is often dry and tasteless. If you're going on a grapefruit diet, do it in the winter.

## HORSERADISH

*Farmers: usually in August, very little*
*High stalls: year-round, irregularly —*
*always in the fall and before Passover*

Horseradish is a bitter herb, revered by some, totally ignored by others. It is incredibly strong. Horseradish root is sold by the piece. It is often grated and served raw, but most people make a sauce of it to serve specially with red meats. It is frequently combined with other ingredients (beets, for example) to tone its flavor down a bit.

## JERUSALEM ARTICHOKES

*High stalls: irregularly during winter*

The reason for the name Jerusalem artichoke is a mystery, since the small, knobby, potatolike tuber bears no resemblance or relation to Jerusalem or artichokes. It is native to North America and is the tuberous root of a perennial sunflower.

Jerusalem artichokes have a thin skin, usually a brown or yellow shade, and crisp, white flesh; they have a sweet, nutty flavor, and if you lack sugar in your diet they have some nutritional value. Their three main components are dextrose, sucrose and levulose—all sugars.

If you decide to try these "artichokes," choose ones that feel firm and heavy, and avoid those with signs of mold. They should be stored like potatoes. They also may be cooked like potatoes and adapt well to most white potato recipes.

## JICAMA

*High stalls: unpredictable, infrequently*

Jicama is a tuber, something like a sweet potato, from Mexico. It is brown, like a russet, with a crisp but bland white flesh, and it is about the size of a baking potato. It can be used like a sweet potato or may be sliced raw for salads, where it has a texture something like water chestnuts. It is popular in some Latin foods and is more readily found in markets in Spanish communities than at the Market.

## KALE

*Farmers: September to November*
*High stalls: September to April*

Kale is another member of the large cabbage family, one of the hardiest members. It has very long, curly leaves with ruffled edges. Kale has a strong flavor and is extremely healthful. The robust flavor stands up better than other greens to red meats. Creaming kale tones down its flavor and makes a pleasing vegetable dish. Remember when cooking it that kale, like collard, needs to cook longer than other greens.

## KIWIS

*High stalls: year-round, peak summer and early fall*

The kiwi is a lovely, green, tropical fruit native to China. Its correct name is Chinese gooseberry (a kiwi is a type of bird) and if you compare the two you will notice the resemblance of their inner structures.

A kiwi is larger than an egg and smaller than a tennis ball, more oval than round, and has a fibrous, brown skin (that also resembles a tennis ball). Inside, it is structured something like a tomato and has tiny black seeds that contrast sharply with its bright, green flesh.

Kiwis peak in the summer and early fall, when they come from New Zealand. Winter kiwis come from California and are not as good or as plentiful as the New Zealand kiwis.

Buy kiwis that are soft to the touch but not mushy. Kiwis pair well with other summer fruits, especially the strawberry. Peel and cut a kiwi into wedges and toss lightly with sliced strawberries for a beautiful, bright, and delicious summer dessert or salad. Serve with cream.

## KOHLRABI

*Farmers: August to December*
*High stalls: September to March*

The kohlrabi is a vegetable you probably never heard of as a child but now will find frequently in the Market. It is another part of the cabbage family, popular in Europe. The name is German and means cabbage turnip. It is bulbous like a turnip but grows above the ground rather than below, and it has a mild turnip flavor.

A kohlrabi bulb is rather funny-looking, with shoots for leaves growing up from it. It is a pale green color and firm and crisp like a turnip. For best flavor buy the smallest ones, no more than three inches in diameter. The large kohlrabies get tough, and sometimes mealy, losing the sweetness the smaller ones have. When they are small, kohlrabies are good raw either in salads or cut julienne and served with a vegetable dip. Steamed and tossed in butter, kohlrabi is a tender vegetable with a robust flavor, a good side dish for heavy meat dishes.

## KUMQUATS

*High stalls: peak summer; winter, irregularly*

This is a small, tart relative of the orange. Usually kumquats are about the size of large grapes. They have a spongy orange skin and a very bitter, acidic flesh. Lovely to look at, they taste terrible. But they do make good preserves. Those who do not appreciate them use them as a pretext for very poor puns like "kum quat may."

## LEEKS

*Farmers: September to February*
*High stalls: September to April*

The French call leeks the asparagus of the poor. They must be cheaper in France than they are here. One bunch of leeks costs

about the same as one pound of asparagus in season and doesn't go as far. But like fresh asparagus, leeks are one of those things we should treat ourselves to when they are available.

Leeks look something like oversized green onions. They are among the mildest of onions and are the richest nutritionally, high in vitamin C and minerals.

Leeks have been the national symbol of Wales since A.D. 604 when, with leeks in their hats to distinguish themselves from the enemy, the Welsh won a battle against the Saxons. To this day, on the first of March, all good Welshmen wear leeks in their hats.

Leeks are a winter crop and are available from September to April. Aside from the roots and the tough upper parts of the leaves, the entire leek is eaten. They must be washed very carefully. Unlike most onions, which have tubular leaves, leeks have flat leaves, and dirt settles between them. With your knife, split the leek lengthwise almost in half and wash thoroughly between layers. Then trim the tops and cut off the roots close to the stem. Save the tough, green tops for your soup stock.

Leeks are pleasing to the eye and make a lovely vegetable dish when cooked whole and topped with a vinaigrette, cream, or cheese sauce. The French prepare leeks this way:

Clean leeks and tie them together in bunches of 3 or 4 as you would asparagus. Either cook in salted boiling water or steam in vegetable steamer over salted water until tender, about 15 minutes. Remove and drain thoroughly. Chill well and lay on serving platter. Sprinkle with coarsely chopped, hard-cooked egg mixed with finely chopped parsley and chives. Serve ice cold with a vinaigrette sauce. (This may also be served as a hot vegetable. After cooking the leeks, drain, place on platter, and serve immediately with the eggs, chives, parsley, and a warm vinaigrette sauce. Or omit the sauce and cover with chives and parsley sautéed in lemon butter.)

For creamed leeks au gratin, cook the leeks in the French method, drain, cut into inch-long pieces, and place in a baking dish. Cover with a rich cream sauce. Sprinkle with bread crumbs and a generous amount of grated Parmesan. Brown in a hot oven and serve immediately.

## LEMONS

*High stalls: year-round, peak summer*

Lemons are always available but fluctuate in price and quality. The best time of year for them is summer, beginning about May. Look for lemons that are firm and glossy, that feel heavy, and that have a smooth skin. A rough lemon usually has a thick skin and will not be juicy. Also avoid green-tinged lemons; they tend to be excessively acidic.

The Greeks, who have a countryside full of lemon groves, have developed a whole cuisine around them. A favorite, both hot and cold, is lemon soup.

---

## Lemon Soup

1/2 cup rice                          4 eggs
2 quarts rich chicken broth           juice of 2 lemons

Cook the rice in broth until tender, about 20 minutes. Remove broth from the heat. Just before serving, beat eggs until light and frothy. Slowly beat the lemon juice into the eggs and dilute the mixture with a few cups of the rice soup, beating constantly until well mixed. Add the diluted egg-lemon mixture to the rest of the soup, beating constantly. Bring almost to a boiling point; do not boil or the soup will curdle. Serves 6.

---

### LETTUCE

*Farmers: leaf begins late May, head in mid-June, both through October*
*High stalls: year-round*

There are four basic types of lettuce cultivated commercially, and most of the time they are all available. Only size and price varies with the seasons anymore. In summer, when local lettuce is available, quality is high and price is low. In winter we usually have a good supply of moderately priced, nice-looking lettuce from California. If there is a bad time of year for lettuce, it is springtime, especially April and May, when the crop that is planted around Christmas is harvested. If California has a rainy, cold winter, supplies in the spring are low, and prices can go quite high. Luckily, the arrival of local lettuce puts a quick end to the shortage.

The most common variety of lettuce is the crisphead, often called iceberg. When someone in the Market talks of lettuce, this is what he is referring to. Other varieties are called by name.

Part of the reason crisphead lettuce is so common is that it travels well. It certainly is not because it tastes best. Most crisphead lettuce is bland. A good crisphead lettuce is heavy for its size, compact, and firm but not hard.

Butterhead is another variety of head lettuce. It has a smaller, looser head, with soft delicate leaves rather than crisp, firm ones. The most common butterheads are the Bibbs and Bostons.

Bibb lettuce, named after its first producer, has a delicate, buttery flavor and soft, tender leaves. It is dark green. Boston has a bit larger head with lighter green leaves; sometimes the leaves have a reddish tinge.

Limestone lettuce is available sometimes. The best is grown in limestone soil in Kentucky. It is a special variety, very small, joined like a looseleaf lettuce but with extremely tender leaves like a butterhead. It is worth the price occasionally, but only if you can get the real thing. Some have tried growing limestone varieties hydroponically, but they are not as good.

The looseleaf lettuces do not head. Instead, their elongated leaves join at the base to form a loose bunch. There are many varieties: red leaf (not to be confused with reddish Boston lettuce), curly leaf, and many in-between. They are quite delicate and tender and do not travel or keep well. They should be used no later than the day after they are bought. Because of their perishability, it is especially important to seek out the locally grown.

The best lettuce variety for tossed salads is cos, or romaine. Romaine is versatile, keeps well, and has an excellent, crisp, fresh taste and texture. It is bunched like the looseleaf varieties but has larger, longer leaves and a more tightly closed head.

## LIMES

*High stalls: year-round, peak summer*

Fortunately, limes are most available in summer when the need for them is greatest. What is a gin and tonic without lime juice? And how do you properly enjoy a mango without a squeeze of fresh lime?

Limes get scarce and their price quite high after Christmas; it often doesn't come down until summer. To make matters worse, the quality of the off-season, high-priced limes is often very low. They may be very small, hard, dry, and yellow-skinned.

A lime is best when it is a glossy green color, firm and heavy for its size, but not hard. Once home, limes should be stored in the refrigerator. Citrus fruits do not need further ripening like other fruits often do. They will go bad quickly at room temperature, especially in summer.

## MANGOES

*High stalls: peak summer*

The mango is an extremely aromatic tropical fruit, shaped something like a small football. The best mangoes come from Florida and are available in early summer. They are an orangish yellow color and have a flavor reminiscent of both peach and cantaloupe. The mango flesh is much like that of a juicy peach, and it has a large pit.

Mangos should be served sliced, slightly chilled, with a squeeze of lime juice.

## MELON

*High stalls: almost year-round, peak April to October*

There are melons available most of the year in the Market. Mexican watermelon comes in January, canteloupe in February, but the season doesn't really get underway until April, and it is June before the really superb cantaloupes arrive.

There are five major varieties of melon in the Market. In mid-summer and early fall they are almost always all available.

Cantaloupe, the most widely available melon, arrives as early as February and can stay nearly until Christmas. It is not very good during the extremes of its season and can get quite expensive. The California cantaloupes peak in July, get very inexpensive, and are simply superb. Half a cantaloupe makes a lovely breakfast or lunch on a summer day. Eastern Washington supplies some cantaloupes, and they are available in August and September.

When buying cantaloupes look for ones that have no bruises or cracks in the skin. Take a good whiff at the stem end. A ripe cantaloupe will have a fresh smell. Bad ones can be sniffed out. Their aroma is overripe, and often there will be mold at the stem end.

Persian melons, often sold as muskmelons, are very similar to cantaloupes; they have the same netted skin but are a bit larger.

Crenshaw melons are quite large; they can weigh six to eight pounds. They are a golden color when ripe and have a lengthwise ribbing. Crenshaws are not as sweet as the very ripe cantaloupes

# The Honey Tables

*Beekeepers set up on the farmers' tables throughout the year. They give generous samples, and it is difficult to resist the proffered stick dripping with rich, amber honey.*

*There are five major types of honey gathered in western Washington. Hives are moved into an area as each type of flower blooms and its nectar is high. The first honey to be gathered is maple, in the early spring. Then comes huckleberry, from the Olympic Peninsula and, later in the year, from Mount Rainier. During June and July, blackberry honey is gathered, primarily from the Kent Valley. Snowberry comes from the high Cascades between Snoqualmie and Ellensburg. The last flower to bloom is fireweed, between July and September; fireweed honey comes mainly from the slopes of Mount Rainier.*

*There are other kinds of honey on the beekeepers' tables. Each beekeeper has a special time of the year when he moves his hives to special (even secret) areas where a less common "honey" flower is in bloom. These unusual honeys—star thistle, holly, desert sunflower, mint—are all delicious, but the supply is likely to be limited. If you are looking for a particular seasonal honey, it is best to ask early.*

*You can buy liquid honey in jars or cut comb honey in boxes. Other products from the local apiaries are beeswax, honey soap, candies, and bee pollen. This last is from the bees' knees (truly!), dusted from the worker bees as they return to the hives and collected and dehydrated by the beekeeper. Bee pollen is used in cooking, and many people sprinkle it over salads.*

*Honey is being used more and more as a substitute for sugar. The Market beekeepers have pamphlets and books with recipes and honey hints. There is even a recipe for honey hand lotion.*

or honeydews; they have a deeper flavor. Their flesh is a dull orange color. Crenshaws are available from about April until October.

Casaba melons are another fairly large, golden-colored fruit. They have more defined ribbing than the Crenshaws and share the same season.

Honeydew are pale yellow, almost cream-colored melons. They are extremely sweet when ripe and a bit watery. They have a pleasant, green flesh that, when good, is very firm and flavorful. Bad honeydew can be mushy and grainy.

Watermelon is an American summer favorite. Difficult as it is to imagine, you can eat fresh watermelon in January. They come from Mexico, and the quality is generally quite high.

Watermelon, really all melon, can be very good or very, very bad. It is difficult to tell a good watermelon when it is whole; you are much safer buying halves. Avoid melons with a streak of white flesh up the middle. Check also to see that ripe-looking watermelons aren't too ripe; their texture can be very mealy.

All ripe melons will smell fresh and, when pressed at the blossom end, will give a little.

Melons should be served chilled to bring out their best flavor. They combine well with so many other fruits that the variations are endless and the color combinations (cantaloupe and straw-berry, Crenshaw and kiwi) beautiful. The classic Italian combi-nation of melon and prosciutto makes a lovely afternoon snack. Cantaloupe also pairs well with raspberry sherbet for a summer dessert.

## MINT

*Farmers: June through August*

Mint is an herb so closely associated with summer that it is difficult to imagine warm weather without it. It is used in any number of ways: mint juleps, iced tea with mint, mint with spring lamb, cool mint desserts, and mint garnish on many summer vegetables, starting with peas in June.

## MUSHROOMS

*Farmers: wild mushrooms, September and October, irregularly*
*High stalls: cultivated, year-round; some wild, fall*

Fresh mushrooms are always better than canned, and they are no longer a luxury item, so buy fresh.

A good portion of your mushrooms are brought to you by Ostrom or by Dole, the same people who bring you pineapple and bananas. The mushrooms are cultivated in trays of compost in large buildings; agriculture on a very big scale.

Mushrooms are expensive, but you may have noticed that the prices don't fluctuate as they used to. The only time (almost) that mushrooms are inexpensive nowadays is when they are getting old. Mushrooms are quite perishable and must be moved fast. After a few days, the creamy white caps begin to go brown, the caps open to expose the gills, and a slimy film develops on the mushrooms. This is when the price drops, because in another day or so the mushrooms will have to be thrown out. These older, less expensive mushrooms are a great buy, but use them in soups, stews, and casseroles.

Mushrooms to be used raw should be bought when very fresh, when they are dry and firm, have tightly closed caps, and an unblemished creamy color. Size is no indication of quality.

Wild mushrooms, mostly chanterelles, come to the Market in the fall, usually late September and October. Once in a while we see a few morels in the spring. The chanterelles usually carry an outlandish price tab, but if you tramped around in the wet woods to gather them, you wouldn't sell them for nothing, either. For those who really appreciate the chanterelle, the price doesn't seem to matter.

Chanterelles, like all mushrooms, do not keep long. Use them the day you buy them. They are exceptionally watery. If they are going into a dish or sauce, you might sauté them first (or steam them in the butter a few minutes) to draw off liquid. Chanterelles *must* be cleaned before use. The gills can be quite dirty and riddled with pine needles. Wash them quickly under running water and dry thoroughly before using.

## MUSTARD GREENS

*Farmers: June through October*
*High stalls: June through April, irregularly*

There are innumerable varieties of mustard greens that appear on farmers' tables throughout the year. Cut mustard greens are most commonly marketed under this name. Cut mustards come in large bunches and are excellent buys. They are hardy greens with a strong yet pleasant individualistic flavor. Cooked briefly until just done, they are excellent. They also make good soup.

# Mustard-Green Soup

2 bunches mustard greens　　1 cup Romano cheese, grated
4 quarts rich chicken stock　salt and pepper
8 egg yolks

Wash greens thoroughly and cut off ends. Parboil the leaves. Drain, chop, and set aside. Place the stock in a large kettle and bring to a rolling boil. Add mustard greens and boil for 10 minutes. Beat the egg yolks, add the cheese, and blend well. Remove the soup from the stove and add the cheese mixture gradually, stirring until the soup thickens slightly. Season with salt and pepper to taste and serve hot. Serves 8.

## NECTARINES

*High stalls: mid-June to September*

Most nectarines come from California. There are some grown in Washington, but not enough to meet the demand, and they arrive in the Market in mid-August. Though related to the peach, nectarines are not a recent result of hybridizing. They have been a distinct variety for thousands of years and come to us from China. Nectarines should be eaten one of two ways: straight, or in large bowls with cream.

## OKRA

*High stalls: July to October*

Okra is a strange little vegetable—sort of finger shaped—with pointed ends, a dull green color, and hairy skin. Appetizing. Actually, okra is very good. It's the viscous consistency that presents problems for the uninitiated.

Okra is the fruit of a tropical plant that originated in Africa. How it came to the southern states is unknown, but for a long time Americans have associated it with southern-style cooking. Demand for it in the Northwest has been limited at best. But that is changing, and now okra is a regular late-summer to early-fall feature in the high stalls.

Okra is always cooked, usually in a gumbo or in combination with corn or tomatoes. Okra is not particularly nutritious and some consider it an acquired taste. If you've never had it, begin with this gumbo. It is certain to make you appreciate okra.

## Chicken Gumbo

4 cups rich chicken broth (and more to add to gumbo, if necessary)
1/2 to 3/4 pound chicken legs and thighs
1 medium onion, diced
2 stalks celery, diced
1 clove garlic, diced
1/2 green pepper, diced
2 tablespoons butter
8 small pear tomatoes, skinned and chopped
1 teaspoon grated lemon peel
1 teaspoon sugar
1/4 teaspoon thyme
1 bay leaf
2 sprigs parsley
1/4 teaspoon cumin
salt and pepper
Tabasco Sauce or red pepper flakes, to taste
1/4 pound cooked ham, diced
3/4 pound okra, sliced
4 to 6 sausage links, cooked and sliced
2 ears corn, cut from the cob
1 teaspoon filé powder

Cook chicken parts in stock until meat comes easily from the bones. Meanwhile, in a large pan sauté onion, celery, garlic, and green pepper in butter until soft. Add tomatoes, lemon peel, sugar, thyme, bay leaf, parsley, cumin, salt and pepper, and Tabasco Sauce or red pepper flakes; simmer for about 30 minutes. Add 4 cups broth, ham, and okra and simmer 45 to 60 minutes. Add sausage and chicken meat and cook another 30 minutes. Add corn and cook for about 10 minutes. Remove from heat and stir in the filé powder. Serves 4.

# ONIONS

*Farmers: June through November*
*High stalls: year-round*

Onions probably offer more to a wider variety of cuisines than any other vegetable. They are universally appreciated. The onion family is large and versatile, part of the reason for its tremendous contribution to cooking. It can be mild, it can be strong, it can be sweet. Chives, leeks, green onions, scallions—these are the fresh, young, immature onions. The arrival of potted chives in the Market is a sure sign that winter is drawing to a close. Chives are quite mild and may be snipped onto salads and soups, used almost like parsley to garnish vegetable dishes.

The prized local onion variety, the Walla Walla sweet onion, arrives on the farmers' tables in June, not long after the first green onions. The Walla Walla sweet is a bulbous fresh onion with green tops. It is sweet enough to eat raw and is wonderful sliced thinly and combined with sliced tomatoes and cucumbers. Even if raw onions bother your stomach, you'll find Walla Wallas easy to digest. Walla Walla sweets continue through August, after which there are some dry Walla Wallas available at the high stalls.

Dry onions come in many varieties, but most common are the sweet red Italians (used in salads), the white Bermudas (nature's gift to hamburgers), and the yellow or brown Spanish onions, the variety used for most of our cooking.

There are many special onion varieties. In the fall come the tiny pickling onions, tedious to peel, but of good flavor. Boiling onions are another special crop—mild, young, fresh onions about two inches across. These come in early summer. Dry boiling onions are available year-round. In June, boiling onions, fresh sweet peas, and new potatoes are an unbeatable combination.

Onions keep well if they are stored well. Fresh onions should be refrigerated. Dry onions should be kept in a cool, dry place, not, repeat NOT, in the same cool, dry place you store potatoes. The moisture in the potatoes will cause the onions to go bad.

## ORANGES

*High stalls: year-round, peak in winter*

Oranges are the brightest and the best produce available in the Market in winter. There are so many varieties of oranges and tangerines that they are impossible to keep straight. Every year, it seems, someone comes out with a new hybrid.

There are, basically, two kinds of oranges, navel and Valencia. The Valencia is a summer variety coming from California. It comes here in about May and stays until November. Valencias are good juice oranges.

The rest of the year we have navel oranges. If produce people could do it, we would have navels year-round. They are good eating oranges and they are seedless. The quality of California navels has been excellent the past few years. Here in the Northwest we do not buy many Florida or Texas oranges. There are, of course, variations on the standard Valencias and navels. There are small navels with thin skins called juice oranges, usually sold by the dozen. And then there are the endless varieties of mandarins: Satsumas, tangerines, tangelos, mineolas, honey tangerines, kinnows, and others.

The mandarin is a lovely little tree from China that has been hybridized to death. Not that it is bad; we have benefited greatly from it. We have crossed it with oranges and grapefruits and come up with some superb varieties.

The classic and original mandarin is a yellow to reddish orange, loose-skinned fruit. You've probably never seen one. Closest to the original is the Satsuma, the Christmas fruit the Japanese made famous. Unfortunately for the Japanese, California is now raising Satsumas to rival and often better them. Satsumas and tangerines begin in early November. After Christmas, Satsumas are gone but are quickly replaced by the equally good seedless mineola. Mineolas last at least a couple of months and then the kinnows, yet another variety, arrive. Someday—it is certain—some variety of the mandarin will be available year-round. It will be sweet, juicy, seedless, and easy to peel.

One of the sweetest varieties available in winter is the honey tangerine. Unfortunately, it has seeds in it, but if you squeeze your own juice, you can't beat it. Try it in combination with navels. Be the first person to produce a honey tangerine without seeds and you and all of your descendants can retire.

## PAPAYA

*High stalls: year-round, peaks early summer and late fall*

This tropical fruit has become quite common in recent years. Papaya is a large pear-shaped fruit, part green, part yellow when ripe, with a dense, creamy, golden flesh. The center of the papaya is filled with small, black seeds. When ripe, papaya will have a pleasing fruity aroma and be a bit soft. An unripe papaya will ripen best left at room temperature.

---

# *Papaya, Avocado, and Strawberry Salad*

The combination of papaya, avocado and fresh strawberries makes a good salad course for a light June meal, when they are all in season.

*1 ripe avocado (Black Haas preferred)*
*1 ripe papaya*
*1 head butter lettuce*
*1 pint strawberries*

*2 parts olive oil, 1 part lemon juice*
*1 green onion, minced*
*salt, pepper, and chili powder to taste*

Alternate slices of avocado and papayas on lettuce leaves. Top with strawberries (whole if small, sliced if large). Mix dressing well and pour over salad. Serves 4.

---

## PARSLEY

*Farmers: June through September*
*High stalls: year-round*

Parsley is an indispensable kitchen herb, and its most common form, curly leaf, is always available. Unfortunately, the other, far superior kind of parsley, the Italian, is not as readily found. Italian flat-leaf parsley has larger, flatter leaves that have a stronger taste and a higher vitamin C content than the curly leaf; it also keeps and dries much better. Italian parsley is available only in summer when Market farmers bring it in. Because of this, it is worth growing at home, where it can be kept out-of-doors in summer and indoors in winter.

Chinese parsley is often available from farmers in summer. It is not a true parsley, but it is a relative. What you are buying is cilantro or coriander leaf. These are dark green leaves, more feathery than Italian parsley leaves, and they have a most distinctive, unparsleylike flavor.

All of the parsleys are best used fresh. There is no substitute. Frozen parsley is a disaster and dried parsley lacks flavor. If you must dry parsley, use the Italian variety.

## PARSNIPS

*Farmers: September to November, stored through February*
*High stalls: September to April, limited*

Parsnips are a vegetable you either love or hate. If you don't love them, there is no reason to force yourself to learn to like them; they are not all that good for you. Almost pure carbohydrate, parsnips contain no significant amounts of vitamins or minerals, so you see, it is not true that all vegetables that you dislike are good for you.

Parsnips look like large, tan carrots. They can be prepared like carrots, cooked whole or sliced, and should be peeled either before or after cooking. Parsnips have a distinctive flavor, not unlike the turnip or rutabaga in strength. They should not be restricted to soups; parsnips make a nice vegetable dish when tossed in butter and well seasoned.

## PEACHES

*High stalls: June to September, limited imports February to May*

This succulent fruit has been known and loved by mankind for thousands of years. The peach comes from China and was introduced to the United States in the 1800s. Peaches are a summer fruit—even the California varieties don't arrive before June. (We do get a few peaches and nectarines from New Zealand and Australia in the late winter and early spring. They are usually of good quality and priced by the piece—one costs about as much as a gallon of gas.)

Washington peaches are very limited but of high quality. Most of them, Red Havens from Wenatchee, are semifreestone peaches, excellent for eating. There are also Hales and Elbertas from Yakima around Labor Day. These are freestone varieties and if you want to can peaches, these are the ones to get.

Most California peaches are yellow-fleshed and -skinned with a red blush. The most unusual variety is the Babcock, a white-meated peach with a more subtle flavor than most peaches. It is not tangy but does have the sweetness of other peaches. Babcocks come in midsummer. They always run from ten to twenty cents higher per pound than other peaches.

Peaches make excellent summer snack food. They are high in vitamin A, low in calories, and are a good detergent fruit if you need help in that regard. Serve peaches and cream for breakfast.

Peaches should be bought fairly firm but not hard. Avoid soft or brown spots, signs of damaged fruit that won't last long. Actually no ripe peach will last long; they are delicate and should be handled accordingly. Don't purchase hard, green-tinged peaches; they will not ripen well in your home. Buy them when you are ready to eat them. Enjoy them fresh.

## PEARS

*High stalls: September to April*

Pears are a fall fruit, and most of the ones sold locally are grown in Washington. More than half of the pear crop are Bartletts; the three other major varieties are Bosc, Comice, and d'Anjou. The Washington d'Anjous are excellent; unfortunately, not many Bosc or Comice are grown here.

Comice are large, juicy, green pears, in season from late fall through the winter. The d'Anjou pear is more yellow-skinned and has a crisper texture than the Comice. It shares the same season.

Another winter variety, the Bosc pear, is a spring-green color and has a very crisp texture, the firmest of all the pears. Bosc pears often have rough spots on the skin that do not affect the flavor.

Pears are picked green. They ripen well in a cool, dry place. When ready to eat they are just slightly soft to the touch. Ripe pears combine well with soft French and blue-veined cheeses for a light, healthful dessert. Serve with port.

## PEAS

*Farmers: June and July*
*High stalls: March through July, some Mexican in January*

Peas mean spring in the Market. In February peas are planted, in March California and Mexican peas come to the high stalls.

But the moment we wait for is the arrival of the first farmer with local peas.

The fresh green pea is a minor miracle. It is, especially when picked young, the sweetest, most flavorful vegetable to be found. Fresh peas and new potatoes, common-sounding as it may be, are one of the most superb vegetable combinations one can have in June in Seattle. Combine this with a spring-run chinook salmon and you are providing yourself with a real treat, as good as anything available in the Northwest.

The only way and, unfortunately, the most common way to ruin a fresh, green pea, is to overcook it. This is an abomination, an insult to food, and unforgivable. After shelling your peas, wash them in a colander. Put them in a saucepan with a very small amount of cold water. Bring the water to a boil and turn the burner off. Green peas do not need to be cooked, just heated.

Which brings to mind the purchase of peas. The best way to tell if peas are good is to taste one raw. If it is good, sweet, and tender, buy some. Peas that do not taste good raw, whose sugar has begun to turn to starch, and that are too large, will never be great cooked. There are supposed to be a lot of tricks to make peas better, like cooking with a lettuce leaf. Fresh peas do not need a lettuce leaf. Exactly what the leaf does is not clear, but it does seem to help frozen peas. Nothing can help canned peas.

### Sugar Snap Peas

Sugar Snaps first appeared in the Market in 1978, the result of experiments designed to strengthen pea pods. Technically, they are an entirely new vegetable, much like a snap bean. The pod and peas are extremely sweet and can be eaten whole—raw or cooked—like a Chinese pea pod, or the peas can be shelled and served like regular green peas. If you do not shell the Sugar Snaps, make sure to pull their strings before cooking.

### Edible Pea Pods

Called sugar peas, snow peas, or Chinese pea pods, these are the third variety of peas available in the Market. These tender pods with tiny peas inside of them should be bright green and crisp when you buy them. They are even more perishable than sweet green peas and should be used as soon as possible. Don't snap the ends off until you are ready to use them. Simply boil them as you would sweet peas, or sauté or stir-fry them. Whatever you do, do it briefly.

One more comment. Snow peas are often available out of season. It is quite likely that you will find them at at least one high stall in December if you really want them. The price is generally outrageous, but if you want them badly enough, they are there.


## PEPPERS

*High stalls: year-round, peak fall*

Peppers here refers to sweet bell peppers. If you're looking for something more pungent, you'll find it under Chiles.

There are two kinds of peppers available on the market, green and red bells. Actually they are the same thing. The bell pepper is green when mature and, if left on the vine, turns a beautiful red. All peppers turn red if left long enough.

In Seattle, green peppers are, for some reason, more popular than red. In southern Europe you will find the opposite to be true. The red pepper is sweeter than the green but their use is the same. Both are tasty in green salads, but the red has the added benefit of adding color contrast.

Bell peppers should be bought when they are firm and have a glossy sheen. Watch out for soft, watery spots and bruises, and don't buy the shriveled ones. While bell peppers are available year-round, they are not always a good buy. Some months they are small and grossly overpriced. Fortunately, they are not a staple and can be avoided at these times. The best time of year for red peppers is the late fall, October and November. Greens peak a little earlier, in September, but continue to be quite good through November.


## PERSIMMONS

*High stalls: September*

Persimmons are brilliant orange fruit, shaped like pine cones and about the size of apples. They are delicate, very soft when ripe, with flesh similar in texture to a ripe apricot. Buy them when they are soft to the touch but not too mushy. They have quite a distinctive flavor and, like mangoes and papayas, are loved by some and not cared for by others. They are a great detergent fruit, perhaps even more effective than prunes. Look for them, up from California, throughout the fall.

## PINEAPPLE

*High stalls: almost year-round, peak summer*

The best pineapple continues to come from Hawaii, though pineapple does come in from Mexico and other places. A sweet pineapple makes a wonderful summer dessert by itself or in combination with other fruits. It is a versatile fruit. It can be dressed up or it can be eaten with the fingers like watermelon, and its own shell makes a lovely serving dish.

Buying pineapple should not have to be a trial-and-error experience. If you are unsure of yourself, tell your produce man when you want to eat it and let him pick your pineapple accordingly. A ready-to-eat pineapple can be smelled. Take a good whiff at the bottom. If there is a sweet, pineapple aroma, the fruit is ripe. If your pineapple has been stored standing up, and most are, a few hours before serving cut the leaves from the top and place the pineapple upside down on a plate. This will allow juices that have settled to the bottom to redistribute themselves throughout the fruit.

The source of the following recipe is unknown, having been passed through many friends, but it gets hearty endorsements from those who have tried it.

---

## *Pineapple with Tarragon Dressing*

| | |
|---|---|
| *1 fresh pineapple* | *3 tablespoons tarragon vinegar* |
| *sugar* | *2 tablespoons sugar* |
| *lemon juice* | *3 tablespoons cream, lightly* |
| Dressing: | *whipped* |
| *1 large egg* | |

Cut the pineapple in two lengthwise and carefully remove the core. Cut the flesh away from the shell, slice it, and replace neatly in shell. Dust with sugar and sprinkle with lemon juice. Leave to stand while preparing dressing.

Beat the egg; add vinegar and sugar with a pinch of salt. Set the bowl in a pan of simmering water, or use a double boiler, and stir mixture until it thickens. Transfer to a cool container. When cold, fold in whipped cream and adjust seasoning. Spread dressing over pineapple just before serving. Serves 8.

---

## PLANTAINS

*High stalls: unpredictable, only on occasion*

Grown in the tropics, plantains look something like bananas but are longer, thicker, and less sweet. They need to be cooked like a vegetable. As it ripens, the plantain's peel, like a banana peel, turns from green to yellow to black. Unlike bananas, plantains are best when they are black.

Unknown to most of us, plantains are a staple to many in the tropics. Like our potato, they may be boiled, fried, baked, or sautéed. If not dressed up a bit they are rather bland. But they are essential to the cuisines of the West Indies, parts of Africa, and Latin America; so, when available, they provide you with an opportunity to try a new kind of ethnic cooking with the proper ingredients.

## PLUMS

*High stalls: June to September*

Most of the plums grown in the States are of Chinese origin and are eaten fresh. The European varieties, damsons and greengage especially, are used mostly for commercial canning or are dried and marketed as prunes. The best fresh plums are the Rosas (early and late Santa Rosas, Queen Rosas, La Rodas), Nubianas, Friars, and Wicksons.

The Santa Rosas come to the Market in early June. These plums have crimson red skin and a deep golden flesh. They can be outstanding but sometimes are a bit too firm. They can also be quite tart. When buying plums, check to see that they are soft enough to "give" a bit. Plan to use them immediately, because plums very quickly become overripe and mushy. If you buy fully ripe plums, refrigerate them as soon as you get them home.

Nubiana plums have been quite visible in the Market in recent years. These are large, very dark plums, and they can be really sweet. The Wickson plums are the yellowish green variety, also very sweet.

Plums are low in calories (only 25 in the average plum) and are a good healthful answer to the sweet tooth in summer.

## POMEGRANATES

*High stalls: peak September and October*

Pomegranates, though considered an exotic fruit by most Americans, have been cultivated for many, many years. They are actually berries, but the average one is the size of an orange. Pomegranates have a red, thick skin and are filled with moist yet crunchy ruby red seeds.

## POTATOES

*Farmers: June to March*
*High stalls: year-round*

The potato has become such a staple in our diets that most of us do not give much thought to it. It is indispensable but rather dull.

The potato went to Europe with Spanish explorers in the late sixteenth century. They had discovered it among the Indians of Peru. Once abroad, the potato quickly became popular and spread through northern Europe. The peasant population embraced it. On a small plot of land a farmer could grow enough potatoes to feed his family all year. A grain crop would take from four to six times as much land. Potatoes also, because of their nutritional value, could keep people alive if other crops failed.

Potatoes are still a staple for many of us, but there is no need to stick with boiling russets; there are many varieties of potatoes and many ways to prepare them.

There are four basic potato varieties that you see on the farmers' tables throughout the summer and fall: reds, russets, Finnish (and Swedish), and German purples.

You have seen "new" potatoes. A new potato is not a variety but any potato that is dug before the vine dies down. It has a softer skin than the later potatoes. Locally, new potatoes come in mid-June and continue through September, depending upon when they were planted.

Red potatoes come in many varieties, but the most common are the Norland, an early-season potato (called little reds), and the Pontiac, a midseason, somewhat larger potato. They are both white potatoes with red skins.

Russets are the most common potato variety. Washington is one of the nation's largest potato producers, and russet Burbanks make up the largest part of the crop. The russet harvest begins in October after the vines die down. The Norgold russet comes in first, followed by the russet Burbank (the baking potato).

The Finnish and Swedish varieties are yellow potatoes. The Swedish are elongated (shaped like fingers), and the Finnish are round. Harvest is in full swing in October, though some new potatoes are brought in earlier. If you are looking for the tiny, almost marble-size, red or yellow potatoes, you will find them in summer (June and July). They are not always brought in; it is far more profitable to leave them in the ground and let them mature. However, they are fantastic, and if you really want them, it is worthwhile to ask a farmer to pull some for you.

The German purple has got to be the most interesting potato variety. It turns blue when cooked. It is used most often as a salad potato and shares the late fall season with the russets.

When buying potatoes, look for a firm vegetable that has not sprouted. Do not buy a potato that shows even the slightest amount of green; it is likely to be bitter.

A late-crop mature potato will keep up to three months if stored properly in a cool (50° F.), dark, and dry place. Do not store any bad (even slightly bad) potatoes; they will spoil the rest. White potatoes store better than other varieties.

No matter how well you store them, the chemical composition of potatoes changes with age; the starches turn to sugars. You can remedy this by taking potatoes out of storage a week before use and letting them sit at room temperature. This will reverse the process, and the starch content will rise and the chemical composition return nearly to what it was when the potato was dug. After a week, though, the potato will begin to sprout; so make sure you eat it when it's ready.

Many believe that potatoes are starchy and fattening. Not so. A medium-size potato contains only ninety calories and, at the same time, contains one-third of your daily requirement of vitamin C plus some vitamin B1, niacin, and iron. The fatteners are the butter and sour cream.

## PRUNES, ITALIAN

*High stalls: September to early October*

A real Northwest product, Italian prunes are hardly grown anywhere else in the States. If you are new to the area, you may have not seen them fresh before. Italian prunes look like small plums. They have a lovely, purple blue color with a silvery blush.

Italian prunes are freestone plums. They can be tart or sweet, depending on the degree of ripeness. The skin can be quite acidic, even more so than other plum skin.

Fresh Italian prunes make a good snack food. Like dried prunes, they are very good for you. They are very rich in iron and vitamins, and their calorie count is almost negligible.

When buying prunes, pick ones that yield slightly to pressure. If they are rock hard, they will be bitter. Also avoid very soft prunes; they will quickly go mushy and take on a rotted flavor. Stay away from broken skin and brownish discoloration, signs of rotting.

## PUMPKINS

*Farmers: September through October*

Pumpkin is not a squash, though many consider it one. It is a berry—a fruit—but we use it as a vegetable; so we call it one.

Pumpkins have the honorable distinction of being the most local vegetable in the United States. Just about everyplace has its local pumpkin farmer and 80 percent of all pumpkins never leave the immediate area they are grown in.

Market farmers bring scads of pumpkins in the fall. It is a crop high stalls generally do not carry. You can find the very smallest (under four-inch diameters) and the very largest pumpkins in town at the Market.

No one needs to be advised on how to pick out a pumpkin. Any eight-year-old can do it. It must be firm, with a good shape (many are partial to round faces) and a bright orange color, free of scars and bruises. Only one more thing. Buy pumpkins with at least a couple of inches of stem still attached. Like berries and squashes, the pumpkin needs its stem so it won't deteriorate. Once the stem is broken off, the pumpkin goes fast.

If you are buying your pumpkin for pie, you may not be concerned about its shape; but do purchase a relatively small one. It will have more tender flesh than the large ones that make great jack-o-lanterns; they can be tough and stringy.

## QUINCE

*Farmers: September, sometimes*
*High stalls: November, quite rare*

Quince are sometimes available in the fall, though they are not in high demand. Those who do demand them feel quite strongly about them. Quince make fine jelly, and there are those who cannot face the winter without it. Sometimes a farmer with a quince tree in his backyard will bring a few in. This is not something one plans on; one happens upon it. Usually around Thanksgiving at least one high stall will bring in Oregon pear quince. There is California quince available, but it is usually hard and not good, and rarely does anyone carry it. The Oregon quince is quite good but is not available in great number; so buy it as soon as you see it come in.

A quince looks something like a lumpy pear. It is yellow when ripe and is fragrant when ready to use. Quince are extremely high in pectin and set up well as jelly without additional pectin being added.

## RADISHES

*Farmers: May to September*
*High stalls: year-round*

Not exactly one of your glamour vegetables, radishes are commonly used but rarely used in uncommon ways. To most, they are a salad vegetable. Their crisp texture, mildly pungent flavor, and lovely, red skins blend well with greens.

Radishes grow fast, taking about six weeks from planting to harvesting, and so are always one of the first crops brought to the Market by farmers. Because of their rapid maturing, successive plantings are made, and radishes continue to be brought in through the fall.

The summer radishes are the round red ones and the long, thin, white icicles. They are both good in salads. The red radish is especially good as an hors d'oeuvre (try it raw with butter and salt) and as a garnish (see recipe for Cold Cucumber Soup). The winter radishes available in the Market on the farmers' tables are daikon (see Daikon) and black Spanish. The latter is a very large, round radish—the size of an average cantaloupe—with a purplish black skin and a crisp, white, spicy flesh.

## RASPBERRIES

*Farmers: late June through July*
*High stalls: June through July*

A summer berry, the raspberry is an exceptional local treat. Raspberries, which rarely appear in supermarkets in Seattle and never appear in them most other places, are brought to the Market in late June and continue for about a month. They make the best jam in the world.

Raspberries do not keep well and need to be carefully handled and quickly eaten. When you purchase them, check the bottom of the carton. It should be dry and show no signs of staining. Raspberries, though a soft berry, should be firm and fully ripe with no stems attached. Take them home and refrigerate immediately. If they get too warm they will turn mushy. Do not wash raspberries until you are ready to use them; even then, be careful not to soak them. Don't worry about any little bugs. You won't even taste them.

The season is short; so enjoy them fresh while you can, and don't stand around waiting for the price to go down. It won't. Commercial raspberries are scarce and never, never cheap.

## RHUBARB

*Farmers: outdoor, late April to early June*
*High stalls: hot house, February*
*outdoor, April to June*

The first local crop to come to the Market in the spring is rhubarb. Rhubarb is a very large crop in western Washington, and we supply most of the western part of the country. This plant enjoys the rich soil and cool, moist weather that the Puget Sound region has in such abundance.

The earliest rhubarb is forced. The roots are dug after the fall frost but before the ground freezes. It is then stored in dark cellars or greenhouses and is ready in about February. Forced (or hothouse) rhubarb has smaller leaves than the outdoor, and the stalks are lighter pink and less acidic. It is also not quite as flavorful.

Rhubarb is always sold without the leaves, which contain oxalic acid and should not be eaten. They do, however, have one useful purpose. If you have discolored aluminum pots, boiling rhubarb leaves in them will make them look good as new.

When buying rhubarb, pick firm, crisp stalks with good color. Rhubarb has many uses; the most common is, of course, pie. It also makes an excellent sauce that is good served cold or at room temperature for breakfast or dessert. All you need to do after it is trimmed and washed is cut the rhubarb into half-inch pieces, cook it down (slowly, so you don't have to add water) for about twenty minutes, and sweeten to taste.

## RUTABAGAS

*Farmers: September to January*
*High stalls: September through March*

Rutabagas are a winter vegetable of the cabbage family. They are one of those vegetables kids do not like, and many adults never get over their early feelings about them.

Rutabagas look something like turnips but are a golden color. They are solid, quite heavy for their size, and have a thin, smooth skin. They are not a delicate vegetable but have a distinctive, almost zestful flavor. It adds a welcome sharp flavor to vegetable soups and is also nice on its own, served steamed and buttered. Rutabagas should be peeled and the crowns cut off. They will keep a very long time if you store them, like potatoes, in a cool, dark, dry place.

Fresh rutabagas are on the farmers' tables in September and October; stored rutabagas are available throughout the winter.

## SHALLOTS

*Farmers: September through December*
*High stalls: year-round, peak fall*

Shallots are not onions or garlic but have a flavor reminiscent of both. They are mild little bulbs, related to the onion, that grow in small clusters, something like garlic.

Buy shallots as you do garlic: look for firm, dry bulbs with good shape and no signs of shriveling. Store in a dry, cool place and a well-ventilated container (such as a wire garlic basket).

Shallot braids are sold in the Market in the fall just like garlic braids. They are lovely, but the same cautions apply to both braids. Hanging in a sunny, humid kitchen is not the way to store shallots. Unless you use a lot of shallots in a very short time, don't expect these to remain good. They will become ornamental only. Realize this when you buy them and you won't be disappointed. Shallots make lovely gifts for cooks.

## SPINACH

*Farmers: April to November*
*High stalls: year-round*

Of the great variety of greens on the farmers' tables, spinach is the most common. It is also the earliest, arriving sometimes as early as April, and one of the latest, holding on until November most years.

Spinach has been popular for centuries, especially in the first half of the twentieth, when it enjoyed lots of positive advertising from Popeye cartoons. Then came the oxalic-acid scare, and spinach's popularity declined rapidly. Oxalic acid is the substance found in concentrations in rhubarb leaves that makes them toxic. It was found to interfere with the body's ability to absorb calcium. But spinach contains oxalic acid in amounts comparable to those in the rhubarb stalks we eat, and spinach is no longer considered harmful.

Spinach's other source of unpopularity is its tendency to collect sand and grit between its leaves. This is an especially bad problem when we have heavy rains in the weeks before and during harvesting. It can be difficult to wash out, and if it isn't done, the grit between your teeth is very unpleasant. The only way to be truly successful at ridding yourself of it is to wash the leaves one at a time. Another fairly successful method is to fill a large tub with lukewarm water, swish the leaves through it a few times, and let them stand awhile. Most of the sand will sink to the bottom. Repeat the process once more, but with cold water.

Spinach has the advantage common to all greens of being low in calories and high in valued nutrients. Unless you put butter on it. If you want to spare yourself the cholesterol, cook the spinach with lemon juice and lots of freshly ground pepper.

When spinach is very fresh, the leaves well formed and free of bugs, it makes an excellent salad green. Remove the tough stems. In the late spring, before local lettuce arrives, spinach provides relief from the now traditional outrageous spring lettuce prices.

## SPROUTS

*Farmers: year-round, but not every day*
*High stalls: on occasion, alfalfa and bean sprouts only*

Mow your own. Local sprout farmers can be found with trays of fresh sprouts most any time of year in the Market. No prepackaged stuff here; your wheatgrass is clipped to order.

You will find tremendous variety, a sprout-lover's paradise, and plenty of free advice on sprout cultivation and use. Some of the sprouts usually available from farmers are: wheatgrass, alfalfa sprouts, bean sprouts, radish and lentil sprouts, buckwheat greens, sunflower greens, fenugreek, watercress, and comfrey.

## SQUASH, SUMMER

*Farmers: July to October*
*High stalls: some varieties year-round, peak May to October*

The term summer squash used to mean something, but with modern marketing methods it has come to mean less and less. Zucchini is available year-round, and other summer squashes—straightneck, crookneck, patty pan, and cocozelle—

continue well into the fall. But the local summer-squash season is still a predictable three to four months, overlapping briefly the beginning of the winter-squash season.

The five major summer squashes listed above are always in the Market during the summer. And there are a few oddballs brought in by farmers who favor them (like the patula and

tabungaw). All summer squashes have some common characteristics that enable them to be readily substituted for one another in most recipes: their seeds are small and edible, their rinds are tender and edible, and they may be eaten raw.

Zucchini is by far the most common summer squash. Its dark green skin and white flesh make a lovely addition to salads and raw vegetable hors d'oeuvres. Zucchini is best when very small, no more than eight inches long and two inches in diameter, but it can grow to be huge.

Straightneck squash is a slender, club-shaped squash with a creamy yellow color. Its close relative is the yellow crookneck, a curved version of straightneck. Both can be used just like zucchini.

The cocozelle squash is very similar to zucchini, having the same cylindrical shape, but it has a smooth, light green skin.

The most interesting of the summer squashes is the patty pan, a small (five inches across), squat, pale green or white squash with deep ribbing that gives it a scalloped edge.

All of the summer squashes are tremendously versatile. They may be eaten raw; they may be cooked. They may be baked, sautéed, boiled, broiled, stuffed, or fried (try fried tomatoes and zucchini in combination).

---

## Zucchini with Sardo

2 tiny zucchini
  (6 inches maximum)
juice of 1/2 lemon

2 tablespoons butter
1/2 to 3/4 cup Sardo cheese,
  freshly grated

Parboil the zucchini until just (or just under) tender. Drain well. Leave whole (or cut in half lengthwise if slightly bigger than tiny), drench with lemon juice and melted butter, sprinkle with Sardo, and bake at 400° until the cheese browns. Serves two.

---

## SQUASH, WINTER

*Farmers: September through December*
*High stalls: September through March*

Winter squashes are some of the most exceptional vegetables if prepared well. They are larger than most summer squashes, with large seeds and hard shells. There are five major varieties that are brought to the Market: acorn, spaghetti, butternut, buttercup, and Hubbard.

The acorn squash, known also as Danish or table queen, has a smooth, dark green shell that is widely ribbed. Its flesh is pale orange, tender and moist, and is excellent split in two and baked, plain or with a spicy sausage stuffing.

Spaghetti squash is fun. It is a large, oval squash with a yellow rind. Bake it whole for about one-and-a-half hours (you may boil it first to cut down on baking time), split it down the middle, discard the seeds, and remove the insides with a pair of forks. You'll find strings just like spaghetti. Toss with an herbed butter and serve.

The butternut squash is another large, yellow-skinned squash with a bulbous base and cylindrical shape. The flesh is fine and yellow and has a good flavor. Because of its size, it is a good idea to cut it into pieces for baking and season with only salt, pepper, and a dribbling of butter.

Buttercup squash is squatty looking and has a turbanlike cap at the blossom end. It is dark green, with a thin, hard shell. The flesh is orange and rather dry, and it has a fine texture. Buttercup also should be cut up for baking. If you are going to put brown sugar on a squash, this is probably the one you should do it to. It is good baked or steamed in serving-size chunks.

Hubbard squash is the largest of the squashes—ten to fifteen inches long—and has a very hard shell. The flesh is orange and thick and can also be quite dry. But it has a sweet flavor, and if properly prepared, either with moist heat or baked with butter, it can be excellent. Hubbard is usually sold in pieces.

Winter squashes combine especially well with pork—baked

with pork chops, stuffed with ground pork, or simply served
with it.

## STRAWBERRIES

*Farmers: June*
*High stalls: peak April to July; some arrive as early as January*

Local strawberries arrive in June and are a matter of local
pride. They are quite different varieties from those shipped here
from California, Mexico, and Florida. The local berries are
juicier and sweeter than any others you've tasted.

Local commercial berry production has become increasingly
difficult in recent years, and the major problems are labor and
competition from California and Mexico. Prior to the midfifties,
strawberry production in California took place on scattered,
small-acreage plots that produced berries in summer for local
consumption. The same was done here. Strawberries were considered a specialty item and not big business. At that time,
growers in California harvested around five tons an acre, about
what Northwest berry farms yield today. California growers now
harvest close to twenty-five tons an acre.

The tremendous change is due to a lot of research that has
resulted in a high-yield berry with a longer fresh-shipping season, a better appearance, and an ability to be shipped and stored
well. These berries, firm and not very juicy, can be machine
harvested. The problem with this is that the berries are tough
and solid and the sweet taste of earlier varieties had to be sac-
rificed. Local berries sell because of their sweetness and juici-
ness. Set side by side, the two berries do not compare at all. But if
you are a supermarket with centralized warehousing and dozens of stores, the local berries are simply too perishable for you to
handle. Hence, even most local supermarkets carry California
berries at the peak of the Puget Sound harvest.

The most common local strawberry varieties raised by Market
farmers are Hood and Rainier. The Rainier is a new berry. The
Hood, the most popular berry available, was developed in the late
sixties to replace the Marshall. The Marshall, the best berry ever
marketed, was wiped out by disease in the midfifties. The Hood
is the closest thing to a Marshall and is more disease resistant.

The Hood and Rainier berries have the best flavor. Another
excellent-tasting variety is the Shuksan, but there are many
other local varieties. If you are buying late in the season, you will
more likely find Puget Beauty, Quinault, Olympus, or Northwest

berries. These varieties produce larger berries, but they are not as flavorful.

Aside from being delicious, local berries are good for you. One cup of fresh strawberries contains more than enough vitamin C to see you through the day.

Strawberries should probably be served plain, but they are exceptional with raw cream (or try sour cream and brown sugar).

When you purchase strawberries, look to see that the caps are attached and the berries are still firm. Avoid white spots; they will never turn red. Don't remove the berry caps or wash the berries until you are ready to use them. Store them unwashed and loosely covered in the refrigerator.

On a warm summer day, this cold strawberry soup makes a good luncheon dish served icy cold in chilled bowls.

---

## Cold Strawberry Soup

2 cups fresh strawberries, sliced
6 tablespoons sugar
1 cup water
2 teaspoons cornstarch mixed
   with 1 tablespoon cold water

1 cup dry white wine
2 tablespoons lemon juice
2 teaspoons lemon peel, grated,
   plus some for garnish
cognac

Combine strawberries, sugar, and water; simmer until berries are soft. Stir in cornstarch and cook and stir until thickened. Purée in blender. Add wine, lemon juice, and peel. Chill thoroughly and season to taste with cognac and additional lemon juice. Garnish with lemon peel. Serves 4.

---

### SWEET POTATOES AND YAMS

*High stalls: late October through December*

Sweet potatoes and yams are not at all related to potatoes or to each other. Sweet potatoes are members of the morning-glory family and are native to America, and yams belong to a group of tropical and subtropical herbs and shrubs and are native to Africa and Southern Asia.

Yams are sweeter and juicier than sweet potatoes but nowhere near as good for you. They are almost all starch. Sweet potatoes are one of our richest sources of carotene (from which the body produces vitamin A), while yams have only a trace of it. Sweet potatoes also have three times the vitamin-C content of yams.

For cooking purposes, sweet potatoes and yams may be treated in the same manner—boiled, baked, or sautéed. If you are boiling them, do so with the skins on; they will be easier to peel after they are cooked.

One of the reasons many Americans never grow to appreciate sweet potatoes has got to be that they were brought up on that whipped-marshmallow abomination. Where that got started is uncertain, but it was a horrible idea. Sweet potatoes have an appetizing flavor and a natural sweetness that should not be overwhelmed. They really are best either sliced and sautéed in butter or boiled whole, sliced, and tossed in butter.

---

## Sweet Potatoes with Rum

You will find that the rum and sugar combination in this recipe will satisfy your sweet tooth without spoiling the natural flavor of the sweet potatoes.

*6 sweet potatoes, peeled and cut      2 tablespoons butter*
*  crosswise into 1/2-inch slices      1/2 cup sugar (scant)*
*1/4 cup butter                        1/2 cup Jamaican rum*

Sauté potatoes in 1/4 cup butter, turning often to prevent sticking. When they are light brown and tender, transfer to a chafing dish in which you have melted the two tablespoons butter. Sprinkle with the sugar and stir lightly. Add the rum, tip the dish, ignite, and baste the potatoes in the syrup. Serve immediately. Serves 6 to 8.

---

### TOMATOES

*Farmers: August and September*
*High stalls: year-round*

Tomatoes got off to a very slow start with most Europeans, and if it were not for the French and Italians, we might still be following the advice in the 1860 edition of *Godey's Lady's Book* to cook all tomatoes at least three hours before eating. And that, after having them for three centuries. The English transferred their fear of tomatoes to America, where the Puritans denounced them. It was largely Thomas Jefferson's advocacy that gave them a chance at respectability. Actually, tomatoes originated in America, probably in Mexico or Peru. These countries are still the source of many of the tomatoes we eat today.

Tomatoes are available year-round, but because of the distances they travel, most of the year they are barely edible. Consumers want tomatoes year-round, and in order to meet that demand, suppliers "follow the sun." In late summer we have local tomatoes, but the rest of the year they come from California, then Florida and Mexico, then Chile and Peru, New Zealand and Australia.

Because tomatoes are soft and bruise easily, they cannot be shipped ripe. Most are picked green after they have reached full size but are still hard with a tough skin. They are shipped, then ripened in storage. Even those you see in winter and spring called vine-ripened are picked at the pink stage. There is no way to provide consumers with a truly vine-ripened tomato unless it comes from a local field. Here at the Market that happens in August and September. The only exception is a hydroponic tomato grown in a local greenhouse. These exist and are worth looking for, but there are not many. The Market has been fortunate to have one hydroponic farmer.

Italian plum tomatoes were developed for use in sauces and stews, but if you insist on slicing tomatoes into a green salad, Italian plum tomatoes are a good choice because they are firm and not watery. In winter, however, they are often grainy so it is best to ask your produce man before buying. The overall best choice for salads is the whole cherry tomato. Beefsteak tomatoes, which are huge, look nice, and have good flavor, are so full of water that they tend to wilt lettuce and dilute dressing, so they're best used for slicing or in combination with cucumbers and onions.

When local tomatoes are in, you can purchase ripe, slicing tomatoes or green tomatoes. Try sliced tomatoes in combination with thinly sliced Walla Walla sweet onions, an unbeatable pair. Green tomatoes are excellent breaded and fried by themselves or alongside red tomatoes. They also make good green-tomato pickles.

If you get a tomato that is not ripe, place it in a cool place—like a basement, not in the refrigerator—until it ripens. You do not have to put them on a sunny window sill; in fact, you really shouldn't. Tomatoes will turn red in the shade if the temperature is right, but if it gets too hot, they will blister.

## TURNIPS

*Farmers: September to December*
*High stalls: September to April*

Turnips are yet another member of the large cabbage family, a winter vegetable, whose appearance on the dinner table is dreaded by most small children.

Turnips have a distinctive flavor with a bit of a bite to them. They are best when very small, about three inches across, but are often marketed much larger. Turnips are white with a purplish crown. Their flesh is firm and crisp and is good raw as well as cooked, an excellent low-calorie snack if you can get used to it. They have a thin skin and the large ones should be peeled before using.

## WATERCRESS

*Farmers: June to October*
*High stalls: year-round, local in summer, California in winter*

Watercress is still largely a wild green that grows in streams. It has half-inch-diameter, rounded leaves that grow on short branches. Watercress is highly favored as a salad green because of its mildly pepperlike flavor. It is a member of the mustard family and is very nutritious, much more so than lettuces.

Fresh watercress is bright green and has crisp stems. Yellow-leaved watercress is old and can have a disagreeable flavor.

# SEAFOOD

During the 1920s and '30s there were eleven fish markets within the Pike Place Market. They were small—People's Fish shared with Hastings Grocery and Angel's Butter and Eggs a space on the main arcade that today is occupied by only one high stall—and the others were as compact, tucked into every level and area of the old Market.

The names of the businesses were resolutely New World—Philadelphia Fish, American Fish, State Fish Market, Olympia Fish and Oyster Company—while the names of the fishmongers were a roll call of the Sephardic families who had come to Seattle from the Mediterranean area in the early years of the century. Calderon, Bensussen, Ovadia, Cohen, Amon, Levy—lots of Levys. There was Dave "Good Weight" Levy and Isaac "Red" Levy. In fact, there were at one time five Isaac Levys in the Market, and on one memorable day they were all working at the fish market in Stall 9. A present-day Levy remembers the occasion well. "We'd go by all day and yell 'Hey, Isaac,' and watch five heads turn."

Things have changed since those days when a whole silver salmon cost twenty-five cents. The fish markets are fewer—there are three—but bigger, and the price of fish is certainly higher. But much has remained the same. The fresh fish is still displayed on ice in open trays. (Indeed, when it seemed that all the fish would have to be displayed inside glass cases to meet health-code requirements after the fish markets were renovated, a special performance ordinance was passed by the City of Seattle to keep the fish on ice and out in front.) Fresh-cooked crabs are carefully piled one on top of the other to form a perfect mosaic of bright orange and cream. There are glistening layers of whole salmon and rainbow trout, the tiny silver flashes of smelt, and the pink of shrimps cooked in the shell. Barrels of the fishmongers' own pickled herring stand open, next to trays of oysters and mussels. A whole sturgeon (perhaps the ugliest fish in the fish market) is occasionally brought in and displayed out front in a wheelbarrow. The slithering mass of a giant octopus, caught in Elliott Bay, spills over the rim of a bucket, another in the gallery of uglies.

Inside the cases are the more delicate fillets of fish, the squid, the raw shrimps, and scampi. There are fish heads and bones for rich court bouillons and fish soups, jars of shucked oysters and clams, and salt cod. Smoked salmon and black cod are here, as well as kippered salmon and long strips of squaw candy. Dried stock fish for lutefisk hang from strings high above the back counters.

Selling fish at the Pike Place Market is as much a show and an art as the display of the fish. The cries of "Fresh fish, EVERYBODY buy!" resound through the arcades until the cadence is firmly caught in the mind like a catchy commercial. Crowds gather as a tourist stocks up on crabs. The fishmongers chant "one and TWO and THREE" as the front man slings the crabs over the counter. The show is on, and the cameras come out.

There is, however, much more to the fish markets than flash and showmanship. The fishmongers know their fish. They go down to the docks at least twice a day to pick personally the best of the fresh local catch. They are on the phone constantly, checking with fish brokers about live Maine lobster, bay scallops, or Florida pompano. They are expert at filleting a paper-thin petrale sole—with no waste (and at no cost). They will clean a crab, gut a salmon, even dismantle a geoduck. And they are quick with advice—how much fish to buy for a party of six, the best way to fillet a king salmon for baking—and with recipes. They know the best way to cook skate wing and will happily share the family recipe for baked lingcod with tomatoes, parsley, and garlic—lots of garlic.

The rule at a Market fish market is *ask*. For advice, for recipes, and sometimes just for a very good fish story.


## WHAT TO LOOK FOR WHEN BUYING SEAFOOD

If you know how to pick out fresh fish, you will probably never get a bad buy in the fish markets. The signs of deterioration are clear and you should learn to recognize them. The flesh of a

# Filleting Fish

Watching a Market fishmonger fillet a fish may lead you to believe that it is quite simple. Actually, the method is simple, but it takes many tries to get the hang of it. Don't expect your first attempt to be an overwhelming success, and don't save it for a company occasion. Begin on a salmon or true cod, not a flatfish, or you may be discouraged for life. Take it slow and easy, keep in mind (cheerfully) that botched fillets make good fish chowder, and, most important, use a very sharp knife.

1. Make the first cut at the base of the head, knife at a slight angle, moving toward the head. Cut to (not through) the backbone.

2. Starting at the tail, move your knife toward the head, keeping the blade along the rib cage, but not cutting the bones. Cut along the backbone; then advance the knife through the whole fish (cutting above the bones).

3. Now, beginning at the head, move your blade toward the tail, separating the first fillet.

4. Turn the fish and make a cut at the back of the head, as on the first side (Step 1). Make the same cuts on this side as you did on the first, but reverse the order.

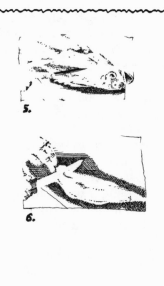

5.

6.

5. *Move the knife from head to tail along the rib cage, then cut toward the head, separating the second fillet.*

6. *Place the fillet skin side down. To skin the fillet, make a small cut about one inch into the tail section. This first cut gives you something to hold on to as you skin the fish. Turn the knife away from yourself and move it along the skin, keeping the blade turned to the skin at a thirty-degree angle.*

whole fish should not be separated from the bone. Give the skin a gentle poke; it should be firm, not soft, and your finger should not leave a dent. The gills should be red and free from slime. The eyes of a fresh fish are bright, shiny, and full. (Eyes are a good indicator of freshness because they are the first thing to go as a fish ages; they turn cloudy and hollow-looking.) Smell is important in both fresh and frozen fish. A fresh, mild smell is what you are looking for. If there is a strong, fishy odor, the fish is old. Inside the body cavity, the fish should show no discoloration. This is always something to check for in salmon. They, especially, need to be gutted quickly; if they are not, the flesh will discolor and, when eaten, will have a bad taste.

If you are buying steaks or fillets, the cuts should look fresn, with no sign of browning or drying around the edges, and the meat should have a firm texture. The same odor requirements apply as for whole fish. Some fish, most often halibut, large salmon, and sablefish, are sold in chunks (sometimes called roasts). These also should be freshly cut and have a good smell.

Frozen fish, if handled properly, can be very good. In the Market, sometimes the fish will still be frozen solid, sometimes it will be nearly or completely thawed. Be aware that a fish that has been frozen and thawed must be used immediately. If it is refrozen, a lot of moisture and flavor will be lost. Buy a "thawed out" fish only if you are planning to have it the same night. If the fish is frozen solid, you may take it home and keep it in your freezer until you are ready to use it.

As with fresh fish, check frozen fish for good smell. You cannot tell anything by looking at the eyes after freezing, because they will always be dull, lifeless, and sunken.

Shellfish deteriorates rapidly and should be chosen with great care. Mussels, oysters, and most clams (exceptions: geoducks and razors) should have tightly closed shells. If the shells are open, the clams should respond to a slight touch by snapping shut. If the shells remain open, the clams are dead and should be discarded. The large geoduck should react to a gentle poke and, as with fish, have no strong odor.

Crab meat should be firm and fresh looking, it gets mushy when it is old. A live crab should be active when picked up; a cooked whole crab should have been cooked within the last day or so. (You'll have to ask.)

If you have questions, ask your fishmonger. He should be able to tell you just how fresh a fish or shellfish is, when it came in, and whether or not he recommends it.

What cut of fish you buy depends on the number of people you are serving and the recipe you are using. A whole fish is usually the best buy *per pound,* but consider also the best buy *per serving.* A salmon has a lot of meat on it and very little waste, so the whole fish, if you have enough people to eat it, will always be your best buy. If your recipe calls for a fillet, buy the whole fish and have your fishmonger fillet it for you; keep the head and skeleton for stock. Salmon steaks and fillets are economical for one or two persons, but they really are not worth the price when feeding a crowd.

Other fish, especially rockfish and flounder, have a lot of waste, a lot of bones. Fillets of sole may seem much more expensive than the whole sole, but remember that only about 35 percent of the sole is retained after filleting. The rest is head, tail, and skeleton. Unless you are planning to steam or bake the fish whole, fillets are often the better buy.

## Guide to the Fish Markets

There are close to one hundred different species and varieties of seafood in the Market fish markets throughout the year. Many are local, some are flown in; most are available fresh, some are always frozen. There are five species of salmon that come to the Market under no fewer than ten different names, there are literally dozens of rockfish varieties, and there are the unfamiliar species, the talapia and gaspergoo.

To add to the confusion, there is the practice of labeling a particular local fish with the name of another from a different region. The hake at the fish markets is not the hake you bought on the Costa Brava, two kilos for fifteen cents. The red snapper here is a Pacific rockfish, not the delicate and very expensive Gulf fish. And the Dover sole at the fish markets is a local flounder, not the true Dover or Channel sole from England.

This guide covers just about everything you'll ever find in the Market fishstalls, from abalone to walleye pollock. The descriptions are brief, with added notes on seasons, origin and availability. The guide is meant to help you shop for fish knowledgeably and enjoy more variety.

## ABALONE

This is a marine mollusk with an ear-shaped shell and a pearly interior. There are two species of abalone in Washington: the northern (or Pinto) and the California red. Sport harvesting of northern abalone is allowed, but neither species may be commercially harvested in Washington. Abalone in the fish markets is from California, Mexico, or British Columbia and is frozen. It is fairly expensive and not often available.

## ALBACORE

This marine fish, found from southeastern Alaska to lower California, is relatively fat and has the white meat of the tuna family. It is one of the smallest of the tunas and the only one found locally. Taken in Washington by the coastal troll fishery, albacore average nine to twenty-five pounds. The catch is taken from July through October and is available fresh during those months.

## ANCHOVY

The northern anchovy is found from Baja California to Queen Charlotte Sound. The population in Washington is fairly small. Its principal use is as bait for the albacore fishery.

## BASS

You will see signs for black sea bass, striped bass, and sea bass in the fish markets. None is really a member of the bass family; they are rockfish.

## BLACK COD. See Sablefish.

## BONITO

One of the tunas, but not local. This fish is related to the mackerel and at times is available fresh from California.

## BOTTOM FISH

Exactly what you would expect, these are all fish that live on the bottom of the sea. The group includes all cods, greenlings, sablefishes, lingcods, rockfishes, soles, and flounders.

## BUFFALOFISH

This is a North American fresh-water fish, similar to carp, but distinguished by a humped back. A very popular fish in the Midwest, it is caught in the Mississippi River and flown here fresh from Wisconsin almost every week of the year.

## CARP

A large, fresh-water fish bred in lakes and ponds, carp can weigh up to sixty pounds. It is not available here often and is almost always frozen when it is.

## CATFISH

This fresh-water fish, abundant in the Midwest and South, is sometimes available here fresh, skinned and dressed, from lakes in Idaho and Montana.

## CLAMS

There are many clam varieties in Washington. Listed here are only commercially important ones you will find in the fish markets.

### Pacific Razor Clams

Dug on ocean beaches, razors are exceptionally meaty. They are long, narrow soft-shell clams. Razors are best in the winter months and are sold live in the shell or fresh and shucked, in jars.

### Butter Clams

These hard-shell clams have fan-shaped, gray-white shells. Found on sand-gravel beaches, a large portion of the commercial catch is canned. They are available most of the year but are especially good in winter. At the Market, they are sold live in the shell and, sometimes, fresh and shucked, in jars.

### Geoducks

The king of local clams, geoducks are hard-shell clams that average six inches in shell width and weigh better than two pounds. They make good chowder and are available on and off throughout the year, live.

### Native Littlenecks

These medium-size, oval-shaped clams are very important commercially. Their color is cream or gray; the shells close tightly. They are best steamed open and dipped in butter.

### COD

Members of the true cod family in Washington waters include hake, pollock, tomcod, and Pacific (often called true) cod. Pacific cod is the only one marketed extensively; the others are occasionally available but not as popular. Sablefish (black cod), rockfish, greenling, and lingcod are *not* cods. See each name for further information.

### CRABS

The only crab of commercial value in Washington is the Dungeness. The red (or rock) crab is another good local species, but it is not as abundant and does not have a lot of meat. Other species available at the fish markets include the Alaskan king crab and the snow crab.

### Dungeness

This is a large, hard-shell crab, measuring up to ten inches across the back and weighing from one and one-half to three and one-half pounds. This crab is best in the winter months when it is fresh. From October to December the smaller, Puget Sound crabs are in, and from December until March you find larger, ocean-caught crabs.

### Alaskan King

These giants are found in very cold waters. Most of the catch is taken in the winter and early spring when the crabs move to shallower water to spawn. King leg pieces are sold frozen year-round. Most of the body meat is canned.

### Snow

Snow-crab harvesting is a new industry compared to other crab fisheries; it began on a large scale only in the late sixties. The snow is a member of the spider crab family, so-called because its legs are long and spindly and its body round. In the Market, the meat is sold frozen. It is, frankly, an ugly crab and does not market well whole. It is also a very tedious job to free the meat from the shell.

### CRAWFISH (or crayfish)

The crawfish found in the inland waters of Washington are considered delectable. They reach about six inches in length. They are not often available, the catch being dependent on warm-water temperatures. Cook them as you do crabs, and eat them dipped in butter or mayonnaise.

### FINNAN HADDIE

This is haddock that has been smoked and salted. The name is Scottish, after the fish and a town, Findon. Finnan haddie is imported and available most of the year.

### FLATFISH

Flatfish, or "sole," is distinguished by its flat body shape and the position of its eyes—both on the same side of the head. None of the sole landed in Washington is true sole, but belongs to the flounder family. Principal species here are halibut, petrale, English, and Dover sole. Also available are starry flounder, rock sole, turbot, and sand sole. See also Sole.

### FLOUNDER

The three types of flounder found locally are halibut, sand dabs (family Bothidae), and our local sole (family Pleuronectidae). All flounder is rather lean fish.

**GASPERGOO.** See Sheepshead.

## GREENLING

This is the common name for a number of fish, including lingcod, belonging to the family Hexagrammidae of the North Pacific. They are *not* cods. The tomcod, a true cod, is sometimes called a greenling because of its green color. Greenling is not commercially fished.

## HAKE

Hake is a member of the true cod family. It is abundant in our coastal waters. Its soft flesh and poor keeping quality have limited its use as food in the past. Its future use will likely be as fish meal.

## HALIBUT

Halibut is a large flatfish belonging to the flounder family. A good eating fish and very important commercially, halibut is best in the summer months when it is available fresh in the Market. Then, it is usually sold in chunks, steaks, or cheek pieces; it is available frozen much of the rest of the year.

## HERRING

Pacific herring is common in Puget Sound, and an average of five hundred tons is taken annually from there for use as bait. It is sometimes available fresh but is more commonly found frozen, salted, or pickled. In addition to local herring, much is sold from Iceland, Holland, Norway, and Sweden.

## LINGCOD (or cultus cod)

The lingcod may be among the ugliest of fish, but it is also one of the best eating fishes our waters produce. Like other bottom fish, it is available most of the year but is best in winter.

## LOBSTER

There are two kinds: Maine lobster (with the big claws), available frozen most of the time and live some of the time; and Pacific lobster, from the warm, southern waters of Mexico, Peru, and Australia. Both are very good, very rich, and not cheap—ever.

## LUTEFISK

This is codfish which is dried for storage, then soaked in lye and rinsed before using. It is available dried, fresh (already "luted out"), and frozen during the Thanksgiving—Christmas season. The best is imported from Norway and Iceland.

## MACKEREL

This marine fish is not regularly available. When it is, it is from Atlantic waters and is sold whole, usually frozen.

## MULLET

Mullet is a tropical and temperate coastal water fish and sometimes is available frozen whole from Florida and California.

## MUSSELS

Two kinds are found in Washington waters: the abundant bay or blue mussel, and the California mussel. Similar to clams in flavor, mussels are available in winter and early spring. The bay mussel is commercially grown in sheltered inlets of Puget Sound and is best in the winter months. Wild mussels are not sold commercially; they are usually covered with barnacles and are not as tender as cultivated mussels. Some cultivated mussels from Oregon are available.

## OCTOPUS

Puget Sound is the home of the largest species of octopus in the world, the Giant Pacific, as well as a few others. Octopus is available fresh, on and off, through the year, because most of it is an incidental catch of the crab and bottom-fish industries. Its taste is similar to shrimp. Octopus is also sold frozen, dried, and smoked.

## OYSTERS

Washington is the leading producer of oysters on the Pacific Coast. The Pacific oyster is most abundant although it is not native but was imported from Japan at the turn of the century. The native oyster is the western, or Olympia; very small, very rare, very expensive, but worth it. Fall and winter are the best times for oysters. They are sold live in the shell or fresh, already shucked, in jars.

## PACIFIC COD

Abundant from Oregon to Alaska, this true cod is the most important commercial species of bottom fish. Although available fresh or frozen most of the year, usually as fillets, this fish is especially good in the spring and fall. There aren't many in summer months when fishermen are looking for salmon.

## PACIFIC OCEAN PERCH

A rockfish, small (always under three pounds), this fish inhabits deep water and is not a true perch. It is sometimes erroneously referred to as rosefish, another rockfish. It has red-colored flesh and is usually labeled rockfish in the Market.

**PERCH.** See Sea perch.

## POLLOCK

This tropical- or temperate-zone marine fish of the Atlantic is sometimes available frozen. See also Walleye Pollock.

## POMPANO

This warm-water fish, found in the Gulf of Mexico and all along the coast of Florida, is small and fatty—available, infrequently, frozen whole.

**PRAWNS.** See Shrimp.

## RED SNAPPER

Probably the most inaccurately named fish in our markets is the red snapper; it is really a rockfish, not the red snapper of the Gulf of Mexico. The body is reddish orange. It is one of the most sought-after of the rockfish, sold fresh, whole or filleted, most of the year. No East Coast snapper is ever available here.

## ROCKFISH

Rockfishes belong to the group of fish called Scorpaenids. Thirty-three species have been recorded in Washington. The body shape of all rockfish is similar, but color can differ dramatically. Rockfishes include Pacific Ocean perch, rosefish, red snapper, canary, and black- and yellowtail rockfish. Rockfishes are often called sea bass, black sea bass, and rock cod. See Perch and Red Snapper.

## SABLEFISH

Also known as black cod, this is an excellent eating fish, rather fatty, sold fresh or frozen as fillets and steaks. The fish attain lengths of more than three feet and average eight pounds. Sablefish is available most of the year.

## SALMON

This anadromous fish is, commercially, the most important in our state. There are five species.

### Chinook or King

The salmon season begins the first of May when this, the largest salmon, begins to run the rivers. Chinook average twenty pounds. Flesh varies from deep red to light pink. Other nicknames given chinook are spring, tyee, and blackmouth.

### Sockeye or Red

The sockeye season begins the first of July. Fish average three to five pounds and have deep red flesh.

### Pink or Humpy

The pinks, smallest of the salmon species, average five to six pounds, have paler flesh than king or sockeye, and begin running Washington rivers in late summer, odd-numbered years only.

### Coho or Silver

These fish average six to twelve pounds and have salmon-colored flesh, though not as deep as the sockeye. They migrate to rivers mostly in September and October.

### Chum or Keta

These begin running in late September. They average ten pounds, have a light-colored flesh, and are not as oily as other salmon species. They are also called fall or dog salmon.

## SARDINES

Any small herring or other marine fish that gets packed in oil gets called a sardine. They are almost always canned. There is no such thing as fresh sardines in the fish markets.

## SCALLOPS

There is such a thing as a local scallop, and you will occasionally find it in the fish markets. There are not sufficient concentrations to make commercial harvest feasible. Two varieties are available year-round, frozen only (they are too perishable to travel fresh), both from the East Coast. The bay scallop is the smallest, and usually preferred. The meat is only about half an inch across. Sea or ocean scallops are larger and are taken from deeper waters in Nova Scotia and south to the middle Atlantic states. The meat is about two inches across.

## SCAMPI

These large shrimps, not among the local species, are often flown in frozen.

## SCROD

A scrod is a young cod or haddock.

## SEA BASS

This name is given to rockfish at the Market; it is *not* a member of the bass family.

## SEA PERCH

A common shallow-water fish found around wharves, kelp beds, and beaches of Puget Sound and of the coast, perch has a compressed body and a silver color. There is a small, commercial, beach-seine fishery in Puget Sound, and the fish is often available fresh in the Market between September and April. It is not related to the Pacific Ocean perch, which is a rockfish.

## SHAD

Shad is related to the herring but is different in that it swims upstream to spawn in fresh water. Abundant along the Pacific coast, it may weigh up to five pounds and is in season from winter through spring.

## SHEEPSHEAD

Often called gaspergoo, this is a fresh-water fish caught in the Mississippi River and shipped here fresh each week. It is sold whole.

## SHRIMPS

There are more nonlocal than local shrimps in our markets, even though we have many local varieties. Louisiana, Gulf, Alaska, tiger, Greenland, and Hawaiian blue shrimps are available most of the year, always frozen. Spot, coon, and side-stripe shrimps are all local and are often considered prawns. The small pink shrimps are what you see the most of, and they are usually available fresh.

## SKATE

This is a flat marine fish, a relative of the shark, with a cartilaginous skeleton. The wings are the only part of the fish that is eaten, and they are marketed by themselves. The flesh is very gelatinous, but the flavor is delicate and makes good eating. Skate is available off and on, especially in winter, and comes from upper Puget Sound. It is not deliberately sought, but is an incidental catch, brought in along with bottomfish.

### Skate Wings

*Skate wings are a bit of an oddity to most of us, but are worth getting to know. They are economical and easy to prepare. The wings have a tough skin and solid skeleton which makes them easy to fillet or skin (you can also buy them already skinned).*

*Skate is excellent broiled with butter and lemon, or it may be sautéed. The flesh is delicate, sweet, and very tender; the flavor is reminiscent of scallops. The cartilage should be cut from the wings before they are cooked and, if you're sautéing, remove the skin as well.*

4 tablespoons butter
1 clove garlic, minced
salt and pepper to taste
dry white wine

fresh lemon juice
1-1/2 pounds fresh skate
  wing, or 1 pound fillet

*In a skillet, melt the butter. Add garlic, salt, and a generous sprinkling freshly ground pepper, a dash of wine, and a squeeze of lemon juice (easy on the lemon). Add skate wings and simmer until just done; be very careful not to overcook. Serves 2.*

## SMELT

These small, silver fish average seven to eight inches. There are two major species in Washington: the Columbia River smelt and the surf smelt. Columbias run from Christmas through March; most surf smelt run between May and September. They are quite oily fish.

## SOLE

None of the sole that you see in the Market is true sole — there is no genuine sole in American waters. Our sole is really flounder. In Washington, the principal sole species are called petrale, English, and Dover. Occasionally, you will also see rock sole, starry flounder, and sand sole. All are fairly lean fish.

## SQUID

Often called inkfish, squid belong to the highest order of mollusks. Rather than external shells similar to most other mollusks, squid have internal shells. They are abundant in Puget Sound, and those in the fish markets that are ten to twelve inches long come from here. The smaller squid, four to five inches long, come mostly from California. The local squid are always fresh, the California always frozen.

**STEELHEAD.** See Trout.

## STURGEON

Sturgeon is both a fresh-water and marine fish. It was plentiful on the West Coast at one time but is much rarer now. The Columbia River is home to some of the best, but it is not often available. The fish is available, on and off, throughout the year, fresh.

## SWORDFISH

This is a large game fish caught off the Atlantic coast. It is said to be in Pacific waters as well, but none is available commercially. Frozen swordfish from the East Coast is available periodically, occasionally fresh from Florida.

## TALAPIA MOZAMBIQUE

Native to Africa, this is a fresh-water fish that looks something like a big, black goldfish. It is raised in warm-water ponds in many parts of the world because it is fast-growing and very high in protein. It grows to about ten inches in length, weighing less than a pound, and is sometimes available frozen whole from a farm in Idaho.

## TROUT

This beautiful wild fish has been domesticated and transplanted to almost every corner of the country. Because it is extensively farmed, it is readily available most of the year, frozen if not fresh. The salmon trout you see on occasion is an immature silver salmon. The silver trout, or kokanee, is a landlocked sockeye salmon, about the size of a rainbow.

A rainbow trout is identified by a broad, reddish band along each side. Rainbow sometimes migrate to the ocean, where they spend several years of their lives. When they return to their stream to spawn, they have acquired a grayish tinge from the salt and are called steelhead. Steelhead are available mostly in the late fall and winter months.

**TUNA.** See Albacore or Bonito.

## TURBOT

Turbot is a European flatfish. There is also an Atlantic turbot, caught on the East Coast, and available here, sometimes fresh and sometimes frozen. It is similar to halibut, but smaller.

## WALLEYE POLLOCK

Sometimes called whiting or big eye (it has tremendous beady eyes), this fish is abundant in Puget Sound but not often available commercially. It has a good flavor, but the soft flesh does not keep well. The walleye is not the same as the Atlantic whiting.

## Smoked Fish

*Smoked fish, especially salmon, is one of the extraordinary things at the fish markets. There are many kinds of smoked fish, and some differ greatly from others. Smoking is like any other preserving process, and the better the fish you start with the better your smoked product will be.*

The really good smoked salmon are rich, oily chinook.

Not all smoked salmon is the same because there are several smoking methods. In the Market fish markets, you will find salmon kippered, smoked, hard-smoked, and made into lox and squaw candy.

Kippered salmon is usually the least expensive. It is a hot-smoked salmon that often has artificial color added. It has a dry, almost crumbly texture. Hot-smoking is a process by which the fish is cooked and smoked at the same time. Columbia River white chinook salmon are used most often for kippering. Kippered salmon is sold in chunks and is delicious with sweet onions and bread or made into a spread with mayonnaise, hard-cooked eggs, and onions.

Smoked and hard-smoked salmon can differ greatly. Some are cured with brown sugar before smoking. Some are chinook and some are chum. The better the fish used, the higher the price usually is. The length of time the fish is smoked determines the "hardness." A very hard-smoked salmon may be smoked for several weeks. The harder the smoke, generally, the better the fish will keep.

Squaw candy is a hard-smoked salmon cut in long, narrow strips. It makes a great snack if you have a grumbling stomach while making your way through the Market. It stores quite well.

Cold-smoking is a method which imparts the smoke flavor to the fish without cooking it. The fire that produces the smoke is usually in a chamber separate from the fish and the smoke passes through a passageway to the fish, which is kept at temperatures lower than 90° F. Cold-smoked fish are usually quite perishable.

Lox is a cold-smoked salmon that is usually soaked in a salt brine and rinsed before processing. Various methods for making lox originated in Norway, Sweden, Germany, and Nova Scotia. Lox is served thinly sliced on bread or bagels and also as an appetizer. It is the most expensive of the smoked salmon.

Canadian-smoked black cod appears in the Market off and on. This is a cold-smoked fish, quite different from other smoked fish. It has not been sufficiently salt-cured *or cooked to be eaten. It must be cooked before eating, and cannot be stored long.*

*Other species of fish are smoked and kippered, too. In late winter, there are smoked Columbia River smelt. These small fish take a lot of smoke for their size and turn out to be very flavorful. The entire fish is edible because the smoking process makes the bones friable.*

*Black cod makes an incredibly moist and flavorful kippered product, not at all dry like so much kippered salmon. It is excellent with black bread and butter. (Do not confuse it with the Canadian smoked black cod; kippered needs no cooking.)*

## Seafood Deserving Special Attention

Of all the varieties of seafood found at the Market, some deserve more attention than others. They are important because they are unique to the Northwest, or because they are abundant, or because they are always available at the fish markets. Some, like oysters, steelhead, and Dungeness crabs, are important simply because they are so good.

The remainder of this chapter is devoted to a few fish and shellfish that people in the Pacific Northwest should know well. Some, like salmon, are already familiar. Others, like octopus and smelt, deserve more attention. They all come from local waters and have a place in the developing cuisine of the Northwest.

### SALMON

There are five species of Pacific salmon available in Northwest waters, and it can be difficult to know which is which. All of them have several common names, and a consumer who doesn't know all the names can be baffled. It is worthwhile to learn the different species and their names, because salmon are not all alike, and some are better than others. Quality is usually reflected in price, but not always. Price is also based on availability (sometimes the cheapest salmon is a bargain, sometimes it is of inferior quality) and on flesh color.

Chinook salmon, the largest of all the salmon, average twenty to twenty-five pounds when mature (three to five years).

Chinook are also known as king, tyee, spring, or blackmouth, depending largely on when they hit the market.

The spring run of chinook begins about the first of May. They are usually the first salmon to come to the Market. A versatile fish, the chinook is rich in oil, has flesh that breaks into large flakes, and ranges in color from deep red to almost white. The white chinook salmon from the Columbia River is one of the most prized and generally commands a high price. With this exception, salmon prices tend to increase with the deepness of flesh color, and many people assume that darker flesh tastes better. It is simply not the case, and if you are willing to sacrifice color, you may get a better fish buy.

The Northwest's most important chinook-producing river is the Columbia, on Washington's southern border. Large numbers of gill-netters and Indian dip-net fishermen operate up the Columbia, and there is an extensive troll fishery on the ocean beyond the mouth of the river. The troll-caught salmon are sold fresh; most of those caught upriver are canned. Sometimes you will see both in the Market, and you will note the significantly higher price on the troll-caught fish. The reason is simple. As salmon begin their trip upriver to spawn, they quit feeding and direct all their energies to the upstream battle, living off fats accumulated in their bodies. Salmon caught upriver tend to be less oily than those still in the ocean, and the flesh is drier when cooked. They also suffer from being caught in the nets. They are packed in like sardines, their flesh is damaged, and they are not usually dressed and put on ice as quickly as troll-caught salmon are.

Troll-caught salmon are individually captured on hooks, pulled aboard the boat, and dressed. This method is not as cost-effective as gill-netting or purse-seining, but the fish are handled better, the product is superior, and the price is consequently higher.

Although chinook are the first salmon to run the rivers in the spring, they are also among the last going upstream. There is an early fall run, and often fresh chinook will be available as late as November or December.

Sockeye, or red, salmon spawn in the lakes and the streams that feed them; the young spend their first year there before migrating to the sea. Some sockeye are landlocked in the lakes. They are known as kokanee, or silver trout, and they weigh only one pound when mature. Kokanee make good pan-fried breakfasts for hikers and fishermen.

Sockeye run the rivers in summer, beginning in June. They average about two feet in length and five to seven pounds. The Columbia River sockeye is usually smaller, about three to four pounds. Sockeye have very red flesh that is rich, oil, and delicious. It is the best of the canned salmons.

Pink salmon, more colorfully known as humpback or humpies, are the smallest of the five species. They are also the most abundant. Pink mature at two years and average five to six pounds when they return to the rivers in the late summer and early fall. The pink is a northern species, rarely found as far south as the Columbia, but common in waters off British Columbia and Alaska. In Washington waters, pink are caught almost exclusively in odd-numbered years. Pink have paler flesh than chinook or sockeye and usually carry a lower pricetag.

Coho salmon, known most commonly as silvers, are very popular with sport fishermen and are fished extensively in Puget Sound. Coho have a deep, salmon-colored flesh and average eight to ten pounds when mature, usually at about three years. The young coho remain in spawning streams a year or so before migrating to salt water, and they never travel the long distances that chinook and sockeye do. Some Puget Sound coho remain in the Sound, never migrating to the ocean. These grow more slowly and are often caught in the three- to five-pound range. They are excellent for barbecuing.

The coho spawning migration is in the fall, usually September and October, but often extends into December. The size of the coho taken in Puget Sound increases in the fall as the "hooknose" coho arrive from the ocean.

Sometimes you will see jack salmon in the Market. These usually are coho (though sometimes they are chinook or sockeye) that mature early and return to their streams to spawn at the age of two rather than three. They are small (often only one or two pounds) because of the short time they spent in the ocean (where salmon attain most of their size). Jack (or jill if it is female) salmon is usually a good buy, largely because consumers, unaware of what it is, don't want it. It is as flavorful as its older and larger relatives and a good size for two people.

Chum salmon are the last to run the rivers in the fall, arriving in the Market chiefly in late October, November, and December. Chum are usually called fall salmon at the fish markets. It sounds more appetizing than its other name—dog salmon. (Back in the days when salmon were more abundant, Northwest Coast Indians used this lowly species as dog food.) Its other names include keta and calico.

Chum mature at four years, averaging three feet in length and weighing about ten to twelve pounds. They are not as oily as other species and are usually the least expensive. Most chum are not sold fresh but are canned.

Salmon are the most highly prized (and commercially important) fish in the Northwest. During the summer months, especially, life in the fish markets seems to revolve entirely around them. They are magnificent fish, and while they are not unique to our area, we have a far greater abundance than most other places.

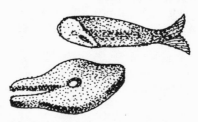

There is such a thing as an Atlantic salmon. The chief difference is that, unlike the Pacific, the Atlantic spawn many times. Pacific salmons are anadromous, that is they begin and end their lives in fresh water, migrating in between to salt water to feed. Most of their lives are spent in the ocean, and when they mature, they travel back to their streams of origin to spawn. For some it is a short distance; others travel as far as 2,000 miles. Wasted by the tremendous battle upstream, salmon die after spawning, and several months later new generations hatch in the streams' gravel bottoms. Streams must have clean, well-oxygenated, cool water for salmon to survive, one of the reasons that pollution of streams and rivers so quickly and devastatingly affects the fish.

One of the five species of salmon is available fresh from May until November, and there are always frozen salmon available. A really fresh salmon is a treat worth waiting for, but a properly frozen salmon may be of high quality, too. If the fish is just in the day you buy it, and if you take it directly home and eat it, it should be unbeatable. But a "fresh" salmon that's been in the fish market a few days and goes home to spend twenty-four hours in your refrigerator is *not* going to be as good as a fish that was gutted on the boat, flash-frozen, and not thawed until you are ready to use it.

When you purchase fresh salmon, look for the qualities you do on all fresh fish—bright eyes, firm flesh, no slimy skin—and also check the belly cavity. Salmon should be gutted quickly after they are caught, and if it has been properly done, you should see a clean-looking cavity with no discoloration.

Salmon is an incredibly versatile fish. It is sold in many forms —whole, steaks, fillets, canned, pickled, smoked, salted—and prepared by many methods (baked, boiled, poached, sautéed, grilled, broiled). Most people have a good idea of how they prefer their salmon. The best advice is to do as little as possible with the fish. A salmon does not need to be "dressed up." There's no excuse for smothering a fresh salmon in a heavy sauce; its own special flavor is enough. Whatever you do, do it lightly.

Dill combines well with salmon and conveniently shares most of its season. You will find it fresh on the farmers' tables from mid-July through September.

---

## Gravlax

This recipe for gravlax is of Scandinavian origin. It is a delicately salted salmon served cold with a light dill sauce and is a perfect choice for a summer picnic.

| | |
|---|---|
| 1/2 cup coarse salt | 1 tablespoon dill seed |
| 1/2 cup sugar | 1 large bunch fresh dill or 3 |
| 2 tablespoons peppercorns, | tablespoons dried dillweed |
| crushed | 3 pounds salmon |

Mix all the seasonings together. Cut the fish in half along the backbone. Lay half in a heavy baking dish, skinside down, and rub half the salt mixture into the flesh. Spread the remainder of the seasoning mixture over the other half, and lay it, skinside up, on top of the first. Now, find something to put on top of the fish to weigh it down (do not use books for this job!). A sackful of small rocks would work fine. Cover the pan with plasticwrap and refrigerate for two days. During that period, you should take it out two or three times and turn the fish. Don't do anything else, just turn it. You will notice liquid accumulating in the bottom of the pan. It is essential: do not throw it out.

When the two days are up, remove the fish from the pan and dry it with paper towels. The fish should be sliced very thin for serving. If you want to be authentic, you have a couple of choices now. You can make smörbröd (open-face sandwiches), or you can serve it with mounds of boiled potatoes. Either way, serve the fish with the mustard and dill sauce that follows.

## Mustard and Dill Sauce

1/4 cup Dijon mustard (or 2
   teaspoons dry mustard)
2 tablespoons sugar
1/4 cup vegetable oil
2 teaspoons vinegar

1/2 teaspoon salt
1/2 teaspoon pepper
1/3 cup freshly chopped dill (or 3
   tablespoons dried dillweed)

Put mustard and sugar in a small bowl. Slowly add oil while blending with an electric mixer. When sauce is thickened, add vinegar, salt, and pepper. Stir in dill. Refrigerate a good 12 hours and check seasoning before serving. Makes about 1/2 cup.

## Pescado Cocho con Juevo y Lemon

This recipe comes from Jack and Esther Levy (City Fish). It is delicious warm or cold, ideal for lovely outdoor meals, as a lunch or light supper, or a first course for dinner. Esther serves it with sliced tomatoes, cucumbers, olives, green onions, and lots of French bread to dip in the sauce. Start with a good quality white fish. White king fillets are Jack Levy's recommendation, although any good, firm, white fish may be used.

1 tablespoon chopped parsley
olive oil
1 tablespoon flour
juice of 1-1/2 lemons

3/4 cup water, salted
2 fillets, approximately 1-1/2
   pounds
2 eggs

Sauté parsley in olive oil for just a minute. Add flour and mix well. Add the lemon juice and the salted water. Bring liquid to a boil, add the fish, cover, and cook until just done, about 10 minutes. While the fish is cooking, beat eggs with a fork. Remove fish from heat and slowly add the fish liquid to the eggs, mixing constantly, until you have a very thin liquid. Pour the liquid back into the pan with the fish and shake to mix. Don't stir; shake gently. Serve immediately, or cool first and serve chilled. Serves 3.

## Manzo-Style Fish

*This method of baking either salmon or white fish comes from Dan Manzo, Market high-staller. The fish is covered with a thick layer of vegetables and baked in tightly closed foil (really steamed). Good straight from the oven, it is even better the next day, served cold.*

*Buy a whole fish and have your fishmonger book-fillet it, leaving in the backbone. (To book fillet means to cut the fish in such a way that the fish opens like a book on both sides of the spine.) The combination of the backbone and wine makes an amber gelatin that sets when refrigerated and tastes sensational. Serve the fish and gelatin with fresh mayonnaise. Superb.*

*To prepare the fish, mix together chopped celery tops, chopped onion, minced garlic, chopped green and red peppers, parsley, and a jalapeña pepper. How much of each ingredient depends on the size of your fish; you want to put a one-half inch covering on it. Lay your fish on a large piece of foil in a baking pan. Cover with the chopped vegetables. Squeeze the juice of one lemon over the top and sprinkle with a tablespoon each of dillweed and sweet basil. Top with one-half cup white wine. Seal the foil tightly. Bake at 375.°*

## BOTTOM FISH

As winter approaches, the flow of fresh salmon to the Market slows. This is the time to discover bottom fish. With the exception of halibut, bottom fish are best and available in the largest quantities in the fall and winter.

There are thirty-three species of rockfish alone in Washington waters, and an abundance of sole and flounder. Still, many of us speak of fish (and prepare it) as if salmon were the only fish around. Here is your chance to learn to shop the other half of the fish markets.

Let's begin with cod. A cod is a cod is a cod, right? Wrong. The practice of attaching cod to the common names of many fish baffles most consumers. A good rule of thumb is that 75 percent of fish with cod in the name is probably not cod. Some greenlings are marketed under the name tomcod, but they are not true toms. The only true members of the cod family available locally are Pacific (or true) cod, hake, walleye pollock, and tomcod. The last three are rarely found in fish markets. Hake have soft flesh and keep poorly. Pollock have much the same problem. Tomcod are good eating, but they are small and are thrown back by most fishermen. If you find cod in the fish markets, it will be Pacific cod, a close relative of the Atlantic cod. Lingcod, black cod, and rock cod are not cods. Which is not to say they aren't good, they just aren't cod.

True cod has lean, soft, white meat with a mild flavor. It is marketed whole or filleted, fresh or frozen, and salted. The whole fish can be very large, as long as three feet, and varies in color from brown to gray.

Cod, like most other bottom fish, is caught almost exclusively by otter trawls. These are large, bag-shaped nets that are dragged along the sea bottom. Fish enter through a large opening at the front and are forced to the back by the movement of the net; there they are trapped in the narrow closed end.

Lingcod is a favorite bottom fish among Northwest fish enthusiasts. It is one of the finest eating fish of the West Coast, but you wouldn't know it to look at it. The lingcod has a long slender body, a large protruding mouth filled with great canine-like teeth, double nostrils, and long deeply notched dorsal fins. A rather mottled dark-brown color with green accents adds to the ugliness of the face. But don't worry; you can buy a fillet and avoid looking at it.

Lingcod is prolific, probably due to its voracious nature, which makes it unpopular with smaller fish. Lingcod can be quite large—the females can grow to five feet—and, although they average only from five to twenty pounds, forty-pounders are not uncommon.

The vast majority of lingcod is caught here in Washington, although it is found from California to Alaska. The fishing is best from October to May. Fresh lingcod makes a special dinner. It has a delicate white flesh with very little fat and is wonderful poached. The whole fish is good baked, poached, or, if you like, split down the middle, boned, and broiled. (If you are not adept at this, ask your fishmonger to do it.)

Sablefish, or black cod, is another favorite. It is not a cod, but a member of the skilfish family. It is caught by off-season halibut fishermen in the fall on set lines, as well as by otter trawlers on the coast. The major fishing grounds lie between Destruction

Island and Barkley Sound on Vancouver Island. It is a very valuable species to otter trawlers. A fat fish, like salmon, sablefish is very rich in flavor. It is sold fresh, chiefly as steaks and fillets, and is good broiled. From time to time you will see smoked sablefish, which is mildly smoked and needs further cooking. It has an excellent flavor.

There are so many rockfishes that it is difficult to know where to begin. Many people have never heard of them, but all have probably eaten them. They are not often marketed under the name rockfish, but as rock cod, yellowtails, sea bass, Pacific Ocean perch, black sea bass, rosefish, or red snapper.

Yes, red snapper. Easterners coming to the West are baffled by the misnomer. This fish is not the red snapper of the Gulf Coast. It is not even closely related, but natives delight in confusing newcomers.

What we call red snapper is the most highly prized of the rockfish. The body is wide and the color a beautiful orange red. And even though it is not Gulf snapper, it is good. It is often available whole and fresh in the fall and winter. As with other rockfish, steaming is a good method of cooking it. Rockfish is fairly bony and difficult for most people to fillet. Even an experienced fishmonger, who gets most of the flesh from the bones, is left with 70 percent waste, counting entrails and head. But steamed, baked, or poached whole, red snapper makes a delightful meal.

Most other rockfish are simply labeled rock cod and marketed as fillets. All rockfish have a similar appearance but are easily distinguished from other fish varieties. Available most of the year, rockfish peak in winter and are generally very good buys.

The last large part of the bottom-fish group is the flounder family. This includes, primarily, halibut, the soles, and starry flounder. These flatfishes all share an interesting body shape that distinguishes them from other fish. Each begins life looking like any other fish, but when it is just a few inches long, its skull begins to twist and one eye moves to the opposite side. At the same time, it begins to swim at a tilt—eventually turning a full ninety degrees, with its eyeless side to the bottom. As adults these fish are quite flat and they swim horizontally. Their skin is the color of the rocky or sandy sea bottom on the top side and a creamy white underneath. This ability to blend with their surroundings is their best protection against predators.

The largest of the flounders is the halibut, a very important commercial fish. The female Pacific halibut may reach a weight of five hundred pounds and live more than thirty-five years. The males are not as hardy as the females, living only twenty-five years and weighing a paltry forty pounds. Halibut mature in about ten years. As they grow, they seem to move to deeper and deeper waters, and many are found at depths of 600 fathoms (that's 3,600 feet, nearly six full Space Needles).

But no one fishes at 600 fathoms for 500-pound halibut. Halibut are caught on set lines, about two thousand feet long, laid out from ten to one hundred fifty fathoms below the surface. A set line is laid on the bottom and anchored at each end. It has a series of baited hooks on it, and lines from each end are attached to surface buoys. The lines are periodically pulled in for harvest.

Halibut is fished almost exclusively in the summer. For a special summer picnic you might order a whole fresh halibut—for a crowd.

The "soles" in our waters are not true soles, but flounders. They are named petrale, English, and Dover, but they are not the same as those fished off the English coast. There are no true sole in American waters.

The petrale, although abundant off our coast, is almost completely absent in Puget Sound. It is the most widely available of the soles and the most valuable commercially. It averages about two and one-half pounds and seventeen inches in length. It is available throughout the year, and there is an especially active winter fishery.

English sole is smaller, averaging less than a pound, and is the most common catch in Puget Sound. It is the most plentiful of the soles in the fish markets in the winter and early spring.

The Dover sole is the largest of the three and is usually most available in the summer. It lives in deeper waters than petrale and English soles and is not very common in Puget Sound.

Starry flounder is what most people catch from their boats on Puget Sound. The water is crawling with them. They are not very important commercially, but they are a good eating fish.

All of the flatfishes have delicate flavor and beautiful white, firm flesh. Many are filleted, but they are usually available whole in winter. Filleting sole—or any flatfish—is a difficult job, best left to experts. Sole is excellent stuffed, too, and you may purchase the whole fish and have it dressed.

## Steamed Fish Saigon

This recipe is from Phuong Pham Nguyen, the owner and chef at Saigon-over-Counter in the Soames Dunn Building. For this recipe, she prefers a whole fish (try red snapper). The dried mushrooms, pickled ginger, pickled onions, and fish sauce are all available at the Oriental Mart in the Corner Market Building.

*12 ounces cod, red snapper, sole,*
  *or halibut fillets*
*4 ounces onions, sliced*
*4 slices pickled ginger (you may*
  *use fresh, but use half as*
  *much and slice thinly or grate)*
*dash pepper*
*1 tablespoon soy sauce*
*1 tablespoon olive oil*

*6 dried oriental mushrooms*
*1 cup rich chicken stock*
*4 stalks green onion, cut into*
  *4-inch lengths*
*1 tomato, sliced into wedges*
*4 pickled onions, thinly sliced*
  *(you may substitute shallots)*
*1 tablespoon fish sauce*
*1 tablespoon sesame oil*

Slice fillets into strips about two fingers thick and marinate 30 minutes with onion slices, ginger, pepper, soy, and olive oil. Wash mushrooms and soak in warm water 25 minutes. Remove stems and cut in half. Cook the mushrooms 5 minutes in stock. Arrange fish in the bottom of a shallow dish. On top, in a decorative wheel pattern, arrange mushrooms, green onions, tomato, and pickled onions. Pour fish sauce and sesame oil over the top. Steam 15 minutes and serve with rice. Serves 2.

To prepare a whole fish, marinate it 15 minutes, just like the fillets. Brush the marinade on the inside cavity and both sides, making cuts in the top of the fish so the marinade will penetrate. You will have to steam a whole fish a bit longer than the fillets.

## Fish Soup

*1 medium onion, finely chopped*
*1 leek (white part only), finely*
  *chopped*
*2 tablespoons olive oil*
*7-8 small Italian plum tomatoes,*
  *skinned and chopped*
*1 clove garlic, crushed*

*2 generous slices orange peel*
*salt and freshly ground pepper to*
  *taste*
*pinch saffron*
*scant 1/4 teaspoon fennel*
*1 pound true cod, cut in pieces*

Sauté onion and leek in olive oil until tender. Add the tomatoes, garlic, orange peel, salt and pepper, saffron, and fennel.

Simmer gently, covered, for 1 hour. Add two cups water and cook for another 15 minutes or so. Remove the peel. Add fish and cook for 15 minutes or until fish is tender but not in shreds. Turn off heat and let pot sit, covered, on the stove for about 10 minutes. (Cooling a bit improves the flavor.) Serve in shallow, wide soup bowls. Serves 4.

## Broiled Sablefish

Sablefish (black cod) is overlooked by many people. It is a fairly fat fish, available most often in steaks and sometimes as fillets. It is a rich-flavored fish and is best prepared simply. Because it is fatty, broiling is a good cooking method.

2 sablefish steaks (about 1 to        pepper
  1-1/2 pounds)                        juice of 1/2 lemon
2 shallots, thinly sliced

Wash the steaks, pat them dry with paper towels, and arrange on a broiler pan. Sprinkle with shallots and pepper. Squeeze lemon juice over the top. Place under a broiler for about 10 minutes. Watch carefully and don't overcook. It is a good idea to take fish from the oven just before it is done; it continues to cook all the way to the table. Serves 2.

## Fish with Rhubarb Sauce

This is a wonderful dish for your first spring picnic, when rhubarb is in season. It is good hot, superb cold. If you are not used to sour sauces you may want to add more sugar; this is quite tart.

2 cups rhubarb cut in small        1/2 cup water
  pieces                              salt to taste
1/2 cup tomato sauce               1 pound fish (salmon, red
3 tablespoons olive oil                snapper, or sole)
2 teaspoons sugar

Wash rhubarb well. Peel off hard skin, if any. Cook all ingredients (except fish) together for about 30 minutes. When rhubarb is cooked thoroughly, add cut-up pieces of fish and simmer until fish is done.

## Codfish Cakes

Salt cod is a favorite of Carol Ludden, the *Notebook's* New England recipe expert (indeed, it was the only kind of cod available during long New Hampshire winters). At the Market you will find salt cod all year (it is one of the few foods in the Market wrapped in plastic; the wooden boxes it used to come in were attractive, but too expensive). Here are a few authentic New England recipes.

| | |
|---|---|
| 2 cups salt cod | 1 cup milk |
| 2 cups hot mashed potatoes | 1/2 teaspoon baking powder |
| 1 tablespoon butter | 1/8 teaspoon pepper |
| 1 egg | bacon |

Soak codfish in cold water for 12 hours (24 hours if exceptionally salty). Change water several times. Drain, cover with fresh water, and simmer until tender. Drain and chop cod (be sure to remove all bones). Add other ingredients, except bacon, and mix; let mixture stand overnight in refrigerator. Mold into cakes about 1/2 inch thick. Fry bacon and then fry codfish cakes in bacon fat. Serve with a fresh tomato sauce. Serves 2.

## Codfish Balls

| | |
|---|---|
| 1 cup salt cod | 1/4 cup milk |
| 3 medium potatoes, mashed | 1/8 teaspoon pepper |
| 1 tablespoon butter | 1 onion, finely chopped |
| 1 egg | |

Follow directions for the codfish-cake recipe, but form into balls instead of cakes and fry in deep fat. Serves 2.

## Codfish with Pork Scraps (or Hog's-Back-Son-of-a-Sea-Cook)

| | |
|---|---|
| 1 pound salt cod | 3 slices raw salt pork, chopped |
| 3 medium potatoes, boiled and sliced | 1 tablespoon butter |
| 1-1/2 cups tomatoes, sliced | pepper |
| 1 onion, sliced | buttered bread crumbs |

Soak codfish in cold water for 12 hours (24 hours if exceptionally salty), changing water several times. Drain and cut into small pieces. Sauté onion in butter (do not brown) and add onion to the fish. Butter a baking dish and layer fish, potatoes, tomatoes, and pork. (There should be enough for two layers.) Top with breadcrumbs and bake at 350° until top is brown (about 30 minutes). Serves 4.

## Traditional Northeast Codfish Dinner

A pound of salt cod will feed two to four persons, depending on appetites and feelings about salt fish. The best rule to follow is to purchase about one-fourth pound *less* per person than you normally do when buying fish.

*1 pound salt cod*
*1-1/2 cups white sauce*
*1 teaspoon Worcestershire sauce*

*2 eggs, hard cooked and*
*chopped*

Soak salt cod 12 hours in fresh, clear water, changing water twice. Boil fish in fresh water to cover for 20 minutes; drain. Add to white sauce the Worcestershire sauce and eggs. Serve boiled fish with boiled potatoes and the egg sauce. Traditional vegetable accompaniments are boiled beets and creamed onions. Serves 2 to 4.

## Gefilte Fish

*1 cup matzo meal*
*5 eggs*
*4 teaspoons salt*
*1-1/2 teaspoons pepper*
*1-1/2 quarts water*
*2 onions, sliced*
*4 carrots, sliced*

*2 pounds raw salmon (save*
*head and bones), ground*
*1-1/2 pounds raw white fish (save*
*head and bones), ground*
*salt and pepper to taste*
*3 large onions, ground*

Mix together the matzo meal, eggs, salt, and pepper; let stand at room temperature 1 to 2 hours. Put into a large roasting pan or stockpot the water (pot should be about one-third full), sliced onions, carrots, fish heads and bones, and a few teaspoons each of salt and pepper. Bring to a boil while you prepare the fish balls. In a large bowl, mix together the ground onions and fish. Add the matzo mixture and more water and salt, if necessary (mixture must be moist enough to hold together). When water has come to a boil, wet your hands and form the fish mixture into balls, about 2 inches in diameter. Drop the fish balls into the water and let them cook for 2-1/2 hours. Remove from heat and cool in the pan for 1 hour. Remove fish balls and strain the liquid. To save some for later use, freeze the fish balls on cookie sheets; when they are solid, transfer them to plastic freezer bags. Freeze the liquid separately. To use frozen gefilte fish, thaw broth and bring it to a boil; add thawed fish balls and simmer 30 minutes. Gefilte fish is usually served cold. Serves 8.

---

## SMELT

With so much attention given to salmon in the summer months, the smelt fishery is generally overlooked. You don't see many gourmet recipes for smelt, and you don't see restaurants advertising them as a specialty. In fact, you are lucky if you can even find them in the supermarket. This all makes little sense, because smelt are prolific in our local waters, and they are relatively cheap to buy, easy to prepare, and very good to eat.

Smelt look a little like miniature salmon, and they are, in fact, distantly related. They are small, slender, silvery fish averaging seven to eight inches in length. The name *smelt* is commonly believed to have come from the Anglo-Saxon word *smoelt*, meaning smooth and shining. But some sources say that smelt is a contraction of the words *smell* and *it*, because fresh smelt smell like freshly cut cucumbers.

There are two major species of smelt in Washington, the Columbia River and the surf. The Columbia River smelt are anadromous like salmon (they are born in fresh water, live most of their lives in salt water, and return to fresh water to spawn and die). These smelt are first seen returning to the river during Christmas week, and they continue running through March. The early ones, brought to the Market in early January, are generally the biggest and the best. They get smaller in size as the season progresses, so watch for the fresh Columbias in January.

Columbia River smelt make up the largest part of the state's smelt industry. Over 4 million pounds are caught each year, half by sport fishermen. Most of this large catch is for human consumption, although there is also a market for smelt as zoo food.

Unlike the salmon, the Columbia River smelt population is on the increase. State fisheries experts believe this is a result of the increased hake fishery off the Washington coast. Hake feed predominantly on smelt, so a decrease in the hake population is resulting in an increase in smelt.

The surf smelt (often called silvers) are not anadromous, but are salt-water fish, found mostly in Puget Sound and around La Push. The majority of them spawn in the summer months, and the Market is always full of these fresh smelt from July to September.

Although commercial fishing for smelt takes place in summer and winter, there are smelt running somewhere in Washington

every month of the year. So if you can't find fresh smelt in the Market and won't settle for frozen, you can always go out and catch your own.

Smelt-fishing is a great sport. During the spawning season, it is very easy and something the entire family can enjoy. On the calm, inland waters of Puget Sound, fishing is usually done with either a smelt rake—a rigid-frame dip net with a five-foot handle—or a smelt jig—nine hooks tied in series on a line.

The best thing about fishing for smelt is that you don't have to go out after them; they come to you. The spawning fish move into waters a few inches deep to deposit their sperm and eggs and may be scooped up in a net quite easily.

Commercial smelt-fishing is done largely with gill nets and trawlers, and commercial fishermen catch the smelt before they move into the water's edge to spawn.

Smelt are an excellent food fish and very easy on the budget. They cost less than one dollar a pound, with between ten and twelve fish in each pound. Most people can eat half a dozen smelt in a sitting; some people put away a dozen. So when buying them, keep in mind your own appetite and your own taste for fish. Three-quarters of a pound per person should be plenty. Smelt have a very delicate flavor and a pleasant oil that aids in digestion.

The standard way to cook smelt is pan-frying. Wash them, coat lightly with seasoned flour, and fry in butter. There's so little in the way of entrails in smelt that it isn't necessary to dress smelt, and lots of people don't. If you do want to clean smelt, you can pull the entrails out by the gills, to which they're attached (this is called gibbing). In any case, leave the heads and tails on. If you find you have a female with a lot of eggs, you may want to slit the belly and wash it out more thoroughly. Be careful when frying smelt. They are small and quite fragile, and they may break up when turned.

Smelt bones are so small and soft that, quite often, they may be eaten. If you prefer to avoid them, lift the head and pull back gently, moving the flesh away with your fork. The head, backbone, and tail will come out, leaving only the meat on your plate.

Smelt are delicious, but they are not particularly versatile. You can broil rather than fry them, you can use cornmeal instead of flour to coat them, or you can squeeze lime instead of lemon on them. That is about it, unless you want to start boning them and covering them with sauces. Northwest Coast Indians used to dry the oily varieties and use them as candles (the nickname, *candlefish*, remains today). Smoke-cured smelt are also popular with those who have the facilities in which to do it, and on rare occasions you will find smoked smelt in the fish markets.

## TROUT

A favorite of sport fishermen and diners alike is the trout, a beautiful fresh-water fish of the salmon family. Wild trout are native to lakes and streams that flow into the Pacific Ocean. If you are a fisherman, you will be familiar with rainbow and cutthroat, steelhead, golden and brown, and the chars (brook, Dolly Varden, lake). But if you buy your trout in the fish markets, you probably have only seen the rainbow and steelhead.

Rainbow trout get their name from a reddish streak that runs down their sides from gills to tail. The bodies are olive green on top, with dark spots and silver bellies. Rainbow have superb cream-colored flesh that is excellent eating.

Rainbow are the most valuable fresh-water fish in the Northwest. The ones you see in the fish markets are from trout farms—they are not the wild rainbow that come from mountain lakes.

Commercial rainbow-trout fishing in streams and lakes is illegal in Washington. Trout are delicate fish, very dependent upon water conditions, temperature, and food supplies. In the wild, very few live to maturity. Commercial fishing could quickly make them an endangered species. As it is, state trout hatcheries produce millions of fish each year to replenish lakes open only to game fishermen. Most of the planted fish are rainbow.

Because trout are raised commercially in ponds, they are available fresh in the fish markets most of the year. They are small fish, three-fourths to one and a half pounds, perfectly suited for a meal for one or two persons.

Rainbow trout that migrate to salt water are called steelhead. In the ocean, like salmon, trout find a plentiful supply of food that helps them attain their larger size, often as much as twenty pounds. The salt water also gives them the gray tinge that gave them their name.

Steelhead are a very popular game fish. Like salmon, steelhead run the rivers, returning to their homes in fresh water. There are both summer and winter steelhead runs, providing sport-fishing nearly year-round. In the winter, steelhead are caught in the ocean and in Puget Sound. In summer, they are found up the state's major rivers, the Columbia and the Snake.

The steelhead that come to the Market are caught by Indians and sold to wholesalers. (Aside from the Indian catch, steelhead are considered a game fish and not available to commercial fishermen.) They usually come in the late fall and winter. Most weigh about eight pounds. Like rainbow and salmon, they are flavorful, versatile fish.

---

## Pan-Fried Trout

The most favored, and unquestionably the best, way to prepare trout is pan-frying. It must be done quickly and carefully to be successful.

2 trout                         butter and oil
flour                           lemon
salt and pepper to taste

After cleaning trout (do not remove heads or tails unless you absolutely *cannot* fit the fish into your pan), coat lightly with flour and sprinkle with salt and pepper. Melt butter in frying pan (with a touch of oil to prevent burning) over medium heat. When pan is hot, add the trout and fry quickly, turning once with a large spatula. Do not overcook. Serve immediately with lemon. Serves 2, generously.

# Stuffed Trout

4 green onions (including tops), chopped
1 celery stalk, finely chopped
1/2 pound mushrooms, sliced
1 clove garlic
3 tablespoons butter
1 tablespoon olive oil, plus a bit for top of fish
salt and pepper to taste
oregano
1 tablespoon fresh parsley, chopped
1/2 cup dry white wine
2 trout, about 1 pound each
1 lemon

Sauté green onions, celery, mushrooms, and garlic in butter and olive oil. Season liberally with salt and pepper and a couple of pinches of oregano. Add parsley and about half the wine. Clean the trout, leaving the heads and tails on. Dry with paper towels. Lay the trout in a pan lined with foil. Stuff the vegetable mixture into the fish. Sprinkle the trout with more salt and pepper and oregano and the rest of the wine; squeeze the juice of 1/2 lemon over each fish and sprinkle with olive oil. Seal with more foil and bake at 400° for 15 minutes.

---

## CLAMS

Almost as if it were planned, when the local produce all but disappears after Christmas, the fish markets blossom. One of the best winter crops is clams. Bins are full of littleneck, Manila, razor, geoduck, and butter clams that provide inspiration for warm, hearty soups and chowders to stay the winter weather. In the spring, summer, and fall, the threat of red tides closes commercial clam beds along the coast and the Strait of Juan de Fuca, and only a few Puget Sound clams are harvested. But in winter the conditions are perfect for clamming, and they are abundant in the Market.

Butter clams are large, hard-shell clams. They have heavy shells marked by concentric rings of a grayish white color. Some butters have shells as large as five inches across, but most of those in the fish markets have three- to four-inch shells. Butter clams can withdraw completely into their shells, leaving only small openings at the necks; they do this when they are disturbed. Butters, like all clams, should be bought in the shell only when they are fresh and still alive. If the shells gape open and do not respond to a good poke, the clams are dead and should not be eaten.

## Steamed Littleneck Clams

*How many clams to buy depends on appetites—and whether you are serving the clams as an appetizer or a main course. For a main course, plan on twenty clams per person; for an appetizer, ten. Scrub the clams well and place in a large kettle with an inch of salted water in the bottom (substitute wine for half the water, if you prefer). Cover the kettle tightly and steam clams just until they open, about five minutes. Discard clams that do not open. Put clams in large bowls and serve immediately with melted butter. Let the broth settle, and then pour it into warm mugs, being careful not to stir up the sand and grit from the bottom.*

*If your guests do not enjoy clam nectar, don't throw it out. Save it for cooking. Some recipes (cioppino and many squid dishes, for example) call for clam juice, which is not cheap to buy.*

Butter clams live on sand-gravel beaches, usually just below the low tideline. At a very low or minus tide they can be harvested by hand. Commercial diggers harvest mechanically in shallow water, using hydraulic conveyor belts. These work from boats that have water jets to loosen the sand and gravel along the bottom, ahead of a blade that passes material onto the conveyor belts. Above, on the boat, the clams are picked off the belt by hand, and the rest of the material returns to the sea. Littleneck and Manila clams are also harvested this way.

The native littleneck clams are smaller—sometimes much smaller—than butter clams and are commonly called steamer clams. You can tell a steamer shell by the ridges radiating from its hinge and its concentric rings. The clams are a dark cream or gray color, and their shells close completely. Like butter clams, littlenecks should be purchased only when their shells close.

Available on an irregular basis year-round, littlenecks are best in winter. Unlike the butters, many of which are canned, most littlenecks are sold fresh. They are best simply steamed and served in their shells with melted butter.

The Manila clams are hard-shell clams, very similar to littlenecks, only a little flatter and longer. They are not native to

Puget Sound but were introduced by accident with oyster seed from Japan. They thrived in Puget Sound and now account for 50 percent of the crop here. They are best steamed like the littlenecks.

Both littlenecks and Manilas are popular with sport diggers. They are found in the higher tidal zones; so a minus tide is not necessary in order to dig them. They are found very close to the surface and may be dug with a small rake or shovel and hands. If you are on a good beach, you can hardly avoid getting your limit: littleneck clams don't run away as you dig.

Razor clam digging is not as easy, but it is a more engaging sport. Razors are fast movers (for clams). They have powerful diggers and smooth, lacquered shells that allow them to burrow at a rate of up to nine inches a minute in sand. A razor is spotted by the hole it leaves on the sand's surface when its neck is withdrawn after feeding. When disturbed, it quickly draws in its neck and digs deeper into the sand. If you happen to be standing over it at the moment, you may get a good squirt in the eye. Razors are defiant creatures. Because the clam won't dig deeper than a foot and does not move horizontally, you are almost assured of getting your prey eventually.

Pacific razor clams are native to our sandy ocean beaches and are often marketed under names reflecting their points of origin, such as Long Beach or Copalis. They are exceptional chowder clams and are generally a good buy; they have more meat and less shell than butter, littleneck, or Manila clams.

Razors are soft-shell clams. Their shells are thin, long, and narrow. They do not close completely. Most razors are harvested when they are about two years old and four to four and a half inches across. On Washington's coast, razors are expected to live about eight years (in Alaska, even longer), but their age comes nowhere near the massive geoduck's, which is believed to live twenty years or more.

The goeduck's average weight is about three pounds, but some clams four times that weight have been found. The geoduck is a hardshell clam with a long neck that looks something like the wrinkled, fleshy trunk of an elephant.

The name geoduck is believed to have come from the Nisqually Indians, and its meaning is unclear. So is its spelling. Some spell it gweduc, some gooey duck, others gwee duk, but geoduck is most common. Whatever the spelling, geoducks are found all along the West Coast but are most abundant in Puget Sound. The clams live from eighteen inches to six feet deep in mud, sand,

and fine gravel. Geoducks reproduce only in shallow, warmer waters close to shore. The larvae float in the water for several weeks before settling in the sand, so a young clam may land miles from where it was bred. Once situated, the geoduck never moves. It only works its long neck to the surface to gather food.

Geoduck digging is great sport, and you are doing yourself a disservice if you have not tried it. Be prepared to get very wet, dirty, and smelly having a good time. It is not uncommon to see a geoduck digger on his knees, head into a hole past his shoulders, ridiculously chasing a clam.

Commercial geoduck harvesters have a much more efficient method of getting their clams. State regulations require them to use only hand equipment and work in water deeper than ten

feet. Divers work from boats that pump water down to them in hoses. A geoduck is usually located by sighting its protruding neck. Grasping the neck in one hand, the diver directs a water jet from the hose into the soil around the clam. This dislodges the clam gently and enables the diver to capture the geoduck without damaging it. A diver can collect between three and five hundred clams a day this way.

Geoducks are available, on and off, throughout the year. Before you buy, make sure the clams are fresh. If one responds to a gentle poke, it is very fresh, but you cannot always count on a reaction from a geoduck. Your best bet is a good sniff; if it has a strong smell, don't buy it. If you have doubts, ask. Your fishmonger should be able to tell you just how fresh the clam is.

A geoduck is rather ugly, and if you are a timid, queasy sort you may be reluctant to try one. Once cleaned, it is not that bad-looking. Cleaning is simple. Drop the clam in boiling water for just a few seconds. This will kill the clam, which should have been alive, and loosen the shell. Pull the shell off, remove the stomach, and pull the skin from the neck. Don't be put off by the slightly offensive smell while cleaning. It comes from the stomach, and once the clam is clean the smell will disappear.

The body of the geoduck may be sliced thinly and sautéed quickly. It makes excellent little clam steaks. The neck is not as tender and is better used in chowder or cut for fritters. For fritters, mince the neck and mix it with crumbled bacon bits, finely chopped onion, salt, pepper, and cracker meal. Add egg to bind. Shape into patties, dip in egg and flour batter, and fry in a hot skillet until browned. Do not overcook.

Preparation of all clam dishes should be quick and easy; clams toughen and dry out when overcooked. The cooking method you use depends on the type of clam you have. Littlenecks and Manilas take well to steaming and stuffing. Razors are best sautéed or in chowder. Butters are also good sautéed, as well as stuffed and baked. There is a lot of flexibility with most clams. Only one sin. Do not fry clams. As James Beard says of fried clams, "These to clam lovers are as tank wine is to lovers of good Burgundies! Murder!"

---

## Sautéed Razor Clams

Razor clams should be cleaned just like geoducks. Drop them first into hot water to loosen the shells, then discard the entrails and skin the digger (neck). The digger is the most tender portion of the razor, but the body meat is good, too. If you have an incredible amount of them, you might sauté the necks and chop the body meat for chowder, but razors are a bit dear these days, so use the entire clam.

| | |
|---|---|
| 4 pounds razor clams | butter |
| flour | lemon |

Dip the clams in the flour and sauté gently in a generous amount of butter. Quickly. They need only be warmed. Serve with lemon. Serves 3 to 4.

## Clams Sicilian

| | |
|---|---|
| 4 pounds small clams or mussels | 2 cloves garlic, chopped |
| 2 tablespoons olive oil | 1 dried red pepper |

Clean shellfish well, scrubbing shells and removing beards if using mussels. Put 1 inch of water in a wide, shallow pan. Add all other ingredients and bring to a boil. Add shellfish; cover, and steam until shells open. Serve with the broth. Serves 2 to 4.

# Carol Ludden's Family Clam Chowder

2 dozen littleneck clams
3 onions, sliced
3 tablespoons butter
2 cups cooked potatoes, cubed
salt and white pepper to taste

2 tablespoons butter
3 tablespoons flour
2 cups milk, scalded
1 cup raw cream, cold

Wash and scrub clams and put into a large kettle with about 1/2 cup water. Cover the kettle and place over low flame; steam until clams open. Chop the clams and reserve the liquid. In the bottom of your stockpot sauté the onions in butter for about 5 minutes. Add the juice from the clams, the potatoes, and salt and pepper. Make a white sauce of the butter, flour, and milk; add to the stockpot. Add the clams and adjust seasoning. Just before serving, add cream (this is available at the creamery in the Market).

---

## CRAB

One of the high points of winter in the Market is the first of December, opening day of commercial fishing for ocean-caught Dungeness crabs. These wonderful crustaceans provide us with one of the best traditional foods of the region—fresh cracked crab. No preparation is necessary. When you buy your crab, have the fishmonger clean it for you. Take it directly home and to the table, where, plenty of napkins on hand, each diner helps himself to a leg. There is no use in trying to be neat. Neat people do not enjoy crab. Roll up your sleeves and dive in. Don't use your best tablecloth. Crab is wet and drips all over. If you have special crab crackers, use them. If not, pass around your nutcracker or a pair of pliers. This meal does not stand on pretense. Provide each diner with fresh lemon wedges and a dish of homemade mayonnaise (the next best thing is the mayonnaise from the Market creamery—almost like homemade), and don't forget a large bowl for the empty shells. Dungeness crabs average two to three pounds each. One-half crab per person should be enough, but it is a good idea to have extra. Serve with crusty French bread, fresh green salad, and a dry white wine.

Dungeness crabs, the only commercially important crabs in Washington, are available in the fish markets year-round. But most of the year they are frozen and expensive. And frankly, they are not worth it. Like strawberries, crabs should be bought in season, when they are fresh. They are *much* cheaper and much better. In fact, the price nearly doubles out of season.

Fished from the Aleutian Islands to Mexico, Dungeness crabs are named after a small fishing village on Washington's coast off the Strait of Juan de Fuca. This is where the first commercial crabbing was done. Our most productive crabbing grounds are along the coast from the Columbia River north to La Push. Throughout the 1970s, the annual catch here averaged nine million pounds. Slightly smaller Dungeness are found in Puget Sound (about one million pounds are taken each year) north of Everett to Blaine. Unfortunately for crabbers, almost all crabs are taken in December, January, and February, when water and weather conditions on the ocean are at their worst.

Crabs have rigid exterior shells, which means they must shed their shells periodically as they grow. This is called molting.

During its first year on the bottom of the sea, a crab molts seven times; in subsequent years, it molts less and less frequently. Most ocean crabs molt for the last time in late summer-early fall, when they are about three and one-half years old. It is during this molting that crabs reach legal size and become the new crop of crabs for the fishery which begins in December. Puget Sound crabs molt in the spring, when they are four years old, and are caught by sport fishermen in the summer and commercial fishermen beginning in October.

Very few crabs ever reach a width of eight inches, largely because 90 percent of the new crop of legal-size males is caught each season. There simply are not many survivors left to grow to old age. In order to protect the species, the female crabs are not harvested.

Another crab almost always available is the Alaska king crab. Actually, the king crab leg is all you will see. Kings average eleven pounds, and they have been found weighing up to twenty-four pounds, with a tip-to-tip span of almost six feet. They come from the cold waters of the North Pacific and the Bering and Okhotsk seas—waters often below freezing and covered with ice.

Kings molt and spawn in the winter and early spring, and to do so, they move into shallow water (60 to 200 feet). In the summer and fall, they retrace their steps to deeper water, sometimes as deep as 1,000 feet. Their life cycle is similar to the Dungeness. They molt and grow new shells as they increase in size and are capable of regenerating limbs lost in struggles with predators.

Kings are caught almost exclusively in crab pots. Only the large males are kept, and they are kept alive in large tanks on the fishing boats until they are cooked for either freezing or canning. At the fish markets, you will find only frozen king crab legs. They are excellent but expensive. Freezing methods are so advanced, and king crabs handled so carefully, that a quality product is now available. Keep the legs well frozen (0°C.) until ready to use. Like Dungeness, king crab legs are best eaten "as is." They are simply delicious served warmed dipped in drawn butter.

---

## Crab Quiche

This is a delicious way to use any leftover crab. The quiche has a mild, delicate flavor and combines well with an oil-and-vinegar-dressed salad. It can also be served as a first course for dinner.

1 9-inch pie crust, uncooked
1 egg white
6 eggs
dash of white wine
salt and pepper to taste

1-1/2 cups half-and-half
1-1/2 cups crab meat
2 tablespoons chopped parsley
paprika

Prepare the crust (preferably a rich one that uses butter), prick with fork, and brush with egg white; chill. Mix eggs with fork; add wine, salt and pepper, and cream; mix well. Layer crab on pastry shell, sprinkle with parsley, and pour in the liquid mixture. Sprinkle with paprika. Bake at 450° for ten minutes; continue baking at 350° until custard is set and a knife inserted in the center comes out clean, about 30 minutes. Serves 4.

Another nice addition, if you have it on hand, is some mild Swiss cheese, grated and added to the custard before baking.

---

## OCTOPUS

Unless you are from the Mediterranean or Japan—or have traveled in those areas—chances are pretty good that you have never tried octopus. You probably think it tastes as bad as it looks. It is ugly. A dead octopus lying in your sink is a limp, slimy mass that defies description. Once it is plopped into boiling water, though, it plumps up like a bicycle tire and looks a bit more appetizing.

The octopus, like the squid, is the victim of too many grade B monster movies that give it the reputation of a vicious animal seeking ships to devour. If this were true, Puget Sound would be a very unsafe place, because it is the home of the Giant Pacific octopus, the largest species in the world.

But the octopus is usually a timid animal, fleeing at the approach of man. It will, however, grasp and cling to any living thing that touches it, and it has drowned men. But those who study and work with the octopus do not attribute that behavior to an aggressive nature. It is usually fear or confusion; when you have eight arms, it is apparently pretty easy to get someone wound up in them. A small octopus can be rather playful, in fact, and divers have a real affection for them.

There are approximately fifty species of octopus. They prefer shallow coastal waters and reefs and are found chiefly in the Mediterranean and China seas, off the coasts of the West Indies, the Hawaiian Islands, and our own West Coast. Here they are found as far north as Alaska and south to central California, but they prefer the inland waters of Puget Sound and the Strait of Juan de Fuca.

The octopus is an inactive animal most of its life. Rather than seek out its prey, it lurks in its rocky lair on the sea bottom or in a cave and waits for dinner to come by. At low tide, in fact, an octopus will remain in its home, surrounded by dry land rather than lose its place to a starfish or sea cucumber.

The octopus is carnivorous, eating only live food, and is primarily nocturnal. It prefers a diet of clams and crabs. It is a mollusk and is classified as a shellfish even though it has no shell. It has a soft, pear-shaped—almost globose—body and a reddish brown coloring that blends well with its surroundings. Extending from the body are eight muscular tentacles, fairly equal in length but not in thickness. They are smooth, fleshy, and elastic. The eyes are set in knobs which stand out from the head so that the octopus can see in all directions.

In Puget Sound there are several species, but the Giant Pacific is the largest and most abundant. The largest ever taken in Puget Sound was 125 pounds, but 100-pound octopuses, with tentacle spans of 20 feet tip-to-tip, are not uncommon.

No one is really sure of the life span of the octopus, but it is estimated to be about three to four years. The male lives only until it mates; then it dies. The female dies after she has laid her eggs.

There is not yet a good way to count the octopuses in Puget Sound, since they are solitary animals that spend most of their time in hiding. Octopuses are now being found in places where they were not previously sighted, though, and fisheries people believe the population is healthy and reproducing successfully.

Because there is not much demand, there is not much commercial fishing for octopus. Most of those you see in the fish markets are unfortunate fellows that got caught in an otter trawl that was looking for bottom fish. About half of our local catch is made by otter trawls off Cape Flattery with the other half coming from Puget Sound. There are a couple of local fishermen looking for octopus here. Modifying Mediterranean fishermen's equipment—they use earthen pots—these Washingtonians are using cedarboard pots. These are strung out along the sea bottom. No bait is used; the octopus does not need to be encouraged to enter small, dark places. Once an octopus has taken refuge in a pot, it is hauled up.

Prior to the midsixties, most of the octopus catch went north to Alaska to be used as halibut bait. It is still used this way, but more and more of it is used for food. Some is shipped to San Francisco markets, and the rest is sold here.

Fish markets on Pike Place sell fresh, raw octopus. It may look a mess when you buy it, but it really is not difficult to prepare. More than likely, you will be buying only part of an octopus—one of the many arms—so you won't have to worry about removing the ink sack because you won't get one.

A Greek cookbook will tell you that the first thing you must do with your octopus is make sure that it is dead by bashing its head against a large rock a dozen times or so. If you buy it in a fish market, you can skip this first step. You may, however, wish to pound the meat as you do an abalone, because it has a tendency to be tough. Cut the tentacles into a few large pieces. Blanch them in boiling water, drain, and peel off the skin. You may need a knife; it is something like skinning a chicken. Another method, faster but messier, is to skip the parboiling, coat your hands with coarse salt, grab each piece firmly, and pull. If luck is with you, the skin will pull off. What you do with your octopus now depends on how you are going to eat it.

---

## Octopus Appetizers

In Greece and Cyprus, the octopus is dried on large rocks in the sun. The tentacles are then cut into smaller pieces, grilled over a charcoal fire, and served with an apéritif, usually ouzo. Since we lack adequate sunshine to prepare this here, try this method.

### Greek style:
5 pounds octopus          pepper
lemon

After cleaning, boil the octopus for 1 hour; drain well. Slice into small rounds about 1/4-inch thick. Place on barbecue rack and grill until edges blacken. Serve hot or cold with a squeeze of lemon and some fresh pepper—and don't forget the ouzo. Serves 6.

### Japanese style:
5 pounds octopus          lemon juice
hot mustard sauce         toasted sesame seeds
soy sauce

After cleaning, boil octopus for 1 hour; drain well. Slice as thinly as you can, at an angle. Serve at room temperature with toothpicks for dipping into sauces—a hot mustard and a soy sauce-lemon juice combination are both good.

## Insalata di Mare Misto (Mixed Seafood Salad)

This recipe, which uses both squid and octopus, comes from La Coppa Pan, the Market's fresh pasta shop. Every region of Italy has its own version of this popular seafood salad, but they all have in common the interplay of textures and tastes of several crustaceans. No recipe is more than a guide for the imaginative cook. Try your own combination of Pacific Northwest shellfish.

1/2 yellow onion
1/2 carrot
1/2 stalk celery
1 bay leaf
salt to taste
pinch of hot pepper seeds
1/2 pound prawns, raw
1 pound small squid, raw
1/4 cup sweet butter
1/4 cup olive oil
salt and pepper to taste
2 cloves garlic, crushed

1/2 cup dry white wine
1 pound small octopus, cooked
2 green peppers
1 large bunch of broccoli
lemon juice
2 tomatoes
4 Calamata string figs
1 pinch crushed mint leaves
1 pinch ground juniper berries
salad dressing, recipe follows
2 eggs, hard cooked (garnish)

Make a court bouillon by boiling 2 quarts water and adding the onion, carrot, celery, bay leaf, salt, and hot pepper seeds. Wash shrimp in cold water and drop into court bouillon; cook for 2 minutes after water returns to boil. Drain, peel, and set aside. Clean squid and save tentacles. Cut bodies into 1/2-inch rings, rinse well, and drain. Melt butter in sauté pan and add olive oil. When oil is hot, add squid rings and tentacles, salt and pepper, and garlic. Sauté briefly; then add wine and cook 2 to 3 minutes or until squid are white and firm but tender. Drain squid and reduce cooking liquid to consistency of gravy; set aside. Prepare cooked octopus by cutting tentacles into 1/2-inch lengths and body into 1/2-inch cubes. Remove stems and seeds from green peppers and roast on a grill in a hot oven until all sides are charred black. Place in bowl and cover with damp towel. When cool enough to handle, peel away charred skin and cut peppers into 1/4-inch strips; set aside. Prepare broccoli by removing stems and parboiling florets in water with lemon juice until just tender; cool and set aside. Cut tomatoes into wedges, and slice string figs into small pieces. Combine all prepared ingredients in a large salad bowl and sprinkle with mint and juniper berries. Toss with dressing to which reserved squid gravy has been added. Garnish with egg wedges. Serves 6.

### Salad dressing

This dressing can be refrigerated and kept for at least one month; it is good on any type of salad.

1 quart olive oil
1 cup red wine vinegar
1 egg yolk
1 tablespoon dry mustard
1 tablespoon chopped Italian

parsley
classic Italian herbs: oregano,
    basil, thyme, and
    tarragon —generous pinch of
    each

*salt and pepper to taste*          *hot pepper seeds, small pinch*
*juice of 1/2 lemon*

Beat all ingredients with a wire whisk until creamy. Makes about 5 cups.

---

## OYSTERS

*"He was a Bold Man that first eat an Oyster."*
*Dean Swift*

For many, it takes an unusual degree of boldness to slide that first raw oyster down the throat. And if by chance it isn't a good one, a person will be turned off forever. But an ice-cold, tiny Olympia oyster—with perhaps just a taste of lemon—is almost sure to win a convert. The oyster liquor tastes the way the fresh sea air smells; it is a rare lover of seafood or the sea that cannot be won over.

Two kinds of oysters are found here, the rare western, or Olympia, oyster and the more common Pacific oyster. The Pacific is not native but was first introduced from Japan in 1902. The native Olympia oyster, once abundant on our coast, was the victim of massive exploitation and now is farmed in only a very few areas.

Washington is the leading producer of oysters on the Pacific coast, and the annual harvest, valued at close to $10 million, accounts for about 10 percent of the total United States oyster production.

The oyster is a bivalve mollusk, distinguished by its dissimilar upper and lower shells. The two shells are hinged together by a complex elastic ligament. The upper shell is fairly flat, while the lower is concave, providing space for the body of the oyster. The two shells fit together to form a watertight seal. Near one end of the shell is the adductor muscle, which controls the opening and closing of the shell.

An oyster is very efficient in converting the abundant, microscopic floating plants of the sea into food that humans can utilize. It feeds by passing sea water through its gills. The gills are covered with small hairs called cilia, which create a current by their rhythmic waving. As the water passes through, minute floating organisms are filtered out and captured in strings of mucous that move the food along the edge of the gills to the mouth. The oyster grows into a food that is very high in protein, vitamins, and minerals.

Oysters spawn in the summer months. (Oysters alter their sex, usually once a year. That is, one may begin life one year as a female, become a male the next, and in its third year revert to being a female.) The female Pacific oyster may spawn up to 200 million eggs in a season. They are expelled into the water, where they are fertilized by sperm from the male. Only a very few of the eggs develop into mature larvae with shells, and even fewer larvae find surfaces on which to live. The larvae float freely with the tide for three to four weeks. Then they instinctively seek clean hard surfaces on which to attach themselves. At this stage, the oysters are called spat and are about the size of pinpoints. By winter, they are visible. The Pacific oyster takes about two years to reach maturity—about four inches across the shell. The smaller Olympia reaches its mature size of one and one-half inches in four years.

Pacific oysters need warm water to spawn and, consequently, our Pacific oyster population has been maintained by imported seed ever since its arrival. Efforts to produce seed locally are meeting with some success, and our dependence on imports is minimized. But our sea water so regularly fails to attain the necessary spawning temperature of sixty-five degrees that it would be difficult, if not impossible, to maintain oyster production without Japanese assistance.

It is commonly believed that oysters are poisonous from May through August—all the months without the letter R in them. This is not true. Oysters are reproducing during the summer, and they are not as good, but they are not poisonous. Because so much of the mollusk's substance is expended in the production of eggs and sperm, the meat is often thin and watery. There is also the threat of red tides in the summer months. These are the reasons oysters are generally unavailable in the Market at this time of year. When reproduction is finished and colder weather cools the water, oysters are brought into the Market in great numbers. Fall and winter are excellent times for oysters; then they are firm, fresh, and have great flavor. After a three- or four-month drought, they are like the fresh peas and new potatoes of springtime.

Wild oysters are all but gone from our coast, and the oysters you find now are farmed on private beaches or on beaches leased from the state. Oyster farming has a long history. The Romans established oyster beds as early as 100 B.C. to insure a reliable supply. The Greeks, too, had been fond of oysters but had collected them as they found them, never developing a farming method. They did, however, use the oyster shell as a ballot. When early Athenians voted to banish a citizen from the city, they put forth their shells, and the individual was "oyster-shelled," or ostracized.

Oyster farming is a complicated process, often requiring several transplantings before mature oysters are obtained. Most oysters are placed on the bottom of sheltered bays to grow and are harvested by hand-picking, dredging, or tonging. There is another growing method, used extensively by the Japanese, which involves rafts that float oysters off the sea bottom. This floating-culture method increases possible production because of the greater surface area available and because deeper water can be used.

Washington has tremendous potential for marine food production. The water of Puget Sound is extremely rich and is considered one of the cleanest, most fertile bodies of water in the world, due partly to its high rate of water movement. The average annual commercial harvest of oysters in Washington has been between 5 and 7 million pounds. An evaluation of the oyster-producing potential of Puget Sound, reported by the State Department of Fisheries, shows that a sustained annual production of up to 6 billion pounds of meat may be possible. This would require adapting the Japanese floating-culture method, but it would also make oysters the Northwest's principal protein contribution to the human food supply.

With the exception of summer, when they are sparse, oysters are available year-round. At the Market you can buy them live in the shell or freshly shucked in jars. If you choose them in the shell, you'll have to shuck them yourself, a formidable chore if you don't know what you're doing. It is not too difficult if you have the proper tools. First, a good thick glove will protect your hand and help you get a good grip on the rough shell. Next, you'll need an oyster knife. This is a two-edged knife with a knoblike handle. (If you are a beginner, you will do well to buy one with a guard between the blade and the handle to avoid a nasty cut.) Insert the blade into the adductor muscle at the end of the shell, and move it back and forth horizontally until the muscle is cut and the shell falls open. Don't let the juice slip out—save it, drink it—it is the best part.

Oysters sell by the dozen in the shell and by weight in the jar. Plan on six to twelve per person, depending on appetites and the size of the oysters. If you are one who thinks oysters are expensive, compare the price per serving with that of better beef cuts. You will find they are cheaper than steak, and shucked ones are all meat—no fat or bone. When they are just in, the oysters in jars are excellent raw. Here at the Market, we watch for the oyster truck, knowing when it drives by that the oysters will be exceptionally fresh that day. If you plan to eat them raw or quickly sautéed, whole, ask for the extra-small ones.

---

## Oyster Stew

There are many ways to serve oysters, but an unquestionable winter favorite is oyster stew. After work on a cold night, this is an excellent choice for dinner—it takes only ten minutes start to finish.

1 pint fresh, shucked oysters,
   extra small
2 tablespoons butter
1/2 teaspoon paprika
2 teaspoons Worcestershire
   sauce

generous pinch cayenne
salt to taste
2 cups milk (or half-and-half)

Cook oysters in the butter with paprika, Worcestershire sauce, and cayenne until the edges curl and the oysters plump. Add milk and heat (do not boil) until bubbles form at the edge of the stew. Serve with Trenton Oyster Crackers (available at De-Laurenti's Italian Market); these are the real oyster crackers, hard all the way through, not a hollow, saltinelike cracker. Serves 2.

## Poached Oysters

If you are serving this delightful quick dish for breakfast, accompany it with fresh fruit and cheese. For dinner, add a large green salad and a dry, or slightly sweet white wine (Chardonnay or Vouvray would be a good choice.)

3 green onions, chopped
1/4 cup butter
1/2 pint oysters (extra small)
1 teaspoon salt

1/2 teaspoon pepper
1 tablespoon Worcestershire
   sauce
large pinch cayenne

*lemon juice*
*1/3 cup white wine*

*2 large slices crusty Italian or*
*French bread, toasted*

Sauté green onions in melted butter. Add oysters, salt, pepper, Worcestershire, cayenne, and a squeeze of lemon juice. Cook until oysters plump, about 3 minutes; add wine. Serve immediately on toasted bread. (The bread must be crusty and sliced thickly to hold the juices without becoming soggy.) Enjoy. Serves 1 or 2.

---

## SQUID

A local delicacy too many people have not tried is squid. Maybe the somewhat slippery body and the tentacles put you off. But if you are interested in economy in the food market, you really can't afford to miss squid. Squid is much cheaper than even hamburger and, like other seafoods, is very nutritious. It is high in protein and phosphorus and contains traces of calcium, thiamine, and riboflavin. Once you learn to prepare it well, you will have a quick, cheap, easy, and delicious dinner at your disposal.

The squid, often called inkfish, is a mollusk. But unlike most mollusks, it has an internal shell. The long body, called the

mantle, is slightly swollen near the middle and tapers to a blunt point. Two fins, which are about half as long as the mantle, are located near this end and are slightly lobed in front. The small head is surrounded by tentacles with tiny suction cups on the surface.

When you go to a fish market to buy squid, you will generally find one of two kinds, and occasionally both. Squid caught in Puget Sound is ten to twelve inches in length and is sold fresh. The more common small squid, four to five inches long, is from California and is frozen. You should buy about one-half pound for each serving.

Once you get the hang of it, cleaning squid is no trouble at all. Rinse one off, get a firm grip on the head, and pull it from the mantle; a good portion of the intestines will come with it. Next remove the plasticlike wand, the quill, that runs like a backbone along the side of the mantle. Now, hold the squid by the fins and run your fingers from end to end, gently squeezing the insides out, just as you would toothpaste from a tube. Rinse it out with water, and your squid is ready to use. You may also wish to remove the skin, which peels off easily.

The tentacles were pulled from the body along with the head. If you want to use them in your recipe, cut them from the head and reserve. The tentacles on small squid tend to be tough, and you probably won't want to use them except ground up as part of a stuffing. The tentacles on the larger squid are more tender and form natural pouches for stuffing.

Squid has a delicate flavor and is delicious sautéed, baked, or stir-fried. The most important thing to remember in cooking squid is not to overcook it. Overcooked squid is very tough and very chewy.

---

## Sautéed Squid

2 pounds squid
2 tablespoons butter
2 cloves garlic, halved

2 tablespoons chopped parsley
1/2 to 3/4 cup white wine

After cleaning the squid, slit it down the middle and cut it into strips. Melt butter in skillet; add garlic and sauté a few minutes. Remove garlic. Add squid and parsley and sauté about 1 minute. Add the wine, blend, and serve immediately with rice for a quick, good meal. Serves 4.

## Stuffed Squid

1 bunch spinach, cooked,
  drained, finely chopped
1/2 cup cottage cheese, small
  curd
2 cloves garlic, finely chopped

white wine
nutmeg
2 pounds squid, cleaned
butter

Mix spinach, cottage cheese, and garlic with a dash of wine and a pinch of nutmeg. Stuff mixture into the squid, being careful to pack loosely so the squid won't burst in the oven. Lay the squid in a casserole lightly coated with olive oil. Pour white wine and melted butter over them and bake at 300° for about 40 minutes. But watch it; don't overcook. Serves 4.

# Sweet-and-Sour Squid

5 pounds squid, cleaned          1 teaspoon sugar
1 tablespoon oil                 salt
1/2 cup vinegar                  pepper
1/2 cup water

Reserve tentacles from squid when cleaning. Slit squid open lengthwise and lay flat. With a knife, make a crisscross pattern in the meat with shallow cuts. This will cause the meat to roll up when cooked. If the squid are small (4 to 5 inches) cut them in halves. If they are large, cut each into four pieces. Place the squid in a hot frying pan with the oil and stir-fry quickly until the flesh firms up and moisture is drawn from the meat, just a minute or two. Be careful not to overcook. Combine the remaining ingredients, heat through, and add to the squid. Toss together and serve with rice. Serves 6.

# MEAT

Do you crave a crown roast of lamb with pastel paper panties on the bone ends? Or a standing three-rib roast aged for six weeks? Or, at the economical end of the meat spectrum, perhaps a lamb's head or fresh pork rind? You will have no problem finding things like these at the meat markets in the Pike Place Market. Specialty cuts and specialty services are their trademarks.

The supermarket boom in the late 1950s hurt the Pike Place Market and especially affected the business of the meat markets. The convenience of shopping in the suburbs and the ease of buying meat already wrapped, labeled, and priced, drew customers away from the downtown Market. Supermarket meat counters were more service-oriented then; a knowledgeable butcher, a meat cutter, would respond to a ring of the bell. Now the swing in the suburbs is toward less service and more pre-packaged meat, and the Market butchers find that customers looking for personal service and more choice are returning.

Very little of the meat you find at the Market is prepackaged. A common sight on Pike Place is a big, refrigerated truck, double-parked while the deliveryman slings another carcass over his shoulder and moves through the crowded arcades. He is quite often followed by a chorus of *ohs* and *ahs* from people who

*133*

have never before been quite that close to a roast on the hoof. The carcasses hang anywhere from a week to three weeks from meat hooks in spacious coolers and then are custom cut. Much of that work is done on a Sunday, the one day the Market is closed and the one day when the butchers can get caught up with special orders.

The Market butchers are not only gourmet meat cutters; many of them make their own sausages, smoke their own meats, or corn their own beef. You'll find homemade chorizos, country and link sausages, Italian sausages (hot and mild), hot links, and pickled tongue at one or another of the meat counters.

The meat markets carry the usual cuts of pork, lamb, veal, and beef, in grades that range from good to prime. What distinguishes them is the range and variety of the meats in the cases. You'll find fresh pork rind for cracklings, slab bacon, and bacon ends and pieces. There are sukiyaki beef, steak thinly cut for rouladen, whole pork tenderloins, and lamb cheeks. Ground veal, pork, and lamb are always available frozen. There are dry-cured hams and fresh pig hocks. Every kind of specialty meat is available: pig snouts, hog maughs, hearts, pig tails and feet, fresh sweetbreads, tripe, beef testicles, kidneys, and lamb tongues. There are marrow bones and veal knuckles for rich, homemade stocks. And you'll find all kinds of sausages, from the homely wiener to potato sausage and all the German wursts.

Market butchers custom-cut and package meat for your freezer. There are locker packages of twenty-five, thirty, and sixty pounds available, all beef or mixes of pork, beef, chicken, sausage, or even wieners. Ask the butchers to put up your own custom package.

All the meat markets are full-service markets. If you don't see what you want, ask for it. A butcher will be happy to make that crown roast for you or to put aside the standing-rib roast to age six weeks in his cooler. He'll cut liver two inches thick, give you a three-inch spencer steak, and saw the ham hock into however many pieces you want. And the butchers, like the fishmongers, are quick to offer cooking tips and recipes.

What follows is in no way a meat dictionary or a meat cookbook. It is a glance, and only a glance, at some of the more unusual cuts you will find at the meat markets. The emphasis here on offal and other strange things does not mean that they are your only choices. They are a few of many. Stick with hamburger if you wish, but dare to try something different first.

## OFFAL

*Offal:* 1. Waste parts, especially of a butchered animal. 2. Refuse; rubbish. (Middle English *offal, ofall,* from Middle Dutch *afval,* "that which falls off."
                                    *The American Heritage Dictionary*

All in all, a rather unappetizing definition of the (does this make you more comfortable?) variety meats that are a feature of the Market meat shops. Offal includes all the innards of an animal—the heart, liver, kidneys, brain, tripe—and everything outside, from the head to the tail to the feet to the testicles. The cuts are economical, they are good eating (and good for you), and they should not be overlooked because of prejudice, ignorance, or a squeamish stomach.

### Heart

One of the best of the organ meats, and the most nutritious, is heart. Even though it is a muscular organ that has had a lot of exercise, it is tender and really does not require the long, moist cooking most recipes call for. (Heart, thinly sliced and quickly barbecued on an outside grill, is excellent.) Heart may be stuffed and baked, pickled, and ground and prepared like hamburger.

---

## *Braised Heart*

One Market butcher prepares heart this way.

1 beef heart, diced into 1/2-inch
  cubes
flour
1/4 cup butter
1/8 cup oil
3 to 4 carrots, diced

1-1/2 medium-size onions,
  chopped
salt and pepper to taste
French bread, cut into thick
  slices and toasted, or biscuits

Dip the heart cubes into flour and coat well. Brown in butter and oil. Add 1/2 cup water, carrots, onion, and salt and pepper; cover and cook until heart is fork tender. Check occasionally to make sure there is liquid in the pan. For a richer gravy, add some cream and swirl in a tablespoon of soft butter. Serve over French bread or biscuits. Serves 5 generously.

---

Lamb's hearts are small and make good individual servings. A calf's heart makes two to three servings, and a four-to-five pound beef heart will feed five easily.

## Liver

Liver is the organ meat most people know best and like least, because most people as kids were force-fed ("eat it, it's good for you") overcooked, thin slices of liver fried to the consistency of shoelaces. The secret of good liver is cook it quickly and serve it rare.

Beef, calf, lamb, and pork liver is all available at the meat markets. All of the livers have the same high food value; they are rich in protein, iron, and vitamins A, B, C, and D. There is no waste in liver, and one pound will serve two people well, or three people adequately. Liver is easy to prepare; just make sure the thin outer membrane has been removed. Beef, pork, and lamb liver is comparably priced; calf liver is more expensive.

Calf liver is more tender than beef liver, and it doesn't have large veins running through it. Many people prefer calf liver, because it is more tender and milder in flavor, but beef liver, well prepared, can be every bit as tender and have the same good flavor as calf.

Forget your childhood prejudices and buy a piece of beef liver one and one-half to two inches thick. (Ask the butcher to cut a piece from the tip of the whole liver—that is the best.) Pan fry or broil it until just rare. Do not overcook. Serve with a rich Béarnaise sauce.

Pork liver has a stronger smell and taste, and it is not a good choice for beginners, though it is excellent in paté. Lamb liver is milder than pork (and extremely tender), but it does have a mutton taste that it will lose if it is soaked in milk.

## Sweetbreads

Sweetbreads have long been considered a delicacy best left to a French chef to prepare. This is unfortunate. Sweetbreads are delicious and easy to fix.

There are two kinds of sweetbreads: the thymus gland, or throat sweetbread, and the heart, or belly, sweetbread. The heart sweetbread is preferred, being more delicate in flavor and more tender; the smaller sweetbreads of veal and lamb are more tender and flavorful than the larger ones of beef.

Sweetbreads come in pairs; buy one pair for two people. They should be very fresh. Do not buy them and refrigerate them for a few days; eat them the same day you buy them.

Many recipes for sweetbreads that call for rich sauces can be very good. But be careful—the flavor of sweetbreads is very delicate and can easily be overwhelmed by a thick sauce.

Soak sweetbreads in cold water for about twenty minutes and then parboil them in acidulated water with a little salt. Simmer them for about fifteen minutes and then plunge them into cold water to firm the flesh. It is then easy to remove the connective tubes and the thin membrane.

---

## Sweetbreads

Marjan Willemsen, chef at Rex's Market Delicatessen, recommends preparing sweetbreads this way.

| | |
|---|---|
| 1 cup white wine | 2 tablespoons butter, melted |
| 1 bay leaf | 2 tablespoons flour |
| 1 teaspoon peppercorns | 1/2 cup Marsala |
| 1 pair sweetbreads, cleaned | 1 teaspoon salt, or to taste |

In a saucepan bring to a boil wine, bay leaf, and peppercorns. Turn the heat to low and add sweetbreads. Simmer for 10 minutes. Remove sweetbreads from the pan and slice into 1/4-inch slices. Strain the liquid and set aside. In a pan make a roux of flour and melted butter. Add the reserved liquid; heat and stir until smooth. Add Marsala and salt. Add sweetbreads to the sauce and heat through. Serves 2.

## Sweetbread Terrine

This recipe comes from La Coppa Pan.

| | |
|---|---|
| 1 pound lean ground veal | 1-1/2 teaspoons spice Parisienne (ginger, cinnamon, clove and white pepper) |
| 1/2 pound lean ground pork | |
| 3/4 pound pork fat, coarsely ground | 1 tablespoon flour |
| | 2 egg yolks |

2 tablespoons sherry
3 tablespoons dry white
   wine
1/3 cup chopped
   shallots
2 tablespoons butter
1-1/2 pounds blanched
   and pressed sweetbreads

salt and white pepper
   to taste
caul fat (special-order
   from butcher)
thyme
2 bay leaves

Marinate ground meats in mixture of spice Parisienne, flour, eggs, sherry, and white wine overnight. Sauté shallots in butter for 1 minute. Add sweetbreads and salt and white pepper. Roll pieces to coat with butter and cook gently, covered, 10 minutes. Thoroughly line terrine with caul fat; leave plenty hanging all around the edge. Place layer of marinated meat on bottom of terrine. Arrange pieces of sweetbreads on top, separated by forcemeat. Continue layering forcemeat and sweetbreads, finishing with a layer of forcemeat. Bring caul fat over top of mixture. Sprinkle with thyme and place bay leaves on top. Cover with a double layer of tin foil, crimping edges around terrine. Bake in a pan of hot water at 325° for 1 hour. Reduce heat to 300° and continue cooking 2 more hours. It is done when internal temperature reaches 145.° Remove from heat and press with even weight overnight while cooling. Cover with plastic wrap; allow to set 48 hours. You may, if you wish, coat terrine with aspic.

---

### Tripe

One of the most popular variety meats is tripe. It is the muscular inner lining of a cow's stomach (although tripe in its larger meaning refers to the edible stomach of all butchered animals). There are two kinds of tripe: the plain, or flat, tripe that comes from the walls of the large, first compartment of the stomach; and honeycomb, from the walls of the animal's second stomach. Honeycomb tripe is more tender and requires less cooking time.

# Menudo

Menudo, a hearty tripe stew, is a favorite of Mexicans who recommend it as a cure for hangover. It is always made for New Year's morning. This recipe is from La Paloma, the Mexican restaurant in the Corner Market Building.

3 pounds honeycomb tripe
2 pig's feet, cut in pieces
2 onions, chopped
2 cloves garlic, mashed
2 quarts water
1 teaspoon oregano
1/4 teaspoon each thyme and
   cinnamon

pinch ground cloves
salt
pepper
2 cups hominy (canned, white or
   gold)

Have the butcher cut each pig's foot into six pieces. Cut tripe into small strips. Cook the pig's feet in salted water for an hour, and then add tripe and all other ingredients, except the hominy. Cook for 5 hours on low heat until the tripe and pig's feet are tender. Add hominy in the last half hour of cooking. Serve with wedge of lemon, flour tortillas and dark Mexican beer. (Menudo is always better reheated the following day.) Serves 6 to 8.

# Tripe à la Mode de Caen

This version of one of the world's classic tripe dishes comes from Betty Cockle, an Englishwoman with a great collection of family recipes for variety meats. It requires long, slow cooking in a sealed earthenware pot to be really perfect.

1 veal shank
4 onions, sliced
5 carrots, sliced
4 celery stalks, sliced

salt and pepper
herb bouquet of parsley,
   thyme, bay leaf, tied
   in cheesecloth

1/4 cup butter
5 pounds fresh
   honeycomb tripe, cut in
   2- by 1-inch strips

1-1/2 cups white wine
1 cup apple juice
chicken broth

Put the veal shank in the bottom of a large pot. Cook onions, carrots, and celery in butter until wilted. Arrange vegetables in layers in the pot, alternating with layers of tripe; sprinkle each layer with salt and pepper, and tuck the herb bouquet in the middle. Add wine and apple juice, and fill the pot with chicken broth. Cover, and seal the lid with a paste of flour and water. Cook at 250° for 8 hours. Remove veal bone and herb bouquet before serving. Serves 10.

---

## Tongue

Tongue is an organ meat whose presentation at table can affect your feelings about it forever after. Don't, for heaven's sake, serve it whole, gagging on a plate, with its roots still attached.

Tongue should be soaked in cold, acidulated water to cover for one hour and then parboiled until the skin can be removed easily (ten minutes for small tongues, up to thirty minutes for the larger ones). Drain, skin, and cook for two to three hours in water with onion, bay leaf, a carrot, half a lemon, peppercorns, celery, and parsley. Slice and serve with a horseradish sauce. Or experiment—tongue is good with any number of exotic sauces.

---

# Escabeche de Lengua

A Mexican dish, very good for a cold buffet, is prepared by Betty Cockle like this.

1 2-pound tongue
2 quarts water
juice of 1/2 lemon
1 small onion
1 carrot
1 stalk celery
2 teaspoons salt
1 sweet onion, sliced paper thin

1 orange, unpeeled and sliced
15 ripe olives, sliced
3/4 cup olive oil
1/4 cup wine vinegar
1 teaspoon salt
freshly ground pepper
parsley, freshly chopped

Cook the tongue in water with lemon juice, small onion, carrot, celery, and salt for 2 to 3 hours or until tender; allow to cool in the stock. Skin and slice. Arrange in a deep platter or shallow dish, putting slices of sweet onion, orange, and olives between the layers of tongue. Mix the oil, vinegar, salt, and pepper and pour this dressing over the tongue; chill for 24 hours. Before serving, sprinkle with parsley. Serves 6.

---

### Kidneys

Kidneys are another very popular organ meat, especially with the English. They are available from beef, calves, sheep, and pigs, and all of them are delicious and economical. They are an unusually good source of riboflavin, and they are high in niacin, thiamine, and iron.

The only problem with kidneys is an unpleasant smell that will turn into a very unpleasant taste if the kidneys are not treated properly before cooking. Beef and pork kidneys should be soaked in acidulated water or buttermilk for about one hour. (Some cooks simply recommend boiling kidneys for a long time.) Lamb and veal kidneys, which are milder, can just be washed well and left for a few minutes in cold water with a touch of lemon juice.

Remove the membrane from the kidneys, split into halves, and remove the white cores and excess fat. (Save any fat from the kidneys for later use—this is genuine suet.) Kidneys should be grilled or sautéed quickly. They will become unpleasantly tough if overcooked.

---

## Deviled Lamb Kidneys

This recipe for deviled lamb kidneys is another from Betty Cockle.

12 lamb kidneys, skinned
1/2 cup butter, softened
1/4 cup minced onion
1 clove garlic, pressed
dash Tabasco
2 teaspoons prepared mustard

2 tablespoons dry sherry
1/4 teaspoon pepper
toast or cooked rice
parsley
lemon slices

Split the kidneys and remove the hard centers. Mix remaining ingredients together (except toast and parsley) and spread on the cut sides of the kidneys. Broil 5 minutes or until tender and juicy. Arrange on toast or hot, cooked rice. Pour pan juices over kidneys and sprinkle with finely chopped parsley. Serve at once with lemon slices. Serves 4.

---

### Brains

Brains are very perishable, so they must be very fresh. Soak them in cold water to cover for thirty minutes, rinse under cold water, and drain. Remove the arteries and the outer membranes, and parboil in acidulated water, simmering for anywhere from five to fifteen minutes. (Veal and lamb brains take a shorter cooking time than beef brains.) Plunge into cold water or allow them to cool in the cooking liquid.

Pork brains are reputed to have a better flavor than beef brains and are accordingly more expensive. They average about one-fourth pound each. A beef brain weighs about three-fourths to one pound, a calf brain about one-half pound.

---

## Sautéed Brains on Toast

Betty Cockle recommends veal or beef brains in this recipe.

| | |
|---|---|
| 1 pound veal or beef brains | 1/2 cup butter |
| flour | lemon wedges |
| 1 egg beaten with 1 cup milk, | buttered toast |
|     dash salt and pepper | 1/4 cup fresh chopped parsley |
| fresh or toasted unflavored | |
|     breadcrumbs | |

Soak brains in cold water for 30 minutes; drain. Bring about 4 cups water (enough to cover brains) with 1 teaspoon salt and 1 tablespoon lemon juice to simmer; add brains, return to simmer, and cook for 10 minutes. (Do not boil or overcook, because this destroys the delicate structure of the brains.) Remove, immediately plunge into ice water to stop cooking. When cool enough to handle, remove and pat dry with paper towels. Remove membrane. Slice into one-inch-thick slices. Roll in flour gently, dip into egg mixture, and roll in breadcrumbs. Sauté in butter, turning carefully, until golden on both sides. Serve at once, with lemon wedges, on hot toast, and sprinkle with parsley. Serves 4. (Sweetbreads may be used this way, but simmer them 20 minutes; proceed as above.)

---

### Bull Fries

Bull fries are beef testicles, and they are admittedly one of the least attractive of the variety meats. Their appearance and their anatomical origin seem to keep most Americans from trying them, but in Europe they are considered a delicacy.

To clean, cut through the sac and push the testicle through the slit. Cut the sac from the testicle and rinse the meat in cold water until the water runs clear. Drain and parboil in salted water for about fifteen minutes. Slice the fries one-half- to three-fourths-inch thick, dip in egg and breadcrumbs, and fry like oysters.

### Rocky Mountain Oysters

Rocky Mountain oysters are sheep testicles. (Sheepherders in the Rocky Mountains would eat the testicles of the castrated sheep. The consistency is much like an oyster's—hence the name.) They are not widely available because they are so small that it takes a lot of them to make a pound, and they are simply not worth the butcher's time. Some butchers do keep a small supply in their freezers, however, so ask for them.

### Pork Offal

Most offal found in the Market is pork, and just about every part of the animal is available. You can buy pig's head, rind, ears, snout, tail, feet, maughs, hocks, and knuckles.

Fresh pig's head is seasonal—most people consider it a holiday item, especially at the New Year—and it is available between

Thanksgiving and the first of the year. (A boiled head eaten on New Year's Day is thought to bring good luck for the year.) Pig's head is used in making scrapple and head cheese.

---

## Scrapple (or Pawnhaas)

You'll note that pig's knuckles are an alternative to the head; this is simply because the knuckles are always available.

| | |
|---|---|
| 1 pig's head, or 4 large pig's knuckles and 1/2 pound lean pork | 1 hot red pepper (optional) |
| | 1/2 teaspoon black pepper |
| | 1/2 to 1 teaspoon sage |
| 3 quarts water | 2-3/4 cups corn meal |
| 1 tablespoon salt | |

Simmer the head or the knuckles and pork in water with salt and red pepper until so tender that the meat almost falls from the bones—about 2-1/2 hours. Remove the meat from the broth, remove bones, and grind meat. Strain broth and skim off fat, if desired. Measure 2 quarts of the broth into a large, heavy kettle. Return meat to broth and add black pepper and sage. Bring to a rapid boil. Mix corn meal with 1 quart of cool broth, add to boiling broth and cook, stirring, until thickened. Place on an asbestos pad over lowest heat and cook, covered, stirring often, about 30 minutes. Adjust seasonings to taste. Pour into two large bread pans; cool, cover, and chill overnight. To serve, cut into half-inch slices, coat with flour and brown in butter or other fat over moderately high heat. Serve with real maple syrup. Serves about 12.

---

Pig's feet are available fresh at the meat markets or pickled at the delis. There is very little meat in the foot, but the flavor is excellent. There is more meat in the pig's tail, although it may not appear so. One way to cook pigs' tails is to cut them into one- to two-inch pieces and simmer in a tomato sauce; you eat them like spare ribs. The pig's snout and neck bones may both be cooked this way. They, too, are fairly meaty and have a very good pork flavor.

There is no meat in pig's ears, just cartilage. Cooked, they make good snacks. With your kitchen shears, cut the ears into thin strips. Place them on a rack in a slow oven to render the fat. The strips become crisp and make a good topping for a baked potato.

Hog maughs are pork stomachs. Their best-known use is in the Scottish national specialty, haggis. (Haggis is a mixture of kidney, heart, liver, and oatmeal, stuffed into a hog maugh and baked.) Maughs are also used by the Chinese in soups and as a casing for headcheese.

## MORE FAMILIAR MEATS

There is much more at the Market's meat counters than pig's ears and sow's bellies. The cases are full of every imaginable cut of meat. The following highlights some of the more familiar, along with choices you might not know about, with recipes to tempt you to try them.

### Sausages

Much of the sausage found at the meat markets is homemade, or, more properly, Market-made, mixed and smoked on the premises. Here are just a few ways to enjoy the variety of sausages you will find here.

---

## Sausage and Red Potatoes

This is a hearty dish and is easy to prepare. It can be served hot or at room temperature.

1 pound Polish or garlic farmer  vinaigrette dressing
  sausage  snipped parsley
1 to 2 pounds small red potatoes
  (unskinned)

Boil or grill the sausage and cut into slices. Boil small red potatoes until just tender, cube, and combine in a bowl with the sausage. While they are still warm, add dressing, toss lightly, and garnish with lots of parsley. Serves 4.

# Sausage and Sauerkraut

1 pound wurst (bockwurst, bratwurst, etc.)
1 onion, chopped
bacon fat

1 quart bulk sauerkraut
1 raw potato, grated
1 teaspoon caraway seed

Serve one of the wursts (either boiled or broiled) with sauerkraut that has been cooked this way. Brown onion in bacon fat and add sauerkraut. Cook for about 10 minutes; add raw potato and caraway seed. Almost cover with boiling water and simmer for 1 hour or so (cook uncovered for first 30 minutes, then cover). Serves 4.

# Sausage and Clams

15 clams
1 pound country sausage
1 egg, slightly beaten

cracker crumbs
lemon slices
1 cup dry white wine

Steam clams until they open (save and refrigerate clam nectar for other uses) and chop coarsely. Mix with the sausage. Add the egg and enough cracker crumbs to bind. Shape into patties, put into baking dish, and top each patty with a slice of lemon. Pour in enough wine to half cover the patties. Bake at 350° for about 40 minutes. Serves 2 to 3.

---

### Pork

The pork tenderloin looks like a pale, small fillet of beef. It is available fresh or frozen at the Market and is a fairly economical cut of pork because there is absolutely no waste. (It is the cut used for Chinese barbecued pork.)

The tenderloin is good simply sliced into half-inch pieces and sautéed in butter; garnish with watercress and serve with fried apple rings.

Salt pork, or salted pork belly, is a staple in southern and New England cooking. The French serve boiled salt pork sliced, with purées of dried vegetables—peas, beans, lentils—and purées of fresh peas and leeks. Other combinations are salt pork with a purée of chestnuts or with Brussels sprouts and chestnuts cooked together.

# Pork Tenderloin with Prunes

This is a fine combination and satisfyingly rich.

| | |
|---|---|
| 1/2 pound large California prunes | flour |
| | 1/4 cup butter |
| 1 cup white wine (Vouvray recommended) | 1 tablespoon red currant jelly |
| | 1 cup rich cream |
| 4 thick slices pork tenderloin | dash lemon juice |

Soak prunes overnight in wine. Pour off a bit of the wine and reserve. Bake prunes in remaining wine at 325,° covered, for 1 hour. Lightly coat the tenderloin in flour and sauté in the butter. (Be careful not to brown the butter.) Add the reserved wine, cover, and cook for 20 minutes. Add juice from the baked prunes and cook about 3 minutes longer; remove pork to a serving dish. Surround with baked prunes. Boil sauce to a thin syrup, add currant jelly, and stir. Gradually add cream to the sauce, stirring it in well. Add lemon juice, pour sauce over pork and prunes, and heat in oven at 325° for 5 minutes. Serves 3 to 4.

# New England Salt Pork and Potatoes

Here is another recipe from the *Notebook's* New England expert, Carol Ludden.

| | |
|---|---|
| 1/2 pound salt pork | 1/2 cup milk, scalded |
| 4 tablespoons corn meal | salt and pepper to taste |
| 2 tablespoons flour | pinch nutmeg |
| butter | 4 or 5 potatoes, boiled and cubed |
| 2 tablespoons flour | |

Cut salt pork into thin slices and then cut into halves (pieces should be roughly 3 inches by 2 inches). Gash the rind. Combine corn meal and flour. Dip salt-pork slices into mixture and fry in butter in a cast-iron or heavy enameled frying pan until crisp, turning frequently, for 30 minutes or more. Remove salt pork to a warm plate and pour out most of the fat. Add 2 tablespoons flour to the drippings, stirring constantly. Pour milk in slowly and continue stirring; add the salt and pepper and nutmeg. Continue cooking and stirring until you have a thick white sauce. Add potatoes. Serve the potatoes and sauce with the salt pork.

---

## Lamb

A leg of lamb boned, butterflied, and grilled over coals until just pink inside is very good. It is also fairly expensive. If you love lamb but feel in an economical mood, don't ignore the other, cheaper, cuts of lamb available at the meat markets. Lamb cheeks, riblets, shanks, and ground lamb all have a good flavor, and they don't cost you a leg and a shoulder.

Lamb cheeks—the least expensive cut of lamb—are excellent for stews and curries. If you buy lamb riblets (or lamb breast) buy the leanest you can find and allow about one pound per person. Marinate overnight in the same oil and lemon mixture as for lamb cheeks, and broil over an outdoor grill. Serve with thick slices of eggplant that have been similarly marinated and broiled.

---

# Skewered Lamb Cheeks

2 pounds lamb cheeks
6 tablespoons olive oil
2 tablespoons lemon juice
1/4 teaspoon rosemary

1/2 teaspoon thyme
1/4 teaspoon pepper
2 cloves garlic, crushed

Parboil the lamb cheeks for 20 minutes. Mix all the remaining ingredients and marinate the cheeks in the mixture, preferably overnight, in the refrigerator. Cut the lamb cheeks into small chunks, skewer, and grill over an open fire. (Do not do these under the broiler; they're just not the same.) Serves 6.

# Skewered Ground Lamb

1 pound lean ground lamb
1 small onion, minced
1/2 tablespoon yogurt

1 teaspoon curry powder
1/4 teaspoon salt
1 teaspoon lemon juice

Thoroughly mix the ingredients together. Form around skewers in long, cigar shapes and cook over hot coals. This is excellent served with marinated vegetables, a Greek salad, and crusty bread. Serves 2 to 3.

---

## Beef

Steaks are beautiful. Consider a two-inch-thick rib steak broiled rare, or a spencer steak pan-fried on a bed of salt. The meat markets have all kinds of steaks—skirt, flank, sirloin and T-bone—and all kinds of roasts—rolled, standing, rib and pot. The butchers will cut your beef as you like. They also carry beef precut for special dishes.

---

# Beef with Asparagus

The meat markets sell a cut they call "sukiyaki" beef, which is usually thinly cut flank meat. It takes little time to cook and is perfect for stir-frying.

1 egg white
1 tablespoon cornstarch
1/2 teaspoon salt
3/4 pound sukiyaki beef
1 tablespoon oil
1/2 pound asparagus, cut
  diagonally into 1-1/2-inch
  pieces

1 green onion, cut diagonally
  into 1-1/2-inch pieces
2 tablespoons chicken stock
2 tablespoons oyster sauce
1 tablespoon sherry
1 tablespoon soy sauce
dash sugar

Mix with your fingers the egg white, cornstarch, and salt. Add the beef and coat it completely. Heat the oil in a wok or frying pan until very hot. Add meat, brown quickly, and remove to a hot platter. Stir-fry asparagus and green onion in wok for 30 seconds, add the chicken stock, cover, and steam for 1 minute. Then add a mixture of oyster sauce, sherry, soy sauce, and sugar to the wok, along with the reserved beef. Cook until sauce thickens and serve over rice. (If too thick, thin with chicken broth.) Serves 2.

**Oyster Sauce**

You can make your own oyster sauce.

1 dozen oysters
3 tablespoons soy sauce
1 teaspoon salt

2 teaspoons molasses
1 tablespoon flour mixed with
  1-1/2 tablespoons water

Cook the oysters gently in their own liquid for 20 minutes. Let cool and then purée in a blender or food processor. Mix with soy sauce, salt, and molasses. Simmer another 20 minutes. Add the flour and water mixture and cook (stirring constantly) until thickened. Bottle and refrigerate. Makes about 2 cups.

# Rouladen

Meat for rouladen is cut from the top or bottom round of beef. This recipe for the German specialty comes from the people at Bavarian Meats.

2 slices rouladen meat (about
  1/2 pound each)
salt and pepper to taste
mustard (German Lion brand
  recommended)

4 slices bacon, uncooked
4 tablespoons chopped onion
4 tablespoons chopped dill
  pickles
butter

Salt and pepper each slice of meat; spread with mustard. Lay bacon strips lengthwise over meat and sprinkle with onions and dill pickles. Roll tightly (like a jelly roll) and skewer. Brown on all sides in butter. Put in a pot, cover with water, and simmer for a good hour, covered. Add more water as needed to keep meat covered during cooking time. For a rich gravy, thicken the broth with a roux and adjust seasoning. (Make the roux by stirring 2 tablespoons flour into 2 tablespoons melted butter over low heat.) Serves 2.

# Bobotie

For those of you who must have hamburger, here is a South African curried beef, passed on by Marjan Willemsen from Rex's.

1 onion, minced
2 cloves garlic, minced
1/4 cup butter
1 pound lean hamburger
1 cup hot Bombay mango
    chutney

1 tablespoon curry powder
1 teaspoon salt
1 tablespoon black pepper
Custard: 2 eggs (beaten) and 1
        cup half-and-half

Sauté the onion and garlic in butter for 10 minutes. Add the hamburger, break the meat up carefully, and sauté for 15 minutes. Add the chutney, curry powder, salt, and pepper. Cook for 30 minutes over medium heat; then drain off fat. Place meat in square baking pan, smooth the surface, and cover with the uncooked custard. Bake, uncovered, at 350° for 30 minutes. Cut into squares. Serves 4 to 6.

---

# POULTRY AND GAME

In 1911, chickens, ducks, and geese—their feet tightly bound, their necks limp—hung from racks in long rows around the various meat and poultry counters in the Market. (In deference to possible squeamish customers, poultry could not be slaughtered or drawn in the Market, so no neck-wringing or blood-letting took place here.) Potential buyers assessed the line of beauties, eyeing skin color, breast width, plumpness, and age. At twenty-five cents a pound (one could eat prime rib for twelve and one-half cents a pound) chicken was a little dear, but it could, by using the carcass, giblets, and feet, be stretched: a good Sunday dinner, and chicken soup for the week.

Health regulations have changed the display at the butcher counters and poultry stand, and methods of production have changed the taste of chicken some. But it is now a much better buy than prime rib, it is still delicious, and it can still, from Sunday's carcass, be made into chicken soup for the week.

## CHICKEN

It's hard to get tired of chicken. Its delicate flavor can be enjoyed on its own—grilled or broiled with just salt and pepper—or combined with vegetables, wine, spices, or stuffings. It's good in salads and makes great soup. The wings, marinated and broiled, make terrific appetizers. It's versatile, it's cheap, and it's very good for you.

Chicken is definitely one of the best buys in the Market, both in protein value and servings per pound. But if you think chicken tastes different today than it used to, you're right. It does.

152

The reasons birds tasted different twenty years ago are varied.

Fryers and broilers were, at one time, slaughtered when they were fifteen to twenty weeks old, ample time to run around the barnyard (some say exercise is what really makes a chicken flavorful), eating tasty bugs and worms. After slaughter, before being sent to market, they were dry-picked; the feathers were removed by hand without immersing the chickens in a hot-water bath. Some out-of-state chickens, mostly those from Arkansas, are advertised as dry-picked and are recognized by their yellow, pebbly skin. Dry-picked chickens may taste best, but by the time they reach Washington, that taste advantage has been lost to distance and cold storage.

These days, commercial growers keep their chickens confined, feed them a diet of high-energy foods to plump them out quickly, and slaughter the birds after a mere nine weeks. Almost

all of the chickens produced in this area are wet-picked and recognized by their white, smooth skin. They are briefly immersed in hot water and sent through picking machines. (These machines were originally designed to husk pineapples.) Early slaughter provides a greater supply of chickens at a lower price because the cost of keeping each chicken is less.

There is no reason to *ever* buy out-of-state or frozen chicken. Chicken does not improve with age and is highly perishable, having a total shelf life of only seven days. Most of the chicken available in the Market comes from local distributors and reaches poultry and butcher counters as little as five hours after slaughter. Nothing destroys the delicate flavor of chicken faster than cold storage. So before you buy, ask your poulterer when the chicken was delivered.

You might also ask whether the chicken is additive free. This means no hormones were added to the feed to artificially plump the chicken and no preservatives were applied to increase shelf life. Don't be satisfied with a blank look or an assurance that all chickens have some additives. They don't.

Chicken is tender, short-fibered meat that is (depending on how it's cooked) low in calories. Broilers and fryers are interchangeable terms. These birds are either sex, weigh two and one-half to three pounds and are perfect for most chicken recipes. Because these are young chickens, quick cooking is preferred so as not to dry out the meat. Your best buy is a whole fryer which you can easily cut up at home. A three-pound fryer will serve four people.

The little packet of giblets found in the cavity of each whole fryer contains the chicken liver, the heart, neck, and gizzard. Each of these innards may be bought separately, by the pound, and prepared in a variety of ways to make good, inexpensive dinners.

The best of the chicken giblets is the liver. Small, dark red in color, these are popular for sautées and make an excellent, inex-

## Cutting Up a Fryer

*When cutting up a fryer, use a sharp knife and remember to cut away from yourself. The chicken has joints which are easily broken back away from the body after the initial cut is made through the skin. You can feel these joints by moving the wing or leg back and forth. Place the chicken on its side, and begin by cutting the wings off. These must be cut first because they tend to get in the way of cutting the legs. After the wings are severed, put the chicken on its back. Pull one leg up, slice deeply into the skin, and pull the joint away from the body until you see the top of the bone. Cut through. Repeat on the other leg. The thigh may be cut away from the leg by locating the joint and cutting through. To separate the breast and back, stand the chicken up on the cavity and cut downward through the ribs. This should cut fairly easily. To sever the joint completely, bend the two halves apart and cut through the bone joining them at the bottom. Do not discard the back or the neck (which come inside the giblet bag in the cavity). These make excellent chicken stock for soups. The giblets should not be discarded either. These can be washed, chopped, and added to the stuffing for extra flavor.*

## Boning a Chicken Breast

*Boning a chicken breast is easy and takes only minutes. The trick is to use poultry shears for most of the work. There is less waste this way.*

*With your boning knife, notch the top of the breast in a V. (The top of the breast is where the wishbone is.) Grasp the breast in your left hand, anchoring your thumb in the middle of the keel bone. (The keel bone is the large bone which runs almost up the middle of the breast and to the right.) Push back on the top part of each side with your right hand, breaking the smaller bones away from the keel bone. Pop the keel bone out and pull it away with your right hand. The cartilage will pull right up with it. Turn the breast over, skinside up. Take your poultry shears and snip the wishbone away from (not off) the meat on both sides. Lay the chicken breast skinside down again, then pull the smaller bones away from the meat. These should pull away easily. Snip the wishbone off at the top of the breast on both sides. If you want the skin off, most of it can be peeled away; the rest, trimmed. This process gets easier with practice. If you don't want to do it yourself, you can usually get boned chicken breasts (for an extra charge) at the poultry counter. If there are none on display, ask.*

pensive paté. If you do not overcook them, they are tender and have a less dense texture than calf or beef liver.

The heart and gizzard are generally used only for the enhancement of stew and the enriching of stock. Some people love them. To be edible they require moist heat and lengthy cooking (or lengthy marinating) to soften their elastic texture.

Although the fryer is a better buy, you may prefer a particular part of the chicken: the breast, wing, drumstick, or thigh. These are available separately and are sold by the pound. Breast, though it seems expensive, is a good buy because of the high meat-to-bone ratio. Chicken wings are relatively inexpensive and have enough meat on them to make a satisfying appetizer or a light dinner.

Boning a whole chicken is possible but it takes a good knowledge of the bone structure of a chicken, incredible patience, and a very good reason. If you absolutely must have a whole, boned chicken, talk to your poulterer. With enough advance notice he can do this for you (it will cost about a dollar more per pound), and you don't run the risk of having a chicken that looks like it's gone through its second slaughter.

Larger and fattier than a fryer is the roasting hen. The roaster is comparable in price per pound to the young fryer. It weighs from five to seven pounds, is six months old, is extremely flavorful, and is good for stuffing. Allow one pound per person. Roasting hens are called roasting fryers when they are three months old. These are slightly smaller, about four to six pounds.

Stewing hens (sometimes labeled baking hens), are generally former egg layers and were once the staple of the stockpot. Althought they are inexpensive, very few people buy them anymore. Stewing hens take much longer to cook than fryers do, but once in the pot they require very little attention. These birds are one to two years old. They're tough; respect that fact and don't try to sauté, fry, or broil them. But because they are mature and have had plenty of exercise, they have a rich, full flavor and can be falling-away-from-the-bone tender with long, moist cooking.

---

## Garlic Chicken

Garlic lovers may increase the amount of garlic to taste. This is a basic recipe; the herbs may change according to your mood and your spice cabinet. Tarragon, thyme, rosemary, and mint are all great with chicken.

*1 3-pound fryer, cut up*
*flour*
*olive oil (short stream)*
*4 garlic cloves, peeled*
*  and cut in half*
*1 to 1-1/2 tablespoons of*
*  your favorite herb*

*1/4 to 1/2 cup white wine,*
*  sherry or vermouth*
*salt and pepper*
*  to taste*
*1 cup finely chopped*
*  mushrooms*

Rinse the fryer pieces, pat dry, and dredge in flour. Heat oil in a large frying pan. Before the oil begins to smoke, sauté the garlic until lightly browned; remove. Add the chicken (careful, the oil will be quite hot and will splatter easily) and brown well on all sides. Add the herbs, wine, and salt and pepper. This will steam up quickly; so be prepared with your cover and stand back. Cover and let cook for 30 to 40 minutes, checking to make sure there is always some liquid in the pan. (If it becomes dry, add some chicken stock or water.) Turn once. Before serving, let chicken cook a few minutes without the cover to dry it out. A pan gravy may be made from the liquid. Add some water, or chicken stock, to the pan and deglaze, if necessary. Add mushrooms. Mix one tablespoon flour in one tablespoon water until smooth. Stir (with wooden spoon) into liquid. Heat over low heat until just boiling. Pour over the chicken and serve immediately. Serves 4.

## Lee's Complete Chicken Dinner

This recipe comes from Lee Spencer, manager of Chicken Valley, the Market's poultry stand. It's a good dinner if you want something hearty but don't have a lot of time to fuss.

| | |
|---|---|
| 1 3-pound fryer, cut up | 2 turnips, cut up |
| olive oil | 3 medium-size potatoes, cut up |
| 3 carrots, cut in chunks | salt and pepper |
| 3 stalks celery, cut in chunks | 1 teaspoon rosemary |

Brown the fryer pieces well in hot olive oil. Transfer the chicken to a large roasting pan with a cover. Add the vegetables to the roasting pan, arranging around the chicken. Sprinkle with salt and pepper and the rosemary. Cover and bake at 325° until vegetables are tender and chicken is done. It is not necessary to add liquid because the chicken and vegetables release enough moisture to create a broth. The broth may be used to make gravy or put in chicken soup. Season to taste. Serves 4 to 6.

## Roast Chicken

This makes a substantial meal and is not that expensive.

| | |
|---|---|
| 1 whole 5-pound roasting hen | 1 tablespoon rosemary |
| 1/2 lemon | 2 parsley sprigs |
| 2 garlic cloves, peeled and | 1/2 onion |
| crushed slightly | 2 tablespoons butter |
| 1 tablespoon tarragon | |

Rinse the roaster, pat dry, and rub the inside cavity with the cut half of the lemon. Truss the bird. Rub the outside with butter and salt and pepper. Put the garlic, tarragon (fresh or dried), rosemary, parsley sprigs, onion, and butter in the cavity before roasting. This imparts a delicate flavor to the hen. It's a good idea to truss a bird even if you are not stuffing it because it holds its shape better. Place on a rack in a roasting pan. (Any roasting bird should be kept out of its own fat.) Roast at 400° for 40 minutes; baste with butter. Roast 20 minutes longer and check for doneness. The leg joint should wiggle easily and juices pricked from the thigh should run clear. Serves 6.

## Tom's Chicken and Beans

This is good for Saturday night. Tom thinks it's just for family, but guests will like it, too. Start it early—it takes all day to cook.

| | |
|---|---|
| 1 whole stewing chicken | 1/2 cup molasses |
| 1 onion, thinly sliced | 1 teaspoon salt |
| 1 pound navy beans, soaked overnight | 1 teaspoon dried mustard |

Take an old stewing chicken; be sure all the feathers are plucked out. Put it in the bean pot and add the onion and navy beans. Mix the salt and mustard into the molasses and add to bean pot. Cover with water. Cover the bean pot with a lid and bake at 240° for 7 (yes, 7) hours. Take the lid off and bake 1 hour longer. Remove the skin and bones of the chicken and break up any large chunks of meat. Arrange on a platter and serve with homemade relishes. Serves about 8.

## Chicken and Dumplings

Here is an old standby that deserves another look. It does take some time to make, so do it some Saturday or Sunday afternoon—or the evening before.

| | |
|---|---|
| 1 stewing chicken, cut up | 1-1/2 cups flour |
| 2 bay leaves | 2 teaspoons baking powder |
| 12 peppercorns | 1/2 teaspoon salt |
| 2 cloves garlic, peeled and cut in half | 1 egg |
| | 1/2 cup milk |
| 1 teaspoon salt | 1/2 teaspoon dillweed |

In a large stockpot, place the stewing chicken, bay leaves, peppercorns, garlic, salt, and water to cover. Bring to a boil and then simmer for about 2 hours or until chicken meat separates from the bones. Blend together flour, baking powder, and salt. Beat egg well and add to milk. Mix into dry ingredients. Add dillweed and mix well. Your dough should be stiff. If it isn't, add flour.

Drop dough by spoonfuls into the boiling stock. (If you wet the spoon in the liquid first, the dough will roll off easier.) As soon as you have them in the pot, put the lid on and leave it on for 20 minutes: steam is essential to good dumplings. Check to see if they are done just like you do a cake, with a toothpick. Serve a piece of chicken, soup stock, and dumplings in each bowl. Be sure to provide your diners with large napkins, knives, forks, and spoons. Serves 4.

## Phuong's Chicken Wings

These wings are delicious, easy (although time-consuming), and make a wonderful hearty appetizer or a light dinner. This recipe is from Phuong Nguyen at the Saigon-over-Counter, who advises, if you like your stuffing spicier, to add more pepper.

| | |
|---|---|
| 1 pound fresh ground pork | 1 egg |
| 4 ounces onion, finely chopped | 3 pounds chicken wings |
| 2 teaspoons soy sauce | 1/2 cup soy sauce |
| 1 teaspoon salt | 1 teaspoon sugar |
| 1 teaspoon pepper | flour |
| 1 ounce bean thread (available at oriental groceries) | salt and pepper to taste |

Mix first seven ingredients together to make the stuffing. Cut the chicken wings at the second joint from the wing tip; you'll be using the piece with the tip. (The cut-off pieces are ideal for the marinated chicken wings in the next recipe.) Pull bones out of the wings and insert stuffing. Mix together soy sauce and sugar; coat wings with it. Roll in flour seasoned with salt and pepper. Bake at 400° for 30 minutes, turning once after 15 minutes. These can be served with a soy dip. As an appetizer, serves 6; as a dinner, serves 4 generously.

# Marinated Chicken Wings with Plum Sauce

2 pounds chicken wings (about a
   dozen)
pepper
2 tablespoons soy sauce
2 tablespoons sherry
2 cloves garlic, crushed

pinch of sugar
1 cup plum jelly
1/2 cup Major Grey's chutney,
   chopped fine
1 tablespoon vinegar
1 tablespoon sugar (optional)

With kitchen shears or a knife, cut the wing tips off and discard. Now cut the wings in half at the joints. Place the pieces in a shallow dish and sprinkle generously with pepper. Prepare a marinade by combining soy sauce, sherry, garlic, and sugar; pour over the wings. Refrigerate overnight, turning once. Make plum sauce by heating plum jelly, chutney, vinegar, and sugar in a saucepan (or buy your plum sauce at an oriental grocery). Broil the chicken wings until done, turning once. Serve hot or at room temperature with the plum sauce. For a tangy glaze, baste the wings with a light coat of plum sauce before broiling. Serves 6 to 8 as an appetizer, or 4 for dinner.

## Sautéed Chicken Livers

1 pound chicken livers
1/4 cup butter
1 tablespoon parsley
1 tablespoon shallots
1/4 cup mushrooms
1 tablespoon flour

1/2 cup dry white wine
1/4 cup chicken stock
1 bay leaf
1 sprig thyme
6 sprigs parsley

Rinse chicken livers and pat dry. Sauté over low heat in butter together with parsley, shallots, and mushrooms. Sprinkle with flour, blend, and stir in wine and chicken stock. Tie bay leaf, thyme (or add to mixture 1/2 teaspoon dried thyme), and parsley in cheesecloth; add to livers. Cover and simmer gently for 15 minutes, stirring occasionally. Serve with crusty French bread. Serves 2.

## Chicken Liver Paté

1 clove garlic, finely chopped
2 or 3 tablespoons butter
1/4 pound mushrooms, chopped

1/2 pound chicken livers
4 tablespoons finely chopped
   scallions

1/4 cup white wine            1/4 cup butter, softened
1/2 teaspoon paprika       salt
2 or 3 drops Tabasco

Sauté garlic briefly in butter; add mushrooms, chicken livers, scallions, and paprika and simmer for 5 minutes. Add wine and Tabasco and cook, covered, for about 7 minutes. Cool. Mix in blender until smooth. Swirl softened butter into mixture, salt to taste, and refrigerate overnight. Serves 4.

---

## CAPONS

The Romans were the first to discover, after much trial and error, how to make the strutting, stringy, inedible rooster into a plump and delectable bird. Capons are the eunuchs of the barnyard. Castrated (surgically sterilized) at three to five weeks, they fatten quickly, growing extra large and tasty. They are really more like small turkeys than chickens. A capon weighs from six to eight pounds and is from six to eight months old when slaughtered. An eight-pound capon will serve ten to twelve people.

The flesh of the capon is extremely tender because its fat is marbled throughout the lean tissue. Capons sell for a higher price per pound than chickens because they require more labor and feed to produce. But they do have a wider breast and more white meat. Although they are carved like turkeys, in cooking, capons are treated much like roasting hens. They are not generally available fresh.

## DUCK

Most people's version of duck is a glazed, golden brown bird set on a platter, surrounded by wild rice and sliced oranges. It should look like this. Duck, prepared well, can be an exquisite dish with crusty skin and rich, dark meat. But too often it is poorly prepared and becomes a fatty, spongy, uncarveable mess.

Because there are few commercial duck farms in western Washington, duck is rarely sold fresh in the Market. Frozen duck, from the eastern and midwestern states, is available year-round. These birds are descendants of the Pekin, which in turn is a descendant of the wild mallard, introduced to this country in 1872.

A four- to five-pound duck is ready for market in three months

## Carving

*Carving a duck can be a bit of a mess. Always use a heavy, sturdy fork to anchor the duck on the platter, or you will be picking it up off the floor. In fact, unless you are an accomplished carver, do the carving in the kitchen. Use a long, sharp knife. Insert the fork into the joint, gently pull away from the body, and cut the leg off, severing the tendons that hold it tightly to the body. Cut off the other leg in the same manner. Remove the wings in a similar fashion, changing the position of the fork when necessary, to hold the duck steady. To slice the breast, begin at the neck and slice across the grain, first on one side of the breast and then the other. A much easier way to serve duck is to halve or quarter it with heavy poultry shears. Arrange pieces attractively on a serving platter.*

*Don't throw the duck carcass away. It can be used (as chicken is) to make a rich stock for soup. Since duck is fattier, chill the stock and skim. Unpeeled vegetables cut in large chunks will absorb less fat than small, peeled pieces when added to the stock for soup.*

and will feed two to three people. If you are having more than three for dinner, consider roasting two ducklings (three and one-half to four pounds each); it's really not much more work than preparing one duck. Keep in mind that less than 25 percent of the duck is edible because of its high fat and bone content.

A duck looks, before roasting, like a doughy and flattened chicken, with tiny front legs and long, thin wings. Under the skin is a thick layer of fat that must be rendered if the bird is to be crisp and succulent. Duck has only dark meat and has a far gamier flavor than any other domestic fowl. The easiest way to prepare it is to roast it.

---

## *Roast Duck with Apricot Glaze*

The most important thing about roasting duck (or roasting anything, really) is to keep it out of its own fat while cooking. This is critical in cooking duck because it is a very fatty bird. Set the duck on a rack inside the roasting pan. There are special cross-racks designed to hold birds or meat, but these are not really necessary if you have anything at all that will hold the bird off the bottom of the pan. Use your broiling pan, if you prefer.

Although duck is often stuffed with a bread or rice stuffing, the fattiness of the bird tends to make the stuffing too wet. Rather than using grain, try stuffing with quartered apples, seedless raisins, and sliced oranges. Discard these before serving the duck.

| | |
|---|---|
| *1 large duck, 4 to 5 pounds* | *1/2 cup water* |
| *salt and pepper to taste* | *1/2 cup honey* |
| *1/2 lemon* | *1/2 cup apricot juice* |
| *1 orange, sliced, or* | *beurre manié: 2 tablespoons* |
| *   2 stalks celery, chopped* | *   flour kneaded with 2* |
| *1 small onion, whole* | *   tablespoons butter* |
| *5 apricots, halved* | |

Remove the giblets from duck cavity; wash and boil with neck in water to cover for 30 minutes. Strain and reserve for sauce. Rinse the duck quickly and pat dry. Rub the outside of the bird with salt and pepper and the cut half of the lemon. Insert orange slices, or chopped celery, and the onion in the cavity. Truss the bird. (If you are basting with butter only, you may want to sprinkle the outside with a bit of rosemary or thyme.) Roast at 325° for 1-1/4 hours for rare duck and 1-1/2 hours for medium rare. A rare or medium-rare duck has a gamier flavor than does a well-done duck (2 hours).

While duck is roasting make the glaze. Cook apricots in the water until soft; stir in honey. Duck lends itself to sweetened glazes, and orange, cherry, plum, or apple may be used instead of apricot. If fresh fruit is not available, used canned fruit preserved in water or a light syrup. If you are not basting with a glaze, a simple butter baste adds crispness and richness to the skin. After the duck has roasted for 40 minutes, prick the skin all over. This releases the fat and makes the skin crunchy. At this point, begin basting with the glaze. Baste every 10 to 15 minutes until duck is fully roasted. Remove the duck from the roasting pan to a hot platter. Skim the fat from the pan. Deglaze the pan with the giblet broth; then pour broth into a small, heavy pan and place over high heat. Add apricot juice. Cook down over high heat. For a thicker sauce, add beurre manié to the hot liquid and stir well until blended. Serve carved duck with this sauce and wild or white rice on the side. Serves 2 to 3.

## GOOSE

A goose is a wonderful change from the standard holiday turkey. Fresh geese are available in the Market twice a year, at Thanksgiving and again at Christmas. The supply is limited and the demand is great, which makes preordering a necessity. Because geese are sold at eight to ten months (unlike chicken, which is ready for Market in two months), they are expensive birds (both to raise and to buy) and are best saved for special dinners. Frozen geese and goslings are available year-round. The best ones come from Sleepy Eye, Minnesota.

Geese should be young (eight to ten months) and weigh eight to sixteen pounds. A ten-pound goose will feed only about six people because, like duck, it has a high fat content and loses much of its bulk in roasting. A goose has all dark meat.

---

## Cooked Goose

1 goose, about 10 pounds
salt and pepper to taste
1/2 lemon

2 stalks celery, chopped
1 onion, sliced
butter

Wash the bird quickly and dry carefully. Never immerse in water. (For that matter, no poultry should be immersed, because the flesh absorbs water.) Rub the outside and inside surfaces with salt and pepper and sprinkle with lemon juice. Put the sliced celery and onion into the cavity to absorb any off flavors. Discard after roasting. Traditionally goose has been stuffed, but it is not recommended. The fattiness of the bird tends to overwhelm the flavor of the stuffing. (If you do stuff, be careful not to overpack. Skewer or sew the openings shut.) Truss the bird even if you are not stuffing it; this helps to keep the shape while roasting. Place goose on a rack in a shallow roasting pan. As with roasting duck, it is important to keep the goose out of its own fat; otherwise the bottom gets spongy. You may sear the goose at 450° for 15 minutes. Continue roasting at 350° for 20 minutes to the pound. When the goose is half-done, prick the skin all over (especially at the leg and wing joints) to release the fat. Begin basting, either with butter or drippings from the pan. Basting is important because it keeps the meat from drying out. Remove the fat from the bottom of the pan with a bulb baster.

Brush butter on the skin and run under the broiler for a few minutes at the end of the cooking time. This will crisp the bird and turn it golden brown. Serves 6.

---

## ROCK CORNISH GAME HEN

Rock Cornish game hens are simple to prepare, relatively inexpensive, and make elegant dinners. They are not stunted chickens and they are not true game hens. They are young, female, broiler-type chicks that are fed a special diet and are slaughtered at about five weeks of age. Cornish game hens are all white meat.

Locally, they are not available fresh, although there are a few farms in western Washington raising similar birds for restaurants. Most of the frozen game hens available here come from Arkansas.

If you plan to serve one bird per person, try to purchase one-pound birds. Larger birds—and they average one and one-half pounds—can easily serve two people because of their small bones and plump (for their size) breasts. What is wonderful about these often overlooked birds is their versatility: they can be stuffed, baked, sautéed, or broiled. They are compatible with a variety of spices (anything suitable for chicken), brown nicely, and, if not overcooked, are extremely tender. Broiling is an easy way to prepare the hens. Just cut them in half with heavy kitchen shears, sprinkle with salt and pepper, a little lemon juice, and some tarragon. Heat the broiler until very hot and place hens about four inches away from it. Broil 20 minutes; turn, and continue cooking until brown and crisped.

---

## *Roasted Cornish Game Hens*

2 game hens, 1 pound each
1/4 cup butter
1 tablespoon lemon juice
1 tablespoon chopped parsley

1 teaspoon rosemary, thyme, or
   tarragon
salt and pepper to taste
melted butter

When hens are defrosted, remove the giblets from the inside cavity, rinse birds, and pat dry. Game hens are not very fatty birds and can be put directly into the roasting pan. A good way to impart the herb flavor to the meat and to keep the meat moist (if you have the time) is to put butter and seasoning under the skin. Here's how. Slip your fingers between the skin and flesh. Do this gently so as not to rip the skin. Work your fingers from the top of the breast and as far down as possible on the legs. Cream the butter with lemon juice, parsley, and one of the herbs. Add a sprinkling of salt and a few grinds of pepper. Insert this butter mixture under the loosened skin, spreading it evenly. Truss the hens and brush with melted butter. If you do not have the time to put the seasoning under the skin, rub the bird inside and out with lemon juice and the parsley, herb, and seasonings. Spread the butter on top of the bird. Truss. Roast at 400° for 10 minutes; baste and return to the oven for another 10 minutes. Reduce the heat to 350°. Baste frequently with butter and roast about 40 minutes longer or until juices pricked from the thigh joint run clear. To get an even browning, turn the birds from side to side while roasting, ending with the breast up. Serves 2.

---

## TURKEY

There was a time when turkey only made it to the dinner table during the holidays. Everyone would admire it, enjoy turkey leftovers for a week, and promptly forget about it again for another year. But things have changed. Americans now consume over a billion pounds of turkey a year. Fresh turkeys are available during the holidays (watch for the "Order Your Holiday Bird" signs at the butcher counters and poultry stand), and frozen turkey is available year-round. If you are interested in only part of the turkey, fresh legs and wings are often in at the poultry counter during the year, and whole turkey breasts, frozen (and occasionally fresh) are now available. In spite of the fact that turkeys are difficult to raise (they're fussy, skittish, and panic easily), there is a healthy turkey industry that keeps us well supplied.

Turkey is excellent eating and the least expensive, per pound, of all the birds. It easily stretches into several meals. Serve it first with stuffing, then sliced for sandwiches. And when almost picked clean, the carcass can be simmered in the stockpot for a rich, hearty soup.

The turkeys we get in Washington, even the fresh ones, are from out of state. Most come from California and Utah, but the larger birds come from Colorado. Turkeys weigh from eight to twenty-eight pounds and are from six to eight months old when sent to market. A female turkey is called a hen and a male, a tom. You will pay more per pound for the hen because of its wider, deeper breast.

When planning to serve turkey, allow about one pound per person. A ten-pound turkey will serve twelve people. A seven- to

eight-pound turkey will serve four to six people well. It is more economical to buy a slightly larger bird; it gives more meat, less bone weight, per pound. When picking out your bird (they are all wrapped in tight, white plastic that is virtually impossible to see through), look for one that has more width than length and has plumpness through the breast and legs. Scrawny, long turkeys make poor eating.

Of the turkey parts, the breast is a remarkably good buy. The breast is all white meat, very little bone, and is uncommonly good for you—low in both calories and cholesterol. Turkey breasts average between four and six pounds. The initial purchasing investment may be high, but one pound of turkey breast will serve two people well. Roast turkey breast has all the fine flavor of a whole turkey but is not nearly as much work. Since it is only the top part of the bird's cavity, it is not suitable for stuffing.

Some turkeys are labeled self-basting. Try to avoid these. They are injected with a butterlike solution that is no substitute for frequent, pan-dripping basting. The whole idea behind basting is to prevent the meat from drying out while allowing the skin to slowly brown and turn golden. But if you have a twenty-pound turkey sitting in a heavy roasting pan, getting it out of the oven every fifteen or twenty minutes is painful. Here are two ways to cut down on your basting time. Fold a large piece of cheesecloth several times. Soak it in melted butter and a little olive oil and place it on the breast of the turkey before putting it into the oven. Leave it on the breast until the turkey is half-done; remove. Continue roasting the uncovered bird, and baste every 15 or 20 minutes with seasoned butter or pan drippings until the bird is done. You can also cut down on basting time by making a tent of aluminum foil to loosely cover the bird. This retains moisture, yet allows even browning. Keep the tent over the bird until half- or three-quarters done. Try to baste at least a few times toward the end of the roasting time. Do not completely wrap the bird in aluminum foil. This will steam the meat and it will taste stewed.

---

## Roast Turkey with Oyster Stuffing

1 cup butter
4 onions, chopped
1/4 cup chopped parsley
2 cups chopped celery
salt and pepper to taste
1/2 teaspoon sage
1/2 teaspoon thyme

6 cups soft breadcrumbs
1 pint oysters, drained and
  chopped
1 turkey, 10 to 12 pounds
1/2 lemon
1/2 cup butter, melted
salt and pepper to taste

Prepare the stuffing first. Melt butter in a large, heavy sauce-pan. Sauté the onions, parsley, and celery. Add the salt, pepper, sage, and thyme. Cook over low heat until onions are tender. Add the breadcrumbs (make sure these are not fine; if they are the dressing will compact too much) and mix well. Add the oysters and mix again. Wash the turkey quickly and thoroughly and pat dry. Rub the cavity with lemon. Stuff loosely and either skewer or sew the opening shut. Truss the bird, rub well with butter, and sprinkle with salt and pepper. Place in a fairly shallow roasting pan or wide baking pan.

Roast, uncovered (or partially covered with cheesecloth or foil, described under Turkey) at 350° and baste frequently with melted butter or melted butter mixed with a little white wine. You may sear the bird (and many people swear by this method) at 450° for the first 15 minutes and then reduce the temperature to 350.° Allow 25 minutes per pound. The thigh joint should move up and down easily. Puncture the thigh joint with a fork to see if the juices run clear. Do not overcook. Serves 12 to 14.

## Turkey Breast

1 turkey breast, 4 to 6 pounds      1/2 cup butter, melted (optional)
salt and pepper to taste

Turkey breast is all white meat and very little fat, so use moist heat, rather than dry, to cook it. After seasoning with salt and pepper, cover with a tin-foil tent and bake, or bake in a clay pot with a tight seal. Bake at 350° for 1-1/2 to 2 hours. Check for doneness by poking a fork through the skin. If red liquid comes out, it's not done. It should be just fork tender, like a chicken breast. Serves 8 to 12.

---

## RABBIT

Rabbit, when it was wild and plentiful in this country, was almost as common on the dinner table as chicken. Although at present it is considered a specialty item, Americans are once again consuming lots of rabbit—almost 50 million pounds a year. At the poultry counter in the Market, you will often see whole, fresh rabbit lying on a bed of ice. The fresh rabbit is raised locally. Cut-up, frozen rabbit from California is available year-round.

More expensive per pound than chicken, rabbit has many tiny bones that, no matter how you cook it, make eating it with your fingers almost mandatory. If you have never tried rabbit and are leery, keep in mind that what you purchase at the poultry stall is a commercially grown, two- to two-and-one-half-pound young fryer that is four to six weeks old. The meat is white and some-what less fatty than poultry. The flavor of the rabbit is delicate but carries most spices suitable for chicken. In fact, you can use any recipe that you use for chicken for rabbit.

---

# Sautéed Rabbit with Pan Gravy

1 rabbit, cut up  
flour  
salt and pepper to taste  
2 tablespoons butter  

2 tablespoons oil  
1 or 2 tablespoons flour  
1 cup milk, half-and-half, or  
  chicken stock  

Rinse the rabbit and pat dry. Dredge the pieces in flour sea-soned with salt and pepper. Heat the butter and oil in a heavy frying pan until hot. Sauté the rabbit until brown and continue cooking at a lower heat, turning frequently, for 20 to 30 minutes or until tender. Remove to a heated platter. Pour all but about 2 tablespoons of the drippings from the pan; return to low heat. Stir flour into the drippings until smooth. Still stirring, add milk and adjust seasoning to taste. Serves 2 to 3.

# Rabbit Stew

If you've never tried rabbit, this is a good recipe to begin with. It comes from David Guren, a friend who prepares rabbit often.

1 rabbit, cut up
cooking oil or a butter and oil
  mixture
1 teaspoon salt
1 teaspoon peppercorns
1 bay leaf

4 medium potatoes, cut up
2 onions, cut up
4 large carrots, cut up
1 large can tomatoes
1/2 cup white wine

Brown rabbit in oil in large skillet; set aside. Add 1 cup water, salt, peppercorns, bay leaf, potatoes, onions, and carrots to the skillet. Simmer for 1 hour or until vegetables are tender. Return rabbit to the skillet and add tomatoes and white wine. Simmer 1-1/2 to 2 hours. Serves 4.

---

# DAIRY PRODUCTS

Most of the butter and egg farmers who came to the Market in 1907 lived in the Scandinavian communities across Puget Sound. Places like Skandia, Pearson, Lemolo, Keyport, Agate Pass, and Bainbridge and Vashon islands. They came in by steamer, gathering on the docks before dawn, their eggs carefully packed in straw baskets, the butter pressed with rose patterns and covered with butter paper. The trip to the Market was a long and often unpleasant one. The early morning fog was chilling and damp, the weather sometimes uncertain. But the trip was worth the discomfort. The butter and egg farmers brought fresh goods, and fresh goods sold well at the Market.

In the next decade, in addition to the commuting farmers, there were several permanent dairy stores. The Liberty Butter Store, the Bee Hive, the Hamilton Butter Store, and the Cow Path Creamery all did a brisk business. A dozen fresh eggs sold for fifty-five cents, a pound of butter cost fifty-eight cents, and Swiss cheese, one of the few imports available, was twenty-five cents a pound.

In 1923, the biggest (and, old-timers say, the best) of the dairy stores opened. The Enumclaw Creamery occupied the entire first floor of the Fairmount Hotel at First and Stewart. Butter and buttermilk were displayed in large wooden vats, and people crowded into the store just to watch the churning. Often, on a busy Saturday, a sign would go up in the window, "All the buttermilk you can drink for a nickel," and lines would form on the street outside. Tired children gladly trekked up the steep hill from the main Market for a scoop of freshly made ice cream.

In the late 1930s, the name of the dairy was changed to the

**171**

Fairmount Dairy and Creamery. During the depression, business slowed, and prices dropped by almost half. A few years later, the war brought controls on the sale of butterfat, and the proliferation of rules and regulations at times overwhelmed the owners, Mr. and Mrs. Graves. The Fairmount was the last of the big dairy stores, and when it closed, the tradition of "butter-

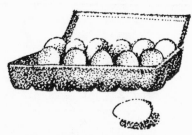

churned-while-you-wait" died. New production techniques and government health requirements meant the end of the small family dairy in the Market.

Still, even today the Market is the place to shop for the freshest of dairy products. You can buy fresh eggs from farmers at the tables (they'll be happy to tell you what they feed their chickens), and you can also buy fresh eggs from other permanent merchants. There is a creamery in the Market, and while the butter you buy wasn't churned on the premises, it does come from local dairy farms. The local farms also provide raw milk, raw cream, and goat's milk. The cheese shops and delis carry a wide range of domestic and imported cheeses.

The Market is the next-best thing to a cow and some chickens in your own backyard.

### EGGS

The best eggs, of course, are those you gather yourself, warm, right out from under the hen. Not many people can do this, but just because you don't raise your own chickens doesn't mean you have to settle for tasteless eggs that have been wrenched from hens whose feet never touch the ground and whose bodies are shot from twice-daily laying.

In the Market you will often see signs advertising eggs from "free-run, rooster-happy hens." Free-run chickens are those that are allowed to run about on the ground. They get exercise, sunlight, and fresh air. They may or may not consort with roosters, but these chickens lead a more natural chicken life. Free-run chickens often have access to pasture or grass. When this diet is combined with a feed of yellow corn or alfalfa, the chickens produce eggs with yolks that are darker and richer in flavor than those of confined hens. Many people believe (and most egg sellers in the Market are adamant about this) that a free-run chicken lays eggs that taste better than the eggs of confined hens. The best way to decide if a free-run chicken produces a better egg is to taste one.

The color of the egg shell does not determine the quality of the egg. Some people swear brown eggs are best; they think that a brown egg has better flavor and are willing to pay a few more cents per dozen. For those who believe, the brown egg does taste better. Nutritively, white and brown eggs are the same. In the Northwest, most white eggs come from white-feathered chickens called Leghorns. Brown eggs come from brown-feathered chickens, either Rhode Island Reds or New Hampshires. Green or blue eggs, often seen in the Market, come from Araucanian hens and can be used in the same way as brown or white eggs.

The freshness of the egg is one of the most important factors in good flavor. People selling at the farmers' tables raise their own chickens. Other Market egg sellers are supplied by local egg producers and receive shipments of eggs several times a week.

A blood or meat spot in an egg is caused by the rupture of a blood vessel on the yolk surface during the formation of the egg. Eggs are examined for this before being sold, but sometimes one gets through. Although unsightly, these eggs are fine to eat.

Egg shells are porous (so should not be washed), allowing water to evaporate from the egg and air to enter. An egg loses a tiny bit of weight every day due to evaporation. Eggs should be stored large end up because the natural air pocket in the egg is located in the large end. If the air pocket is resting at the bottom, it will rise through the egg white, hastening deterioration. Eggs should be refrigerated because they go stale quickly at room temperature.

Cold-storage eggs are eggs that are kept in a cool, controlled atmosphere for thirty days or more. Often they are coated with mineral oil to retard evaporation. These should be eaten only if there are no other eggs for fifty miles.

A fresh egg is heavy; when shaken it should feel full. The yolk should be firm, high, and a deep—almost gold—color. The white should be thick, and when broken into a pan, it should not run in all directions but should stay close to the yolk, making a tight circle covering a small area. The two thick, white, ropelike cords on either side of the yolk are called chalazas. They should be prominent and anchor the yolk well.

Eggs are one of the best sources of protein available because they contain all the essential amino acids (essential amino acids are those which cannot be manufactured by the body.) They are second only to fish-liver oils as a natural source of vitamin D. A large egg has about eighty calories. Eggs do have a relatively high cholesterol content, and people on restricted diets should note this. One dozen eggs weighs about one and one-half pounds. When you figure the price per pound, eggs become one of the best protein buys in the Market. Don't always assume that the largest eggs are best. The best buy is usually the medium- to small-size egg.

## Tips for Cooking Eggs

*There are some basic suggestions for cooking eggs. Everyone seems to develop a preferred method, but if yours are not satisfactory, try these:*

- *Eggs are best used at room temperature. This is especially true when baking with eggs. If you don't remember to take them out in time, don't just plop them into a bowl of warm water to bring up their temperature. Eggs are porous. Instead, break the necessary number of eggs into a bowl and set it inside another bowl filled with warm water.*
- *When scrambling eggs, use a saucepan instead of a frying pan; this will make the eggs stand higher. Don't cook eggs over high heat; this makes them chewier than rubber bands. Use low to moderate heat (this does take patience, especially in the morning) and remove the pan from the heat before the eggs are completely cooked the way you want them. They will continue cooking all the way to the table. Also, don't put salt in your eggs until after they are cooked. Salt draws out the moisture and makes the eggs drier.*
- *To poach eggs, allow the water to come to a boil, stir the water rapidly in one direction, and turn the heat down a bit before slipping the eggs into the water. If you have trouble with this, and you love poached eggs, there is now a kitchen gadget available that resembles a large spoon with a bent handle. It holds the egg whole while the near-boiling water swirls around it.*

- *To hard-cook eggs (eggs are never hard-boiled; this makes unsightly green rings around the yolks), put eggs in cold water and bring to a boil. Remove from heat, cover, and let stand for twenty minutes. Remove immediately from pan, rinse with cold water, and refrigerate.*
- *When beating egg whites, use a cold bowl. Stainless steel is fine, but even better is copper, which will make the whites more stable and cause them to produce more volume. Fresh egg whites, no matter what they're beaten in, will have more volume than cold-storage whites. When the egg is fresh the white is elastic and air can easily be beaten into it. Make sure that the egg whites are yolk-free. A bit of yolk in the whites will affect the volume. Adding a pinch of cream of tartar before beating will make the whites whip better, but if your eggs are really fresh, this is not necessary.*

## Eggs Jex

This is a good brunch recipe because most of it can be assembled beforehand, and it is easy to prepare for a group. It's a rich egg dish that needs only fresh fruit (strawberries, blueberries, and fresh chunks of pineapple) and hot coffee for accompaniments.

| | |
|---|---|
| 2 thick slices French bread, halved | 4 fresh eggs |
| 1 cup grated Swiss or Fjordland cheese | 4 slices crisp bacon, crumbled |
| | 1/2 to 1 cup raw cream |
| | parsley, finely chopped |

Butter a square baking dish. Make a depression in each half slice of bread (this requires tearing bits of the bread out) and place in baking dish. Mound cheese (reserving some for tops) around each depression and slip one egg into each depression. (This is easier to do if you first break the egg into a bowl.) Sprinkle bread and eggs with extra cheese and the bacon; drizzle with cream. Bake at 350° for 10 minutes or until yolks firm over. Before serving, garnish with parsley. Serves 4.

# Brunch Eggs

There are many variations of this way of making eggs. Plan ahead, or just use whatever you have on hand. Ham strips, tomato sauce, cream, grated cheese, and crisp bacon all go well with eggs. It is not necessary to add anything to the egg, but it does make it more special. The basic method is to cook the eggs in a muffin tin or in individual custard cups in the oven. If you are adding liquid (cream, tomato sauce, chili), you can cook the eggs together in an au gratin dish and save on dish washing. This is good for large groups, or just yourself, if you are feeling lazy.

butter
1/2 cup corned beef hash
  (cooked and still warm)

salt and pepper to taste
2 eggs

Butter individual custard cups or muffin tin. Line with hash (or whatever you have on hand). Sprinkle with salt and pepper. Slip an egg into each cup. Bake at 375° until white firms over, about 10 to 15 minutes. Serves 2.

# Easy Egg Sandwich

This is good, easy, and can be eaten with one hand, if you are in a hurry—but wrap the bottom in a napkin or you'll have it in your lap.

butter
1 egg
salt and pepper
1 slice French bread cut in half
Dijon mustard

1 or 2 slices crisp bacon, cooked
  Canadian bacon, or ham
  (optional)
1 slice cheddar cheese

Melt a bit of butter in a pan, break one egg into it, and sprinkle with salt and pepper. Poke the yolk so that it breaks. While the egg is cooking, spread the halves of French bread with mustard. Add any extra items, like the bacon or ham. Turn the egg over and cook 15 to 20 seconds more. Remove and place on bread. Add cheddar cheese and the top half of the bread. Serves 1 but can easily expand to serve a crowd.
VARIATION: If you have more time, this simple variation of the easy egg sandwich can be made into an excellent late-night

supper. Make the easy egg sandwich. Secure with toothpicks if unsteady. Beat an egg with a fork until blended. Dip the sandwich into the beaten egg. Place in a hot frying pan with melted butter and cook until golden on both sides. Serve with a knife and fork, additional mustard, and a spread of relishes and pickles.

---

## MILK

Do you remember when milk came in glass bottles that frosted in the refrigerator and made the milk colder and sweeter than that in any wax-coated paper carton? Milk still comes in bottles, unpasteurized and unhomogenized. And cream, real cream, is still available—cream that is so thick it takes a full minute to come down through the bottle.

Milk, at one time, was simply cooled after coming from the cow and bottled. Today, most milk is pasteurized. Pasteurization is a process by which the milk is heated at increasing temperatures in decreasing amounts of time. Pasteurization, although it protects the consumer against any harmful bacteria, also destroys some of the milk's nutrients and some of the milk's flavor. Pasteurized milk is usually further treated by homogenization. Homogenized milk is milk that is forced through tiny openings

under high pressure; this permanently breaks the butterfat into particles that do not rise as a layer of cream, giving the milk a uniform consistency.

Milk that is not treated is called raw milk. Local dairies that supply the Market must pass rigid inspections of cows, equipment, feed, and employees who handle the milk. The risk of drinking milk with any harmful bacteria is minimal. Herds are constantly checked. Raw milk, because it is not treated, does not have as long a shelf life as pasteurized milk. Buy only what you need for three or four days.

Raw cream is as carefully checked as raw milk. Raw cream is wonderful stuff. It is rich and thick, with a naturally sweet taste that is superb over fresh fruits. Sauces made with raw cream are richer. And if you are whipping it, be careful: a few minutes too long and you are apt to get butter.

Both the raw cream and raw milk are available in returnable glass bottles. Also available in glass bottles are pasteurized, skim, and chocolate milks. For those who don't want to carry the bulk, most everything comes in cartons, too.

There are many dairy items at the Market that are hard to find elsewhere: both raw and pasteurized goat's milk and goat's-milk yogurt, for those who have acquired the taste; mayonnaise, some of the richest outside your own kitchen, made without chemical stabilizers or hydrogenated oils; kefir, cultured milk in all flavors; buttermilk, rich and smooth; cottage cheese, sold in bulk or by the carton; and ice cream, some of the smoothest and best (also some of the most expensive) you've ever tasted. There are many varieties of high-quality butters in the Market: the sweet cream is lightly salted, available at the creamery and in bulk (the best ever) at one of the cheese stalls; unsalted butter, increasingly hard to find, is fresh at the Italian grocery and frozen at the creamery; and soy-bean margarine (no animal fats), good for people on restricted diets, is here, too.

---

## Crème Fraîche

Crème fraîche is cream that is naturally fermented until thick. This is much more like Devonshire cream than sour cream.

1 cup raw cream
1 teaspoon buttermilk or yogurt
  (optional)

Crème fraîche must be made from raw cream. Leave the cream at room temperature for a day or so until it clots and becomes thick (or add buttermilk or yogurt to the raw cream to speed the process). Refrigerate. Serve crème fraîche over fresh fruit or, more unusually, over carrots grated and sautéed in butter or cucumbers sliced with onions and seasoned with salt, pepper, and dill. Makes 1 cup.

# Indian Pudding

5 cups milk, scalded
1/3 cup corn meal
1 cup molasses

1 teaspoon salt
1 teaspoon ginger

Pour milk slowly on corn meal. Cook in double boiler for 20 minutes; add the molasses, salt, and ginger. Pour into a buttered casserole dish, set in a pan of hot water, and bake at 300° for 2 hours. If baked too rapidly, it will not whey. Serve with ice cream or whipped raw cream. This old New England recipe serves 4 to 6.

# Salsa di noce (Walnut Sauce)

This recipe comes from La Coppa Pan. This sauce is served almost exclusively in Recco, a small village in Italy.

1 cup unsalted butter
1/2 clove garlic, chopped very
   fine
1/2 tablespoon chopped parsley
4 fresh basil leaves, chopped, or
   1/2 teaspoon dried basil
1 tablespoon pine nuts, chopped
   fine

3/4 cup walnuts, chopped fine
freshly ground black pepper
1 pint heavy cream (try raw
   cream)
1 cup freshly grated Parmesan
   cheese
1 tablespoon olive oil

Melt the butter very slowly in a one-quart saucepan. Add the garlic, parsley, and basil and cook for 5 minutes. Add pine nuts, walnuts, and pepper, stirring constantly so that the nuts do not burn or stick to the bottom. Add cream and continue stirring until the mixture thickens. (When making cream sauces, always use a wooden spoon. Aluminum tends to turn the sauces an unappetizing gray.) Add the cheese and oil and stir over *low* heat until cheese is thoroughly melted. Remove from heat and add to freshly cooked pasta. Serves 6.

---

## CHEESE

Many of us have been raised on pasty, orange, processed cheese that has as its main attribute an ability to melt easily.

There is a place for this kind of cheese, but to stop there is to ignore some of the finest food in the world. A single wedge of perfectly ripe, crumbly Stilton, blue-veined and slightly aromatic, served on a wooden cheese board, with crisp, green apples, thin crackers, and an especially fine port, makes a wonderful dessert. For a satisfying lunch, try a wedge of runny, creamy Brie spread thickly on a piece of crunchy French bread accompanied by a good ripe pear.

There are well over a thousand different kinds of cheese in the world. Many never go farther than the villages in which they are produced, and many that do get exported are bought quickly and are not distributed widely. In the Market, over 125 different cheeses, both domestic and imported, are sold, and even more varieties are available during the holidays. Some cheeses are available only in the spring and summer; some are available year-round but are best in the winter months. It's a good idea, when trying cheese you are not familiar with, to ask your cheese dealer how to best serve and use them. Advice is free and it can often save you from ruining a good cheese.

Cheese, it is believed, was developed as a way of preserving excess milk. All cheese begins with that single item: milk. What distinguishes the same kind of cheese made in different parts of the world is the quality of the milk: the breed of the cow (goat's or ewe's milk is used for particular cheeses), the soil, climate, and feed all have their effect on the final product. Four-fifths of the protein of the original milk remains in the cheese. It takes about ten pounds of milk to make one pound of cheddar. If made with whole or cream-enriched milk, cheese will be anywhere from 40 to 75 percent butterfat. A cheese labeled double crème will be at least 60 percent butterfat and a triple crème, at least 75 percent. The fat content of butter, in comparison, is 85 percent. Cheese is high in proteins but relatively high in calories as well—on the average, 100 calories per ounce.

The milk, in the initial stages of all cheese making, is warmed. Generally, cheese (especially in this country) is made with pasteurized, rather than raw, milk. Cheeses made with raw milk must be aged for at least sixty days. (This is not true of cheeses produced and sold in Europe.) Although pasteurization of the milk protects people against any pathogenic flora, it does make difficult the full ripening of a cheese. When the milk is warm, to speed the curdling process rennet (an enzyme present in the stomach lining of milk-fed calves or lambs) or a vegetable enzyme is added. Cheese made with the addition of rennet can be aged. Slow curdling, accomplished by the addition of lactic acids rather than rennet, results in fresh, nonripening cheeses such as cottage or ricotta.

When the milk reaches its proper acidic level (and this varies for different cheeses) a starter culture is added. The starter culture is important because it determines, in large part, what kind of cheese will be made.

## Basic Cheese Categories

Surveying the cheese counter can be a bewildering experience. There is a tendency to rely on the favorite stand-bys, Swiss and cheddar. It helps to keep in mind that most cheeses fall into one of four basic categories: fresh, soft-ripened, hard-pressed, and blue-mold.

Fresh cheeses are not ripened. They are generally bland and have a relatively short shelf life. Cottage cheese, ricotta, cream cheese and mozzarella are in this family. The spiced cheeses, Alouette and Boursin, also fall into this group.

The soft-ripened cheeses are not pressed. The flavor and ripening results from the penicillium mold that is sprayed on top of the pie-shaped rounds. Most soft-ripened cheeses are surface-ripened (from the outside crust inward). Ripening takes about a month while the cheese is kept at 90 percent humidity in a curing room. There are a few soft-ripened cheeses in which the curd is cut into smaller pieces before curing begins, which increases maturing time and results in a much stronger cheese. If a soft-ripened cheese is dry and chalky, it is underripe; if it has a strong smell of ammonia, it is past its prime. There are many special cream-enriched soft cheeses such as Explorateur and Boursault.

In making hard-pressed cheeses (such as Swiss or cheddar), after the curd forms in the milk, it is cut into smaller pieces. Most often, the curd is then cooked briefly and stirred constantly at a low temperature. (The higher the temperature and the longer the cooking time, the harder the cheese: Parmesan is one of the hardest.) The whey (liquid left over after the curd is formed) is then drained. If the curd is compacted and molded, cheeses such as Edam result. If the curd is milled (torn and then compacted) cheeses such as cheddar result. The term *hard-pressed* refers specifically to the fact that the curd is compacted. A hard-pressed cheese can be anywhere from semisoft to extremely hard.

The blue-mold cheeses are basically hard-pressed cheeses that have been renneted, cut, and salted. They are either injected or layered with a blue-mold starter. The cheese is often needled to make pathways through the cheese and to ensure even spreading of the blue mold. The blue-mold family includes Roquefort, Gorgonzola, and Stilton.

The last step in cheese making is the ripening. This may take as little as a month or as long as several years. The tendency is toward short ripening time so that the cheese can be marketed sooner. But a four-year-old cheddar, though far more expensive than one that is one year old, is worth the price.

The reason that many cheeses are aromatic (i.e., smelly, foul, absolutely behind-the-barn cheeses) is that, in them, gases are given off by bacteria resulting from the culture used to innoculate the cheeses. This is also, in effect, what creates the holes in Swiss cheese. Because cheese is a living food, its bacteria, when exposed to air, continue to work. Although a cheese will not ripen properly after it has been cut, exposure to air will affect its flavor (often strengthening it) and surface texture. That is why some cheese (like Tilsit) have a thin covering of wax and others are sealed in plastic.

Pasteurized, processed cheeses are made by blending one or more kinds of cheeses together with the aid of heat and an emulsifying agent. This results in a homogenous, plastic mass.

### Serving and Storing Cheese

When you finally decide, from the array available, on your cheese purchase, treat it carefully. It is a good idea to buy only as much cheese as you can use in a week. Do not precut cheese, either before storing or in advance of serving. This dries out the cheese. The best wrap for most cheeses is polyethylene (Saran wrap and other such brands). Semihard cheeses may be wrapped in a cloth that has been dipped into water or a weak brine solution and wrung out. Soft cheeses are best kept in aluminum foil; this protects them from odors and conserves their moisture. Keep cheese in your refrigerator at about thirty-five degrees. In using cheese, remember not to subject it to a warm temperature for a long period of time. After cutting off what you need, return the block to the refrigerator; leaving it near a warm stove or in the back seat of your car during summer will make most hard-pressed cheeses "sweat" out some of the fat that is in the curd. This makes the cheese quite unappetizing. Occasionally, on hard-pressed cheeses, a mold will develop. This mold does not generally penetrate the cheese. It can be scraped, or cut, off and the cheese rewrapped.

Most cheese should be removed from the refrigerator about an hour before serving so that the cheese is about fifty-five degrees when eaten. (Fresh cheeses, however, are served cold.) Soft-ripened cheeses, such as Brie and Camembert, are served when soft and runny, about two to four hours out of the refrigerator. Stilton and many other blue cheeses are served after sitting at room temperature for several hours. Check with your cheese dealer for specific serving suggestions.

Although most cheeses should not be frozen, there are some exceptions. Brie, mozzarella, Swiss, Parmesan, and Provolone, when cut in pieces weighing less than one-half pound and not over one inch thick, and when wrapped tightly, can, if your freezer is zero degrees or less, be frozen successfully. If the temperature is not low enough, you are apt to get a mushy and grainy cheese upon defrosting. When you do defrost, do it in your refrigerator rather than on a counter. Use immediately after defrosting.

When cooking with cheese, remember that it separates at a temperature above 150 degrees (a low to medium simmer) and should not be cooked unless starch is present (a flour or cornstarch base of some kind) to stabilize it. Most cheese should only be melted, not thoroughly cooked. Use wooden utensils when cooking with or melting cheese. If it should curdle, remove from heat and whisk vigorously until cool again.

When selecting and purchasing cheese, the best guide is your cheese dealer. He knows, and will be glad to explain, what a particular cheese is, how it can be served, whether it is especially good or ripe, and whether you can cook with it. If you want more than the usual information (Is the Brie ripe?) don't approach the cheese counter when there is a line three deep. Do your other shopping and get back to the cheese counter when you see that your cheese dealer can take the time to answer all your questions.

# Cheese Guide

This is a basic guide to cheeses available at the Market. There are more (or less) available in different seasons. When selecting cheese, let your own taste be your best guide, but do, before making a costly purchase, check with your cheese dealer and consider his recommendations.

### ALOUETTE *(Domestic)*

This is the American version of Boursin, and although less expensive, it is less flavorful, as well. It is available in herb-garlic, French onion, and other flavors in small, foil-wrapped boxed rounds.

### AMERICAN *(Domestic)*

A generic term more than a cheese, American often includes blends of cheddar or jack. It is sold in loaves and slices, always processed.

### BANON *(French)*

This goat's-milk cheese comes in a small wheel. When young, it is firm and rubbery. When ripened, it has the texture of Brie. It comes wrapped in chestnut leaves and is also available with paprika or herbs.

### BARAKA *(French)*

Actually a Camembert, Baraka is shaped like a horseshoe for easy ripening. With 60 percent butterfat, this is a double-crème cheese.

### BEAUMONT *(French)*

This is a washed-rind dessert cheese from Haute-Savoie. It starts out moist and develops a stronger aroma and flavor as it ages. It has small, irregular eyes in the center and is reminiscent of Port-Salut, but firmer.

### BLUE *(Danish)*

A rich, blue-veined cheese, more open in texture and yellower than the domestic blue, the Danish is a rewarding eating cheese with a medium sharpness. Don't waste this higher-priced, imported blue on salad dressing.

## BLUE *(Domestic)*

This cheese is lighter in color than the Danish blue, with more blue veins. The flavor is acceptable to pretty good, depending on age, and is best at nine months to a year.

## BLUE CASTELLO *(Danish)*

A soft-ripened, blue-and-white mold cheese, Blue Castello is a Danish kind of Camembert with blue veins. It is available in half-rounds that weigh about five ounces each.

## BOURSAULT *(French)*

A wonderfully rich, mild- to strong-flavored (depending on age) triple crème cheese, Boursault should be spread on crackers or on crusty bread and served with fruit. It comes in small rounds with an edible rind.

## BOURSIN *(French)*

Fresh, white, and spicy, this triple-crème, spreadable cheese is flavored with either herbs and garlic or with pepper. It comes foil-wrapped in boxes and is excellent.

## BRIE *(French)*

This mild-flavored, popular, soft-ripened cheese is runny and creamy when just ripe. The thin, chalky rind is edible. Serve it at room temperature, with fruit, for dessert or on crusty bread with a mild, red wine. Varieties are Melun, Coulommiers, and Meux. It does not keep well once cut: four days after purchase is probably the limit.

## CAERPHILLY *(Welsh)*

This cheddarlike cheese is slightly more acidic and tangy than most and lacks a cheddar's usual elasticity. It is a white, moist, and crumbly cheese. Very good.

## CAMEMBERT *(French)*

Camembert, soft-ripened and cream-enriched, is considered a major cheese. It is more aromatic and full-flavored than Brie. Although it is sometimes available from a large wheel, most often it is sold in small rounds of six to eight ounces. Good Camembert makes an excellent dessert cheese. Straw yellow in color, it should be creamy and served at room temperature. When it is young it is rubbery. When overripe, it is wild with an ammonia taste and smell.

CHEDDAR *(Canadian, Domestic, English)*

Depending on age, cheddar can be anywhere from rubbery to full-flavored and crumbly. All cheddars undergo cutting, tearing and milling of the curd, which gives them their texture. The best American cheddars come from Wisconsin, Vermont, and New York. Raw-milk cheddar is also available. It is generally white and has a slightly sharper taste. Aging is an important determiner of quality in cheddar. A six-month-old cheddar is mild. After one year, it is labeled sharp. Occasionally, three- and four-year-old cheddar is available. (Grocery-store prepackaged cheddars may be labeled sharp after aging only three to four months.) When cut, a well-aged cheddar should break cleanly and easily and have a slightly sharp taste. It is available with or without rind and is an excellent all-purpose cheese. Smoked cheddar tends to have a more congealed texture and is often processed.

CHESHIRE *(English)*

An excellent country cheese, Cheshire is like a cheddar but crumblier and softer in texture. When well aged, it is one of the most flavorful of the English cheddar types. The Cheshire generally available at the Market has been aged for a little under a year.

CHÈVRE *(French)*

A goat's-milk (*chèvre* in French means goat) cheese, semisoft chèvre is formed into a sausagelike roll and wrapped with straw (now plastic). When young, it is the mildest of the goat cheeses available. A small chèvre is a chevrette.

COLBY *(Domestic)*

Colby is basically a cheddar in which the curd is not milled—it is stirred and heated. This results in a softer body and a more open texture than that of cheddar. Colby cheese is ripe after one to three months, and because it contains more moisture than cheddar, rather than aging, it spoils if stored longer. This is an unexciting eating cheese but it melts well.

CREAM CHEESE *(Domestic)*

This fresh cheese is popular for cooking and eating. It is available in loaves or in round lengths (like sausage). Some is made without the addition of vegetable gums or preservatives; ask for it.

### Danbo, Low-Fat (Danish)

Small-holed, semihard Danbo is similar to Swiss but with a somewhat elastic texture. It has a mild-to-medium, pleasant flavor, much better-tasting than most low-fat cheeses, and only 20 percent butterfat. To be good, it should be aged at least a year.

### Derby (English)

Pronounced Darby, this is similar to a mild cheddar (but has a higher moisture content). It has a pale color and, when aged, has a crumbly texture and good flavor—most often compared to Double Gloucester.

### Edam (Dutch)

Edam comes (preferably) in one-kilo balls that are then cut into pieces, or it comes in loaves. Firmly textured, mild, and lower in fat than Gouda (to which it is often compared), this cheese has a pleasant, clean flavor. It is either coated in red wax or its surface is colored red and rubbed with wax. Edam is also available in small balls.

### Emmenthal (Danish)

Danish Emmenthal is a pleasant, rindless loaf cheese, creamy, yellowish in color, and moderately dense, with irregular eyes.

### Emmenthal (Swiss)

Although there are many good (and ghastly) imitations, this cheese is excellent. It has a hardened, natural rind and large, irregular holes. Firmer than most Swiss cheeses, it has a distinctive, nutty flavor and is by far the best of its kind.

### Esrom (Danish)

Esrom is a white loaf cheese pocketed with small holes. The medium-to-sharp flavor of this semisoft, part skim-milk cheese is often compared to Port-Salut.

### Explorateur (French)

A triple-crème cheese that is rich and can be pungent, Explorateur should be cream-colored and almost soupy in texture. The rind is edible but bitter if slightly overripe. Sold by the small round, this cheese is excellent, although expensive.

### Feta *(Bulgarian, Danish, Greek)*

A fresh ewe's-milk cheese with a firm but flaky texture, feta is shipped and stored in brine. It is almost pure white and excellent with Greek olives, tomatoes, and an oil-and-vinegar dressing. Bulgarian is good and less expensive.

### Finn Swiss *(Finnish)*

This is a yellow-tinged Swiss with very large holes—sharp and nutty, moist and weepy, when properly aged.

### Finnish Lappi *(Finnish)*

Basically an Edam, packed in plastic, with a moist, sticky texture and mild flavor, this cheese is a good buy. It becomes distinctive with age.

### Fjordland Swiss *(Norwegian)*

This Swiss-type cheese is for Jarlsberg fans who want to pay less for their cheese. Basically a Jarlsberg, it is shaped into loaves instead of large rounds and is sealed in plastic rather than wax, which results in a moister cheese. It has a definite Swiss flavor—medium strength—and is excellent for cooking.

### Fontina *(Italian, Swedish)*

The Italian Fontina is white to creamy yellow, full in flavor, and good for cooking. The Swedish Fontina is an excellent table cheese. Good with beer.

### Gamalost *(Norwegian)*

Gamalost looks very much like a slice of gritty bread that has been toasted until it is a dark, almost caramel color. (It starts out straw-yellow but quickly darkens as it ages.) It has a foul smell and a foul taste; after the cheese dealer cuts it, he has to wash the knife. It is served, by those who enjoy it, thinly sliced on dark, heavy bread.

### Gjetost *(Norwegian)*

For newcomers to this cheese, it is best to get the combination cow's and goat's milk variety, which is less strong. It is made from whey, has a caramel color and is naturally sweet. Ekte is the best, made totally of goat's milk. An acquired taste.

### Gloucester, Double *(English)*

A hard-pressed cheese, somewhere between a cheddar and a

Cheshire in flavor, Double Gloucester is pale orange. It has a crumbly, dense texture and a slightly acidic taste. It should be well aged.

### GORGONZOLA *(Domestic, Italian)*

Lightly blue-veined, with a soft, creamy, pastelike texture and a sharp, distinctive taste, Gorgonzola is excellent served with bread and a vinegar-and-oil-dressed salad or stuffed into cored pears for dessert. The domestic variety is crumblier and tends to be sharper and stronger in flavor.

### GOUDA *(Dutch)*

A wheel-shaped cheese, when aged one year Gouda is dense in texture and yellowish in color, often with small irregular eyes. It's a good general cheese with a slightly salty taste. Serve with firm breads, sliced meats, and beer. Its red wax covering makes it resemble Edam, but Gouda contains more fat. A smoked variety, which comes in loaves or rounds and is processed, is also available.

### GOURMANDISE *(French)*

This is a pasteurized processed cheese spread with a creamy texture, flavored with cherry or walnut. It is primarily a dessert cheese. Some really like it; some find its taste and texture cloying.

### GRUYÈRE *(Swiss)*

Gruyère is pale and dense, with a nutty taste that is distinctive. The natural rind is often thick and tends to get thicker if improperly stored. This cheese is used in making fondue (with Emmenthal, in equal parts) and is a good eating cheese. Don't bother with the processed variety wrapped in foil that is sometimes available.

### HAVARTI, DANISH CREAMY *(Danish)*

Havarti is a cheese with tiny, jagged eyelets and a 60 percent butterfat content. It is the most popular of the imported cheeses because of its semisoft, mild, slightly acidic flavor. It is rindless, has no bacterial culture added, and makes an excellent table cheese.

### HAVARTI, TILSIT *(Danish)*

This is really a different kind of cheese than creamy Havarti. It is the same color but is denser, with more chipping in the texture and a considerably stronger flavor. Because it has less butterfat (45 percent, plus), it is less rich. It has a thin wax coating and gets sharper and more aromatic with age.

### JARLSBERG *(Norwegian)*

This highly advertised Swiss cheese has a mild, good pleasantly sweet flavor with a satisfying, rubbery texture. It is covered with a yellow wax rind and is the second most popular imported cheese.

### KASSERI *(Domestic, Greek)*

This sharp cheese is less dense than a Parmesan and slightly less salty. It makes a good eating cheese and goes well with green grapes or pears. The Greek kasseri is made of ewe's milk and ages much better than the domestic.

### LANCASHIRE *(English)*

Soft and mellow in flavor, this cheese is very good for cooking, as well as for eating. It melts well and retains its flavor. It is somewhat similar to Cheshire and has an almost crumbly texture.

### LEICESTER RED *(English)*

Leicester Red is actually a deep orange. It is dry and flaky but has enough moisture to make slicing easy. Slightly tangy.

### LEYDEN *(Dutch)*

This firm cheese (resembling Gouda) is spiced with caraway seeds, cumin, and curry.

### LIEDERKRANZ *(Domestic)*

This creamy, soft-ripened cheese is similar to Limburger and is sharp and smelly when ripe.

### LIMBURGER *(Domestic, German)*

A semisoft, full-flavored cheese, Limburger is an acquired taste. It is almost noxious-smelling when overripe. The domestic version is somewhat milder than the German.

### LONGHORN *(Domestic)*

More a shape than a cheese, a Longhorn is a long cylinder that is widest at the bottom. Generally a cheddar or Colby, it is either waxed or plastic-wrapped.

### LORRAINE SWISS (Domestic)

A mild (almost bland), low-fat, low-salt cheese with tiny chipped holes, Lorraine Swiss is good for people on restricted diets.

### MITZITHRA (Greek)

A kind of pot cheese, mitzithra is ricotta without the moisture, made in part from fresh ewe's milk. It comes in a large, hard ball and is used in cooking.

### MONTEREY JACK (Domestic)

Basically a cheddar, Monterey jack was first developed in California. It is often dense and bland. If made from low-fat milk and aged six months, it is suitable for grating. It is also available with caraway seeds or hot peppers.

### MOZZARELLA (Domestic, Italian)

A soft and compact cheese with a mild, bland flavor, mozzarella is used almost exclusively for cooking.

### MUNSTER, MUENSTER (Danish, Domestic, French)

Munster is a firm white cheese with a smooth texture. The French version is aromatic, very strong, and comes in small packets. The Danish variety is medium soft and also quite strong. The domestic variety is bland and similar to Monterey jack cheese.

### NOEKKELOST (Norwegian)

Somewhat like an Edam, Noekkelost is a mild cheese studded with cloves and spiced with cumin. It is 30 percent butterfat.

### NORVEGIA (Norwegian)

This is a slightly soft, rindless, mild-flavored Norwegian gouda.

### PARMESAN (Domestic, Italian)

This hard-pressed, somewhat salty-flavored dense cheese is well known for its use in cooking. It melts beautifully. A young Parmesan is good as a table cheese. The domestic versions (considerably cheaper) are good, although sharper and saltier. Stella makes a good consistent Parmesan.

### PONT L'EVEQUE (French)

This yellow-paste cheese is strong in flavor and has an orange rind. It is seldom available except in spring and early summer. It comes in a container about four inches square.

### PORT-SALUT *(French)*

Port-Salut was first made by Trappist Monks in 1815. It is a mild all-purpose cheese, often served as dessert because of its creamy, dense, appealing flavor and texture.

### PROVOLONE *(Domestic, Italian)*

This white, smooth, mild cheese is sometimes bland from inadequate aging. If well aged, its taste ranges from sweet to sharp and is always flavorful. The domestic variety is tasteless. Provolone is available rindless or with rind.

### RACLETTE *(French)*

This pungent cheese should be placed near an open fire, scraped as it melts, and eaten warm on crackers or crusty bread. Serve it with a bright, young red wine. Buy only the amount you want to eat in a single sitting.

### REVIDOUX *(French)*

Semisoft Revidoux is similar to Pont L'Evêque, but not quite as strong. This ripening cheese has a brownish-red rind and is 60 percent butterfat (double crème).

### RICOTTA *(Domestic, Italian)*

Most ricotta is domestic. It is fresh cheese, resembling cottage cheese, but with smaller, drier, and denser curds. It is used in cooking and as a filling in some desserts, such as cannoli. It is also great on a warm crumpet with a dollop of raspberry jam.

### ROMANO *(Domestic, Italian)*

This hard grating cheese has more bite than Parmesan. The Italian Romano is whiter than the yellow-tinged domestic version. Pecorino Romano, also Italian, is a sheep's-milk cheese with more of a sharp flavor and kick than the others. All are used in cooking.

### RONDELÉ *(Domestic)*

Rondelé is a fresh cheese that has an almost whipped texture and is always spiced. If you like this kind of cheese, you'll like Alouette better and Boursin best.

### ROQUEFORT *(French)*

This salty, crumbly, blue-veined, ewe's-milk cheese is made exclusively in the Causses area of France and is aged in the caves of the Colombau Mountains. It is an excellent dessert or special table cheese. It has some bite and a rich, creamy flavor. Roquefort is a registered name and no other blue cheese may be called by that name. Look for the red seal visible on the top edge of the round. Considered one of the major cheeses.

### SAINT ANDRÉ *(French)*

A triple-crème cheese that is rich and flavorful, creamy and buttery, Saint André has an edible rind and usually comes in an eight-ounce packet wrapped in an oak leaf.

### SAINT MONTRACHET *(French)*

This medium-strong cheese is made of a combination of goat's and cow's milk. It is a good dessert cheese but is not always available.

### SAINT PAULIN *(French)*

Similar in taste and firmer in texture than Port-Salut, this cheese is stronger flavored.

### SARDO *(Argentinian)*

This excellent grating cheese, somewhat salty, has more of a tang than Romano. In fact, it can be used like Parmesan or Romano and is considerably cheaper.

### STILTON *(English)*

Stilton is considered one of the great cheeses of the world. Blue-veined, creamy, with a rich flavor. it is best served as a dessert cheese with fine port. (If exposed to the air for very long, it dries out, so protect it.) On a cold night with a warm fire, Stilton is at its best. Serve with tart green apples, if you wish.

### STRING *(Domestic)*

This is appropriately named because it pulls apart in long, thin strings. It is really a whole-milk mozzarella, and is more of a novelty than a tasty eating cheese. Used for cooking.

### SWISS *(Domestic)*; see also Emmenthal

Firm and mild, domestic Swiss is often bland, wet, and undistinguished.

### TILSITER *(Danish, Finnish, Norwegian)*

Many countries make this cheese. It is cream-colored, firm, and has small eyes. The Danish is the most moist; the Finnish is the strongest.

### TURUNMAA *(Finnish)*

Turunmaa has a taste comparable to a cross between creamy Havarti and Finnish Lappi, although it is not as buttery.

### TYBO *(Danish)*

This firm-textured, brick-shaped cheese has a generally medium to strong flavor. There is a caraway Tybo that is nutty and smooth and does not contain cumin (a spice usually added with caraway seeds).

### WENSLEYDALE *(English)*

A white, rindless, cow's-milk cheese, Wensleydale is crumbly, moist, and mild. It has, like most of the English cheddar family, a slight tang. The blue variety of this cheese (not often available) is often favorably compared to Stilton.

# PRESERVING AND PICKLING

## A Month-by-Month Guide

Preserving food by canning, freezing, drying, or pickling is not something people do to save money any more, unless they grow or catch the food themselves. But you cannot buy pickled onions as good as your own, and commercially frozen strawberries can't touch local ones for flavor. Sometimes you can get an exceptional buy on a crate or case of produce, which does make preserving economical.

There are some crops that, for one reason or another, simply aren't worth preserving: greens, celery, eggplant, leeks, onions, pumpkin, summer squash, and most cabbage-family and root crops (kohlrabi, turnips, rutabagas, cabbage, carrots). Unless preserved in special dishes, like sauerkraut and pickled onions, some of these items do not keep well; others are available fresh year-round at fairly stable prices.

Canning is a lot of hot work and takes a lot of time.* Make it worth it. Keep three things in mind—these go for freezing, drying, and pickling, too. 1) Preserve only what you like. If your family won't eat prunes, there is no sense in canning them. 2) Preserve only the best-quality produce and seafood. Nothing gets better in the can or freezer. 3) Preserve only foods that keep well. You may freeze eggplant, but the quality loss is so high you will have to disguise it well in a casserole to use it.

Each food should be preserved at the peak of its season, when quality is highest and price is lowest. You may be surprised to find that every month of the year some kind of food in the Market is perfect for canning. Plan your preserving year well, and you

*If you are a novice and want reliable information on preserving techniques, call your county cooperative extension service or the USDA.

will not go mad. You will have your pantry and freezer stocked with the very best the Northwest has to offer. The preserving year begins in spring, in April.

## APRIL

The Northwest's first spring crop is *rhubarb*, the pie plant. But the season is short — six to eight weeks — and only so many rhubarb pies can be consumed in six weeks. Rhubarb is something that is not available out of season, and if you especially like it, it is worth preserving.

Rhubarb can be canned or frozen with or without sugar. If you freeze it, it will last longer and taste better prepared with a sugar syrup or dry sugar pack. Without sugar, rhubarb keeps only a few months before becoming tasteless and stringy. Rhubarb sauce keeps very well. Cut the rhubarb into small pieces and cook it down slowly. Sugar to taste. Pour into freezer containers, cool, put the lids on, and freeze. Rhubarb sauce is delicious hot or cold.

## MAY

Local *asparagus* finally arrives in May, and prices begin to drop. Canned asparagus is one of the best of the canned vegetables. Use straight jars, rather than those with shoulders, so your stalks can stand up in the jars. Trim stalks all the same length for a nicer looking product. Because it is a low-acid vegetable, asparagus must be processed in a pressure canner to be safe to eat. The long cooking time required for safety sometimes leaves asparagus mushy. If you have this problem, you probably should opt for freezing.

Asparagus is easy to freeze. After trimming and washing, blanch it for two to four minutes (depending on the thickness of the stalks), chill, and freeze in rigid freezer containers.

## JUNE

Summer is now under way and some excellent candidates for preserving are ready: peas, cherries, and berries.

Canning *green peas* is an abomination. They must be cooked so long to be safe to eat that they are neither palatable nor do they resemble the lovely peas you began with. But peas freeze well and easily. You must shell them, blanch for one and one-half to two minutes, cool, and pack into containers. They keep well and retain their sweet flavor. Snow peas, the Chinese pea pods, also freeze well and require only thirty seconds of blanching.

Why blanch? The major reason is to inactivate enzymes in the food. Enzymes help fruits and vegetables to ripen, but they continue to work after produce is picked, resulting in softening, toughness, loss of nutritive value and flavor, and the changing of

sugars to starch. Freezing food will slow enzyme action but won't stop it. Blanching—steaming or immersion in boiling water— inactivates the enzymes. Fruits, however, should not be blanched because blanching damages fruits and destroys their vitamin C. The deterioration caused by enzymes results in browning, but this can be prevented by the use of sugar syrups or ascorbic acids.

*Cherries* only come once a year; so if you want excellent pie later on, do your preserving this month. Cherries retain most of their flavor and vitamins if you freeze them. They also can well. The major difficulty in preserving cherries is pitting them. The person who breeds the first pitless cherry will be very, very wealthy. Actually, you don't need to pit your cherries, but if you don't, the pits will impart an almond flavor to the fruit. Another thing to consider is color. Cherries will lose some color when frozen or canned. Adding ascorbic acid to each container will help retain color. Some people add red food coloring, but the effect is rather ghastly.

Cherries freeze best in a light sugar syrup or dry sugar pack. You can freeze them without sugar, but they will not keep long, only about three months. Canned cherries also taste best if processed in a light sugar syrup but, as with all canned fruits, sugar is not necessary. You cannot can cherry pie filling. Can the cherries without sugar, and make your pie filling from them as needed. The density of cherry pie filling, resulting from the added flour or cornstarch, is too great to be safely canned. However, you can freeze pie filling safely.

The first strawberries in June announce the arrival of *berry* season, a time of year that for many people does not last long enough. In quick succession come the currants and gooseberries. In July raspberries and blueberries (and their cousins the huckleberries) arrive. If you are lucky, you might get some of the wild berries: blackberries, blackcaps, boysenberries, loganberries, or nectarberries. Because the season of each one is short, the temptation to preserve berries for later use is great. You may simply freeze them, or you may wish to preserve them in a jellied product.

Freeze berries whole on cookie sheets and then pack them into cartons; they look better this way. If you are going to put them directly into containers, remember to leave head space; berries expand when frozen.

Jellied fruit products are a good choice, especially if you have overripe fruit to deal with. Jelly is made from the juice of fruit. It should be clear, and firm enough to hold its shape. Jam is made from crushed fruit; so it has seeds in it. It is not as firm as jelly but should retain some shape of its own. Preserves are whole fruits. The fruit is cooked with pectin and sugar to form a thick syrup, slightly jellied. A marmalade is similar to a preserve, but the fruit is cut into pieces that are distributed evenly throughout the product. Marmalades often contain citrus. Conserves are jams containing a combination of several fruits with nuts or raisins. Butters are made from pulp that is pressed through a sieve and cooked with sugar to a very thick consistency.

Jams, jellies, and preserves may be made with or without added pectin, depending on the berry. Strawberries and raspberries generally need added pectin. Currants gel successfully without it. The trick to these products is to find a good recipe and stick to it.

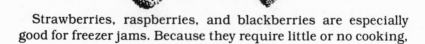

Strawberries, raspberries, and blackberries are especially good for freezer jams. Because they require little or no cooking, they keep their berry flavor and many of their vitamins, and they have better color and aroma than do cooked jams. Better still, they can be made one batch at a time from frozen berries at your convenience. However, freezer jams (all jellied products for that matter) have a lot of sugar in them. Many people run into trouble making jam when they try to cut down on sugar. Usually they end up using their jam for pancake syrup. The amount of sugar called for in the recipes is necessary, and you won't get a good gel without it. Make your jelly the way it should be made, and eat less of it.

---

## Fresh Strawberry Freezer Jam

2 cups finely mashed or
   sieved strawberries
4 cups sugar

1 box powdered pectin
1 cup water

Combine fruit and sugar. Let stand about 20 minutes, stirring occasionally. Boil powdered pectin and water rapidly for 1 minute, stirring constantly. Remove from heat. (Liquid pectin may be used instead of powder. In this case, substitute 1/2 cup liquid pectin for powdered pectin and water. No heating is necessary.) Add the fruit and stir about 2 minutes. Pour into freezer containers, cover with lids (paraffin is not needed), and let the containers stand at room temperature for 24 to 48 hours or until fruit gels. Freeze. Makes about 6 cups.

## Fresh Raspberry Freezer Jam

3 cups finely mashed or
   sieved raspberries
6 cups sugar

1 box powdered pectin
1 cup water

Follow the directions for Strawberry Jam. Makes about 9 cups.

## Red Currant Jelly

2-1/2 quarts currants
1 cup water

4 cups sugar

About one-fourth of the currants should be underripe and three-fourths fully ripe. Underripe berries have a higher pectin content and will help you get a good gel. Sort, wash, and crush the currants (without removing them from the stems) in a heavy pan. Add water, cover, and bring to a boil quickly. Reduce heat; simmer 10 minutes.

Extract juice by putting the prepared fruit in a jelly bag or several layers of cheesecloth and letting it drip from the bag into a pan. (The clearest jelly comes from fruit left to drip without pressing, but you will get more juice by squeezing the bag and then restraining the juice.) Measure 4 cups of juice into an enamel or stainless-steel kettle; add sugar and stir well. Boil over high heat to 220° F. The proper temperature is very important. Remove from heat; skim off foam. Pour immediately into hot jars and seal with paraffin or two-piece canning lids. Makes 5 or 6 six-ounce glasses.

## Blackberry Chutney

4 pounds blackberries
1/2 pound apples
1 pound onions
1-1/2 pints vinegar
1-1/2 teaspoons salt

2 teaspoons ground ginger
3 teaspoons ground mace
1/4 teaspoon cayenne
2 teaspoons dry mustard
1 pound sugar

Wash berries in lightly salted water; then rinse in cold water. Peel apples and onions and chop coarsely. Put into a pan, along with blackberries. Pour in enough vinegar to barely cover. (For a more exotic flavor, add 1 tablespoon each cardamom pods and coriander seed in a muslin bag. Remove before sieving fruit.) Cover with lid and cook gently for about 1-1/2 hours or until fruit and vegetables are quite tender. Rub mixture through a sieve to remove blackberry seeds (mixture can simply be mashed in the pan with a wooden spoon if you don't mind the seeds). Return the mixture to the pan and stir in salt and spices mixed to a thin cream with part of the remaining vinegar. Dissolve sugar in the rest of the vinegar and add to hot mixture. Cook over medium-high heat until chutney has thickened, stirring as necessary.

Pack hot chutney into hot pint jars. Process in a boiling-water bath for 5 minutes (begin timing when water returns to boil). Store at least 2 months before opening. Makes about 6 to 8 cups.

The biggest item to consider preserving this month is eastern Washington *apricots.* Canned, frozen, or dried, apricots are outstanding. You might consider partially drying them (to about the consistency of commercially dried apricots) and then packaging and freezing them. The only problem with drying apricots is that you lose all of their vitamin C and some of their vitamin A. (But they make great snacks, and home-dried ones cost less than store-bought, which are outrageously expensive.) You do not lose nearly as much in canning and you lose nothing at all if you freeze.

If you do decide to can apricots, hot pack them. This prevents the floating fruit you see in so many jars of home-canned apricots, peaches, plums, and prunes. Canning in a sugar syrup will help prevent discoloration of apricots. If you use plain water, your product will taste good, but the fruit will turn a little brown and will be less firm. Apricots have free stones and so are easy to pit. You don't have to do it, but the pits will give an almond flavor to your fruit if left in.

---

## Norsk Frukt Suppe

If you dry apricots, you might like to try this recipe (you may also use your own dried prunes and red currants) for fruit soup, a Scandinavian classic. It makes a wonderful dessert after a heavy, wintertime meal. It is rich, but the fruit makes it seem light. It is also good cold for breakfast or served with sherry late in the afternoon.

*1 cup large tapioca (sago)*
*1 pound dried prunes*
*1/4 pound dried apricots*
*1 cup raisins*
*1/2 cup currants*
*1 lemon, thinly sliced*

*1 orange, thinly sliced*
*1 cup sugar*
*1 stick cinnamon*
*2 apples, sliced (Granny Smith best)*
*raw cream*

Soak tapioca, prunes, apricots, raisins, and currants overnight in water to cover. Place all ingredients except cream in a large saucepan and cover completely with water. Cook until fruit is tender. Soup should be thick, but not too thick; thin with water, if necessary. Cool. Serve cold with thick raw cream. The soup is really best after it has chilled 24 to 48 hours in the refrigerator. Serves 8.

---

*Basil* is fresh on the farmers' tables this month. The leaves can be frozen (in bags) or made into pesto and frozen in containers. Basil also dries well. Tie it in loose bunches and hang upside down inside a paper bag. Keep it in a well-ventilated room, not in the warm sunlight. When it is dry, you can shake the leaves off their stems and into the bag without losing anything. Store basil in an airtight glass jar in a dark, dry cupboard.

Fresh *okra* will be in the high stalls beginning this month. It is not available year-round, and if you are a gumbo fan, you might want to take time now to put some in your freezer.

*Beet* season also begins this month. If pickled beets are one of your specialties, do them now while the small, tender beets are available in good number. Beets do not freeze well.

*Green beans* are in this month. They may be canned or frozen, of course, but canned beans are not that great.

---

## Dilled Green Beans

This very special product is made from small, fresh string beans.

| | |
|---|---|
| *4 pounds green beans, whole* | *dried hot red peppers* |
| *garlic, peeled* | *5 cups vinegar* |
| *mustard seed* | *5 cups water* |
| *fresh dill* | *1/2 cup salt* |

Wash beans well, drain, and cut into lengths to fit jars. Pack beans into clean, hot jars and add to each jar 1 clove garlic, 1/2 teaspoon mustard seed, 1 head dill, and 1/2 hot pepper. Combine vinegar, water, and salt and heat to boiling. Pour the boiling liquid over beans, filling jars to 1/2 inch from the top. Tighten lids. Process in a boiling-water bath for 5 minutes. Remove jars and set several inches apart on a wire rack or folded towel to cool. After 24 hours, check the seals, remove metal rings, and store in a dark, dry, cool place. Makes 7 to 8 pints.

---

## AUGUST

August is a very busy month in the Market; it's the peak of the local harvest and, consequently, a busy time if you are preserving. There is lots of eastern Washington and California fruit (plums, peaches, nectarines), the local tomatoes arrive, and broccoli and corn are in.

*Plums, peaches, and nectarines* offer pretty much the same preserving options as apricots (see preceding section on July). Discoloration occurs if you do not use sugar, but you can add ascorbic acid to these four fruits to prevent discoloration. (There are methods for pretreating the fruit before drying to accomplish the same purpose; specialized books deal with this subject.) Remember also that plums make good jam.

If you want to preserve *broccoli* (or any other green vegetable), freezing is best. Green vegetables are high in vitamin C, and freezing is the only method by which you will retain any of it.

*Tomatoes* are preserved by a lot of people. They do not freeze well except as juice or sauce, but because of their high acidity, tomatoes are one of the few vegetables that may be canned in a water bath rather than a pressure canner. If you want to can tomato sauce, you should use a pressure canner because of other vegetables in it. However, you may safely freeze the sauce; it keeps well, and freezing is a whole lot easier than pressure canning.

When choosing tomatoes for canning, make sure they are ripe, but not overripe. If overripe, tomatoes lose acidity, making them potentially unsafe to eat if processed in only boiling water. The same goes for tomatoes picked from dead vines late in the season. To make sure your canned tomatoes will be safe, add 1/2 teaspoon citric acid or a combination of 2 tablespoons bottled lemon juice and 1/2 teaspoon salt to each quart jar.

Peeling tomatoes, especially if you have a lot to do, is tedious but will result in a much better-looking product. Dip them in boiling water to soften the skins and they will peel easily.

# Green Tomato Relish

Many people like to pickle green tomatoes. The tomatoes should be peeled and packed into jars, covered with a vinegar brine (1 part vinegar to 1 part water), spices added, and then processed in a boiling-water bath for 5 minutes. You might also want to try this relish recipe.

*8 pounds green tomatoes, finely chopped*
*4 pounds brown sugar*
*1 quart vinegar*
*1 teaspoon each mace, cinnamon, and cloves*

Mix the tomatoes and sugar together and boil until tomatoes are tender. Add vinegar and spices and boil together another 10 minutes. Pack hot into clean jars and process in a boiling-water bath for 15 minutes.

# Tomato Sauce for the Freezer

This is a good basic sauce that freezes well, can be thawed and used as it is, or can be added to. Of course, your favorite ingredients may be added and the seasoning adjusted to your taste. Do not add vegetables that do not freeze well (Mushrooms, for example, should be added fresh when you use the sauce, not put in the freezer) and do not add anything in large pieces.

*2 onions, chopped*
*4 cloves garlic, finely chopped*
*1/4 cup olive oil*
*2 tablespoons butter*
*5 pounds Italian plum tomatoes, peeled and quartered*
*1 bunch green onions, tops included, chopped*
*1 green bell pepper, chopped*
*1 teaspoon salt*
*1 teaspoon pepper*
*1 tablespoon basil*
*1 teaspoon oregano*
*1-1/2 cups dry red wine*

Sauté onions and garlic in oil and butter. Add vegetables and seasonings; blend, and then slowly add the wine. Simmer together 30 minutes or until vegetables are nearly tender and liquid is reduced to a thick sauce. Check the seasoning and adjust, if necessary. Package the sauce in rigid freezer containers and freeze as soon as it has cooled. Makes about 3 quarts.

Local *corn* is superb when it is young and really fresh. Unfortunately, there is no way to completely preserve that juicy sweetness; the closest you can come is freezing. You can freeze corn-on-the-cob successfully. The first rule is to blanch it. No matter what your neighbor or mother-in-law has to say on the subject, corn should be blanched for 8 to 10 minutes. You have heard that corn deteriorates rapidly. It does. What happens is that the sugars in the corn turn to starch. Blanching inactivates the enzymes that cause this deterioration. If you don't blanch, the process will continue even in the freezer, and when you thaw the corn, it will be tough and grainy.

---

## *Fresh Corn Relish*

Corn relish is a long-time favorite condiment. It is especially good with ham, sausage, and other pork products.

| | |
|---|---|
| 16 large ears fresh corn | 1-1/4 cups cider vinegar |
| 4 cups finely chopped cabbage | 5 teaspoons salt |
| 1 cup diced celery | 1 teaspoon celery seed |
| 2 cups diced green pepper | 1-1/2 tablespoons dry mustard |
| 1-1/2 cups chopped onion | 1 teaspoon turmeric |
| 3/4 cup sugar | 1/4 teaspoon cayenne |
| 1/4 cup fresh lemon juice | 1/2 teaspoon garlic powder |
| 3/4 cup water | 3/4 cup chopped pimiento |

Blanch corn, on the cob, in boiling, salted water to cover for 2 to 3 minutes, using 1 teaspoon salt to 1 quart water. Cool corn, cut from cob, and mix with cabbage, celery, green pepper, and onion; set aside while preparing vinegar and spice mixture. Combine sugar, lemon juice, water, vinegar, salt, and spices in a 5-quart kettle. Bring to a boil. Add the vegetables and cook for 25 minutes, stirring frequently. Stir in pimiento and heat. Pack in hot, sterilized jars and process in a boiling-water bath for 15 minutes. Keep 4 or 5 weeks before using. Makes about 3 pints.

---

**SEPTEMBER**

This is another big month for local produce. Pears, grapes, and Italian prunes are the abundant fruits, but this is also the month for pickling items: cucumbers, onions, chiles, cabbage, and cauliflower. Pickle products may be divided into four categories.

There are brined pickles. These are cured for about three weeks and include dilled cucumbers and sauerkraut. They are the saltiest pickle products and may be kept in the crock or canned after fermentation.

Then there are fresh-pack or quick-process pickles. These are brined overnight, for several hours, or, in some cases, not at all. Then they are drained and combined with vinegar and spices, yielding a tart pungent flavor. This group includes fresh-pack dills, crosscut cucumber slices, sweet gherkins, and other vegetable pickles.

The third category is fruit pickles, usually whole fruit simmered in a sweet-and-sour syrup and processed. Watermelon pickles are in this category.

Relishes are the last group and are fruits or vegetables that are chopped, seasoned, and cooked to the desired consistency.

Though cabbage is in season in September, some sauerkraut experts insist that the best cabbage for kraut is picked after the first frost. Those people will be waiting until November for the large Danish cabbages.

---

## Kim Chee

Europeans are not the only ones who make sauerkraut. Kim chee is a Korean dish that is a very spicy, pungent (read smelly) version of sauerkraut. This recipe comes from Ed DeChon, Market craftsman. Ed uses napa cabbage, but he says that any mild cabbage will do, so experiment with savoy.

cabbage
coarse rock or sea salt
garlic cloves, sliced
hot red peppers

dried shrimp
Tabasco Sauce
patis (a fish sauce made from
    anchovies), optional

You must choose your own ingredient quantities and proportions; a lot depends on the size of your crock. Tear the cabbage into small chunks. Put an inch or 2 of the cabbage into a large crock and press it down with your fist. Sprinkle salt to barely cover, add garlic (as much as you want), 2 or 3 crushed hot peppers and 1/2 teaspoon dried shrimp. Sprinkle Tabasco Sauce on top and add the patis (if you wish). Continue layering until the crock is full. Place a weight on top and store in a cool place (preferably 1-1/2 miles from your house). The kim chee will be ready when it stops bubbling, from 2 to 6 weeks. Store in the refrigerator in small jars.

---

Good dill pickles are hard to find, but they are one of the most satisfying things to make yourself, and pickling is easy. The best guarantee of good pickles is to begin with high-quality cucumbers. Cucumbers deteriorate very rapidly—in a matter of hours; so when you buy them from a farmer at the Market, get them early in the morning (before nine o'clock), take them straight home, and get them into the brine before noon.

The other important pickle ingredients are vinegar, salt, dill, and spices. Which vinegar you use is unimportant as long as it is

fresh and has at least 5 percent acidity. Most any bottled cider vinegar will do.

There is some confusion about which salt to use in pickling. The ideal salt is uniodized and contains no anticaking agents. About the only thing locally that fits the bill is kosher salt. Iodized salt will turn pickles black—safe, but unappetizing— and the anticaking agents in "sea" salt and "pickling" salt will turn your brine cloudy.

Fresh dill is a must. Fortunately, it is in season the same time as pickling cukes and is sold alongside them. It is cheap, so use it generously—stem, seed, and head. Other spices used include dried hot peppers, mustard seed, garlic, and pickling spice. Whole spices keep their flavor longer, so use them if you can.

---

## Fresh-Pack Dill Pickles

If you are new to pickle making and don't have an old family recipe, try this one.

10 pounds fresh cucumbers
1-1/2 cups salt
2 gallons water
1-1/2 quarts vinegar
3/4 cup kosher salt
1/4 cup sugar
2-1/4 quarts water

2 tablespoons pickling spice,
 in cheesecloth bag
garlic cloves, peeled
fresh dill
black mustard seed
dried hot red peppers

Wash cucumbers, scrubbing gently with a vegetable brush; drain. Cover with brine of salt and water and let sit overnight; drain. Combine vinegar, salt, sugar, water, and pickling spice and bring to a boil. (You may need another batch; so make sure you have plenty of all ingredients on hand.) Pack the cucumbers into clean, hot jars, tightly, but don't overdo it. To each jar add 2 garlic cloves, 3 heads dill, 2 teaspoons mustard seed, and a red pepper. Cover with boiling vinegar brine to within 1/2 inch of the tops of the jars. Tighten jar lids (you need two-piece canning lids). Process in boiling-water bath for 20 minutes (begin timing as soon as the hot jars are placed in the water). Remove jars and set upright, several inches apart, on a wire rack or a folded towel to cool. When cool, check for seals, remove rings, and store at least 4 weeks before using. Makes about 20 quarts.

---

Many vegetables can be pickled: beans, tomatoes, onions, cauliflower, and chiles.

All chiles—sweet or hot—can be pickled using a standard vinegar brine. Large peppers are cut into pieces, small peppers may be used whole but must be blanched, pricked with a fork or peeled, so that the brine can penetrate the pepper.

Pack chiles into clean canning jars, leaving 1/2-inch head space. Add 1/2 to 1 teaspoon salt per pint (optional). Cover with the hot brine—1 part water to 1 part vinegar (5 percent)—and add a thin layer (1/8 inch) of olive oil.

Process in a boiling-water bath, pints for 15 minutes and quarts for 20. Begin counting time when water in canner returns to a boil.

---

## Pickled Mushrooms and Onions

2 pounds fresh mushrooms,
 small and firm

2 large Walla Walla sweet
 onions, thinly sliced and
 separated into rings

3 cups red wine vinegar (5%
  acidity)
3 cups water
1/2 cup brown sugar

2 tablespoons plus 2 teaspoons
  kosher salt
2 teaspoons dried tarragon

Thoroughly clean mushrooms and trim their stems. In a large saucepan, combine onions, vinegar, water, brown sugar, salt, and tarragon; heat to boiling. Add mushrooms and simmer together for 5 minutes. Remove mushrooms and onions with a slotted spoon. Keep the vinegar solution *hot*. Pack the vegetables into pint jars that are clean and hot. Cover with vinegar solution, leaving 1/2-inch head space. Put on lids and rings and tighten. Process in boiling-water bath for 15 minutes (begin timing when water returns to boil). Cool and store. Makes about 4 pints.

---

## OCTOBER

Most fall crops are either root crops or from the cabbage family and, as said earlier, aren't worth preserving except as pickles. Turnips, rutabagas, potatoes, and kohlrabi turn mushy and grainy in the freezer and never do get expensive enough to merit stocking up on them. There is one notable exception, and that is the Brussels sprout.

*Brussels sprouts* are unavailable for such a large part of the year that, if you love them, it is worth it to put some up. Freezing is the best choice, both for retention of nutrients and ease. Trim the sprouts, making sure the stems are cut away. Soak the sprouts for about thirty minutes in a salt brine (one-half cup salt to one quart of water) to flush out all the tiny insects; then rinse them well before beginning your freezing procedure.

*Bell peppers* are available in October—both green and mature red ones. These don't preserve very well, but they do get outrageously expensive other times of the year. Freezing is the easiest thing to do with them, and peppers are one of the few vegetables that should not be blanched. They will keep best if you freeze them chopped and use them within three months. Their flavor will be good, but their appearance will not. Use them only in cooked dishes.

*Apples* are probably not worth preserving unless you get a good buy on a box of them or you make chutney. If you are going to preserve them, you have several options. Overripe, mushy, or wormy apples should be made into sauce and then canned or frozen. If you want to use your apples for future pies, peel and slice them and freeze immediately. Don't forget to work with a bowl of water with lemon juice at your side. Immersing the cut apples immediately will help prevent browning. If you know you are going to use your apples for pie, consider filling pie pans with the slices and freezing them in the pans. If you need the pans, the apples can be transferred to bags once they are frozen into shape.

Some apples freeze better than others. The Granny Smith, Jonathan, Newton Pippin, Winesap, and Golden Delicious freeze well. Red Delicious is the only variety that will not keep at all; buy only as many of these as you can eat fresh.

---

## Apple Chutney

This is an old recipe. To be at its best, it should sit in the sealed jars several months, preferably six, before being used.

6 pounds apples (Romes are especially good), peeled, cored, and chopped
1 pound onions, chopped
3 cloves garlic, chopped
1 pound raisins, chopped
1/2 pound pitted dates, chopped
1 tablespoon ground allspice

1 teaspoon ground ginger
1 teaspoon paprika
2 teaspoons ground cinnamon
2 tablespoons celery salt
salt to taste
2-1/2 pints malt vinegar
2 pounds sugar

Place the fruit and vegetables in a large saucepan. Mix spices and salt with a little vinegar; then add about two-thirds of the total quantity of vinegar and stir into the saucepan. Simmer gently for 2-1/2 hours or until most of the liquid has evaporated and the onion is soft. Mix sugar with remainder of vinegar and stir into hot ingredients. Cook over medium-high heat, uncovered, stirring occasionally, for 20 minutes or until thick. Pour hot chutney into hot, sterilized pint jars. Process in a boiling-water bath for 5 minutes (begin timing when water returns to boil). Remove, cool, and check for seals. Store in dark, cool, dry place. Makes about 2-1/2 quarts.

---

## NOVEMBER

A popular food item in November is the *cranberry*. Many do not realize that the cranberries we get here are grown in Washington, not on the East Coast. Ocean Spray has a lot of cranberry bogs near Willapa Bay, the same place we get most of our oysters. Cranberries may be frozen plain. Just wash, dry, and throw them into bags.

---

## Cranberry Chutney

This recipe comes from Rex's Market Delicatessen's chef, Marjan Willemsen. It is a wonderful alternative to the traditional cranberry sauce or jelly and goes well with turkey, duck, or goose.

*1 pound package fresh cranberries*
*1 onion, finely chopped*
*4 cloves garlic, finely chopped*
*1 cup white sugar*
*1/2 cup brown sugar*

*1 cup white wine vinegar*
*1/2 teaspoon cayenne*
*1 teaspoon cloves*
*1 cup raisins*

Combine all ingredients and bring slowly to a boil. The cranberries will start to pop as their skins break. Lower the heat, stir, and simmer 1 hour. The chutney will be the consistency of very thick jam. It will keep in your refrigerator about 3 weeks. For longer storage, or if you want to give some jars away as gifts, process the chutney in half-pint jars for 5 minutes in a boiling-water bath. (Begin timing after the water in the canner returns to a boil). Makes about 5 cups.

---

*Winter squash* is another big item this time of year. The best way to store it is whole in a cool spot. Squash can be frozen, but only after it is cooked and mashed, or it will be very grainy. Canning is another possibility, but squash must be pressure-canned, and the final product is not all that great. Better to do without squash.

Winter squash is about the only vegetable that you can store without a root cellar. To store well, squashes (except the acorn) must be cured in the sun, preferably for ten days at about eighty degrees. If this is impractical for you (it is for most people), just put them near your furnace for ten days. This will harden the rind and seal surface cuts. As with all stored foods, no damaged squashes should be stored. If they have worm injuries or bruises, eat them. After curing, store the squashes at temperatures between fifty-five and sixty degrees, making sure they are dry. They should keep a good three months this way. If for some reason they get too cold or too hot, use them as soon as you can.

## WINTER MONTHS—DECEMBER to MARCH

There are not many great buys on produce in the dead of winter, but the fish markets are busy, and you can pick up some very good deals on extremely fresh *seafood*, especially bottom fish and shellfish.

There are even more methods for preserving fish than there are for produce. Fish can be canned, pickled, frozen, dried, smoked, or salted. Often a combination of processes is used.

Freezing is by far the easiest preserving process, and it is also the best for dry fish like cod, sole, and most shellfish. There are three ways to freeze a fish; each has its good points. Whichever you choose, do it carefully. It would be a shame to lose a fish because of freezer burn or because it turned rancid.

The best method for freezing *whole fish*—and also the most tedious, unfortunately—is called glazing. It takes time, but if you have invested twenty-five dollars or more in a chinook salmon, it is worth it. After cleaning the fish, place it in the freezer until it is solid. Take it out and dip it in water and then refreeze. Continue doing this at least five times, and up to twelve if you have the stamina. The more layers you put on the fish, the longer you can keep it in good condition. When you are finished, wrap the fish in freezer paper and label and date it. One additional tip. Water glazes tend to flake off. You will have harder glazes if you dip the fish in a solution of water, lemon juice, and dissolved gelatin.

Another good method for freezing a whole fish is to submerge it in water. This is difficult with a ten-pound salmon but works very well with trout, sole, smelt, and other small fish. Milk cartons make good containers for this job. Just drop the cleaned fish into the carton, fill it with water, and freeze it like a very large ice cube.

If neither of these methods appeals to you, drop the fish in the freezer. When it is solid take it out and wrap it, first in freezer-weight plastic, then in waxed freezer paper.

*Clams* and *mussels* should be steamed open, removed from their shells, and frozen in liquid, preferably in the nectar from the steaming process. Freeze them in rigid freezer containers or wrapped several times.

Cooked whole *crab* should be wrapped twice or submerged in a block of ice. It does not keep long; use within three months. The same goes for crab meat. Freeze it in rigid containers.

Keep in mind that your freezer is not like a commercial one. If yours is running well, it's holding steady at 0° F. A commercial freezer is set at −15° F or lower. Consequently, it can keep fish much longer than yours can. Low-fat fish and shellfish, such as cod, sole, halibut, perch, shrimp, and clams, may be kept up to nine months. Moderately fat seafood, such as rockfish and pink and silver salmon, will keep from six to nine months, and very fat seafood, like oysters, chinook and sockeye salmon, smelt, sablefish, and rainbow trout, can be kept only three to four months.

Never thaw frozen fish until you are ready to use it; then do so rapidly by placing it in the sink and running cold (not warm) water over it.

Salting fish is a wonderful, and quite ancient, method of preserving. If you want to do your own salt curing, it will take about a week. Work with fillets, with or without skin. Cover the bottom of a glass dish with a layer of salt. Lay down a single layer of fish and cover with another layer of salt. Continue layering until all of your fish is covered. Place the top layer skin side up. Refrigerate for one week. Salted fish should be refrigerated or kept in a very cool basement and should never be stored in airtight containers. It will keep several months.

Pickled fish means herring to most people, though any oily fish may be used. You might try shad, sablefish, or chinook salmon. Pickled fish undergoes two processes: salting and brining. You may save yourself the first step (described above) by purchasing salt fish.

---

## Pickled Fish

| | |
|---|---|
| *salt fish* | *pickling spice* |
| *garlic* | *onions, sliced into rings* |

*lemon, thinly sliced*         *vinegar*
*sugar*                    *water*

Soak the fish in cold water for 6 to 8 hours to reduce the salt content. Skin the fillets, if necessary, and cut into 1-inch pieces. Pack the fish loosely (important) into clean glass jars, and to each jar add 1 clove garlic, halved, 2 teaspoons pickling spice, onions, 1 thin slice lemon, and a dash of sugar.

In saucepan combine 1 part vinegar to 1 part water. Bring to a boil, then cool. Pour brine into jars to cover fish, leaving 1/8-inch head space. Let stand at least 24 hours before serving. Pickled fish will keep refrigerated a good 3 months.

---

Home canning of seafood is something that should not be undertaken by a novice. Fish is especially susceptible to spoilage and, if not properly prepared, can contain botulin toxins. If you have a lot of beautiful salmon, take it to a cannery. If you really want to can seafood at home, get the proper equipment, some reliable information, and read up on it.

Smoking fish is another excellent method for preserving it. As with pickling, the fish is usually only partially preserved and must be kept refrigerated. The techniques are beyond the scope of this book. Once, Northwest Indians smoked fish over the fire, but today most smoking is done in controlled smokehouses, either commercial or home models.

## Lutefisk

*Drying fish is not something most people have a great desire to do, but here in Seattle there is a good market for one kind of dried fish: stockfish, usually imported from Norway and used to make Scandinavian lutefisk. Dried stockfish is usually cod and is so well dried that it is hard as a baseball bat. This has got to be one of the most effective ways of preserving fish. It will keep forever. But before it can be eaten, stockfish must be rehydrated or "luted out." Once luted out, the "wet" fish will keep in water a good month.*

*To get stockfish in shape for cooking, start three weeks before you want to eat it. Soak the dry fish in clear water for three days, changing water daily. On the fourth day, dissolve one heaping tablespoon lye in boiling water. Pour into a large bucket and fill the bucket with cold water. Soak the fish in the lye solution for three or more days, changing the solution daily. Keep this out of the reach of children and animals. Next, soak fish in clean water four days or more, until fluffy. This water must be changed three times a day. (If you buy lutefisk already luted out, you may have to soak it a few days at home. Often it is marketed a little firm.)*

*Now that you have edible fish, what do you do with it? There are two schools of thought on cooking lutefisk: baking and boiling. If the fish looks really wet and is not holding together well, bake it. This method is safest, because the fish won't quickly disappear on you, but it can; so don't put it in the oven and forget about it. Place the fish in a covered pan and bake at 350° for 30 minutes. You probably won't need to add any moisture, but if the fish begins to look dry, dribble melted butter over it. Lutefisk has a less fishy smell when baked, so if you are not used to it, you may prefer this method.*

*Here's the boiling method. The first and most important rule is to cook the fish at the very last minute, when the rest of the meal is on the table. Don't think you can do anything else at the same time, or you'll end up with an empty kettle; lutefisk disintegrates quickly.*

*In a large kettle, bring salted water to a boil. It is best if you put the fish in a wire basket that fits into your kettle, because the fish has got to be taken from the water quickly or you may lose it. When the water boils, drop the fish in, bring back to a boil, and then remove from the heat. You may put a lid on the kettle if you dare, but it is probably a better idea to keep an eye on the fish. It should come out in about three minutes. Watch it. This can't be overstressed.*

*Lutefisk is always served with boiled potatoes. The Norwegians serve it with lefse and melted butter, and the Swedes disguise it a bit in a rich cream sauce. Lingonberry sauce is also good with it. But it's a taste and texture you have to get used to. If you were raised on it, you may think its jellylike texture delicate. If you were not, you may think it slimy.*

# WINE

## GRAPE VARIETIES

The most important ingredient in wine making and what distinguishes one wine from another, is the grape. But it is not the grape variety alone that makes a wine distinctive; the soil, climate, vine cultivation, harvesting techniques, and wine-making method all contribute to the final product. A grape variety grown in one region may have very different characteristics from the same variety grown in another region. The care and quality (the balance of sugar, acid, tannin, and fruit within the grape) during the growing season determine the quality-potential and characteristics of the wine. Some grape varieties tend always to be of higher quality than others. Some also age better than others or require aging to be their best. Wines are made sweet or dry (dry referring to the absence of sugar), bubbly, light, or powerful, depending on the winemaker's skill and the grape components.

Following is a list of some of the more important wine-grape varieties, their properties, and where they are produced.

### Red Wines

Most of a grape's color comes from its skin. The skins of red-wine grapes have more tannin than those of white-wine grapes. The tannin acts as a preservative, and makes red wines last longer. It also causes young red wines, high in tannin, to be drier.

*Cabernet Sauvignon.* This is one of the classic grapes, grown mostly in Bordeaux, France, but it also makes very good wines in

Napa Valley, California. It makes medium to dark red wines of sturdy character, is a good wine to age, and usually has elegant flavors reminiscent of wood or flowers.

*Pinot Noir.* This grape, from Burgundy, produces wines of complex flavor. It can be light and delicate with a full aftertaste or rich and heavy with great aging potential. With age, it becomes soft and rich. It is grown extensively in northern climates and also in California. The California Pinot Noir wines have tended to lack character but are improving now.

*Zinfandel.* This grape seems to be unique to California but probably came from Italy. Depending on how it is harvested and where it is grown, it can be light and spicy or rich and full. If rich and full, it should be aged for a number of years. Zinfandel rarely achieves the elegance of the Cabernet Sauvignon or Pinot Noir.

*Nebbiolo.* The Nebbiolo grape became famous in the Piedmont district of Italy, where it produces wines of full, heavy character, for example, Baròlo and Barbaresco. It usually has a high alcohol content and great tannin.

*Gamay.* This grape is made in two styles in the Beaujolais district of France. The nouveau style is light and fruity with a little sparkle. The more traditional style produces wines that will age but that also remain light with good fruit qualities.

*Carignan.* This high-yield grape produces wines that have light body and color but that are usually full flavored. It is used in many wines of southern France and in California as a good blending grape.

*Petite Sirah.* A rich, dark grape, the Petite Sirah is grown extensively in the Rhone Valley of France. It produces powerful, deep-colored wines with an accompanying wild taste. There is confusion as to whether this is the same grape that is planted in California and uses the same name.

*Merlot.* In the Médoc, this sturdy grape of Bordeaux is blended with Cabernet Sauvignon. It produces wines of soft, earthy character, especially in the Saint-Émilion district of Bordeaux, and is well known in northeastern Italy. In California, it makes full, well-balanced wines. It is also being grown successfully in the Pacific Northwest.

### White Wines

Not all white wines are made from white or light-skinned grapes, but the best ones are. For these, the grape skins remain in the fermenting vat with the pulp. White wines, in general, have less tannin than reds and, thus, do not age as well. But there are some great exceptions, notably, Chardonnay.

Most champagnes are made from the Pinot Noir. Other white or pale red wines made from red grapes are very popular with California growers—the Pinot Noir Blanc, White Zinfandel, and Cabernet Sauvignon Blanc.

*Chardonnay.* Wines made from this grape are some of the fullest-bodied whites available, especially those coming from

Burgundy. Classic flavors of butter and nuts dominate when it is mature. This grape produces wines that age quite well. California is capable of making full, rich wines from this grape, as is the Pacific Northwest. It is a hardy grape that does especially well in northern climates.

*Riesling.* Riesling is the grape that has made German wines famous. Its wines can be full and spicy with great fruit flavors, or they can be light and delicate. The grape seems to be best when grown in northern climates, where it attains a balance of good fruit and high acidity. Typically, it is made slightly sweet, but in Alsace, France, Riesling wines are much drier and full bodied.

*Sauvignon Blanc.* This versatile grape produces wines that are dry and crisp with delicate fruit. It is used extensively in Bordeaux but is also grown in the Loire Valley of France and used in wines like Fumé Blanc and Sancerre. It tends to have grassy flavors that offset its high acidity. This grape is often used to make the great Sauternes of Bordeaux, which are almost always very sweet.

*Chenin Blanc.* Vouvray has always been famous for making wines from this grape that are slightly sweet and dominated by citrus-fruit flavors. It is a simple grape that grows well in California and produces soft, fruity wines.

*Sémillon.* This is the prominent grape used in the Sauterne district of Bordeaux to produce wines that are intensely sweet and full-flavored and that demand aging. This grape, like the Riesling, allows a fungus to grow on its skin. The fungus draws juice from the grape, which in most grape varieties is undesirable. But in the Sémillon it results in a wine high in natural sugar and intense flavor.

*Gewürztraminer.* This grape, when grown in northern climates, especially in the Alsace district of France, produces a spicy, pungent wine of good fruit and powerful flavor which is often dry. The hot climate of California produces a grape high in alcohol, and California wineries usually make a slightly sweet Gewürztraminer to mask the bitter flavor caused by the alcohol.

*French Colombard.* This high-yield grape is grown primarily in California for blending. It usually has good fruit but lacks characteristic flavors unless given special care in cultivation. It makes wines that are dry and medium-bodied, but rarely great.

## NORTHWEST WINES

The Pacific Northwest, taken as a whole, is a complex growing region with widely varying geography and climate. There are many different wines produced here, but two characteristics are common to all of them.

The most distinctive feature of Northwest grapes is high acidity, producing wines that are slightly tart. The high acid content is caused, in part, by a long growing season and cool evening temperatures. Because of the tartness, the wines stand up well to local seafood.

The other characteristic common to our wines is their full, fruity quality, also attributed, in part, to the long growing season, in which the grapes develop slowly. This fruitiness balances the

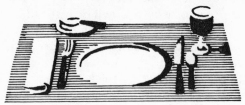

tartness in the wines, and together, these qualities often result in a fine wine that ages well.

It's difficult to discuss Northwest wines as a whole because of the vast differences between viticultural regions. Compare the wines of warm, dry eastern Washington to those of the cool, much wetter Willamette Valley of Oregon. The Washington wines, grown in irrigated, sandy loam soil, tend to be fuller and fruitier than the Oregon wines and have a slightly higher alcohol content. The Oregon wines are delicate in comparison.

Because there are few climate fluctuations in eastern Washington, growers there enjoy consistent growing conditions, and wine quality varies little from year to year. In Oregon, where weather conditions are less certain, wines produced are more unique to their vintage year.

Most Northwest wineries are now concentrating their efforts on making wines from the same grape varieties that are grown in northern Europe, with an emphasis on white-wine grapes, such as Riesling and Chardonnay. This is due, in part, to climatic similarities and to the current demand for more white wines.

The development of red wines in the Northwest is going to be exciting as grapes best suited to the region are discovered. The Pinot Noir, made famous in Burgundy, seems to be doing well in Oregon, and the Cabernet Sauvignon of Bordeaux is making great strides in Washington. More experimentation is needed before the red-wine grapes particularly suited to this region are finally determined.

The Northwest is also producing some fruit wines from produce grown here, especially the rhubarb, peaches, plums, berries and cherries. This should be an interesting area to watch. Probably the most exciting development will be in dry wines intended for use at the table, a welcome change from the sweet, syrupy product that has typified fruit wines in the past.

### SELECTING WINE

Choosing wine can be an adventure or a nightmare, depending on your disposition when you go in the wine-shop door and on whether or not you've let yourself be intimidated by hot-shot wine connoisseurs in the past. Fortunately, the Market has two wine shops, both run by pleasant, normal people who don't care if you don't speak French.

The best approach to buying wine is to ask yourself a few basic questions and then go in the wine shop and tell them what you want. Let them find it for you. The most important consideration in choosing a wine is what you are serving it with and how that food is being prepared. The second most important consideration is how much you want to spend. (Some days this has first priority.) Think also about the quality of wine you want to serve and to whom you are serving it. If you are having guests who are new to wine, they may prefer a white to a red and a light wine to a heavier one, regardless of the food you serve.

Don't be afraid to purchase, or ask for, inexpensive wines. Price does not always indicate quality. The best wines are expensive because it takes time and money to grow fine grapes and to make and age fine wine. But a ten-dollar bottle of wine is not necessarily twice as good as a five-dollar bottle; it's just twice as expensive. Many expensive wines, especially reds, are meant to age before drinking, and the high price indicates the potential of the wine.

Low price does not preclude quality. Some producers have low overhead, have been in business for generations, are family operations, and don't spend money on advertising. Some big producers, as well, can offer standard quality wines at bargain prices.

If you feel totally lost trying to read a wine label, be assured you are not alone. It's not just that you don't speak French or German; even those who do often don't have the slightest idea what the label says. Unfortunately, the very diversity of types of wine and producers that makes it so interesting is the greatest obstacle to most consumers, and they drink the same wine with everything.

## LABELS

Wines are either generic or varietal, and that is indicated by the label. A *varietal* is named after the grape that is predominant in the wine. For example, the word Chardonnay on an American label tells you that the wine has been made with a minimum of 51 percent Chardonnay grapes.

A *generic* wine is made in a particular region and carries the region's name. Wines from the region are made in a similar style, often blending several grape varieties. For example, wines from the Burgundy region of France are usually red, full-flavored and dry. A generic label can also be placed on a wine from another country (usually America) that emulates the wine of the region. California Burgundy is made after the style of the Burgundy wines of France and carries a generic label.

If you find a wine you enjoy, take a good look at the label. If the label tells you the wine is varietal, look for other wines made of the same grape variety. You will find many by different producers in a wide range of prices and styles. Chances are you will enjoy them as well. If the wine carries a generic label, try other wines of the same region or producer.

If you can't distinguish the label at all (don't feel you're alone in this) soak it off the bottle and take it with you next time you buy wine. Your wine merchant can tell you something about the wine and suggest others with similar characteristics and flavor that you may enjoy.

## Wines With Food

The following is meant as a guide to buying wine to complement foods. Many of the wines suggested can be found in a wide price range, so there should always be something here to fit both your menu and your budget.

ANTIPASTO OR HORS D'OEUVRES

A dry or medium white or a light red; Sauvignon Blanc, Chardonnay, Muscadet, fruity Zinfandel, Bardolino, Fleurie; Northwest Riesling and Gewürztraminer when dry.

SOUP

*Bisque.* A dry white with good body—Sancerre, Fumé Blanc, especially the Sauvignon Blanc from Washington; also a dry Riesling, Mosel, or an Oregon white Riesling.

*Clam chowder.* Medium-bodied white with some sweetness—Riesling, Chenin Blanc, Pinot Gris, Mosel, Washington Riesling.

*Consommé.* Dry to medium sherry—Fino, Amontillado; medium Madeira.

*Gazpacho.* Very light and dry sherry—Manzanilla, Fino.

*Creamed vegetable.* Light- to medium-bodied wine with some sweetness—Riesling, Chenin Blanc, Vouvray; Northwest white Rieslings combine good fruit and acidity to complement creamed dishes.

CHEESE FONDUE

Dry white with slight fruitiness—Chenin Blanc, Soave, French Colombard, Washington Sémillon.

ESCARGOTS

Dry red or white with good body—Pinot Noir, Chardonnay, Côtes du Rhône.

PASTA

*With fish sauce.* Light, dry wine—Soave, Sauvignon Blanc, Beaujolais Blanc.

*With meat sauce.* Medium red—Beaujolais, Côtes du Rhône, Gamay, Bardolino; similar light reds from Washington made with the Grenache grape, and from Oregon made with the Pinot Meunier.

*With tomato sauce.* Soft, full-flavored red—Zinfandel, Barbera, Merlot.

*With cream sauce.* Light to medium white—French Colombard, Frascati, dry Oregon white Riesling.

QUICHE

Dry white with medium body or light red, depending on the ingredients—Chardonnay, Chenin Blanc, Riesling, Muscadet, Beaujolais, Gamay, Bardolino; Washington Gewürztraminer and Riesling are excellent choices.

SALADS

Usually a dry white wine—Sauvignon Blanc, Entre-Deux-Mers, Bordeaux, French Colombard. (If vinegar is used in salad dressing, do not serve wine; serve water. You can substitute wine for vinegar in the dressing and then serve wine.)

SEAFOOD

It is true that most seafood dishes require white wine, but use discretion if sauces are used. Light reds, such as Bardolino and Beaujolais, are fine with some seafood dishes.

*Clams.* Dry, crisp, medium-bodied white—Chablis Grand Cru, Chardonnay, Sauvignon Blanc, Graves; an Oregon Chardonnay or a Washington Sauvignon Blanc.

*Crab.* Dry to slightly sweet, medium-bodied white—Chenin Blanc, Vouvray, Pinot Blanc, dry Riesling, Mosel, French Colombard; Northwest Rieslings and some of the lighter Oregon Chardonnays.

*Cod.* Dry, crisp, light to medium white—Soave, Chardonnay, Pinot Blanc.

*Halibut.* Dry, crisp, medium white—Sauvignon Blanc, Sancerre, Macon-Blanc; choose a Washington Sauvignon Blanc, fruity and crisp.

*Lobster.* Dry, medium- to full-bodied white—Chardonnay, Champagne, Sauvignon Blanc, Graves, Riesling from the Rheingau or from Washington.

*Oysters: Raw.* Dry, crisp, full-flavored white—Muscadet, Entre-Deux-Mers, Chablis, Champagne; Oregon Chardonnays combine high acidity with good fruit and stand up to oysters well. *Baked or sauced.* Dry, full-flavored wine—Chardonnay, Mâcon-Villages, dry Washington Chenin Blanc.

*Salmon: Poached.* Dry, fruity, medium white—Pinot Gris, Tokay d'Alsace, dry Riesling, Chenin Blanc, Mâcon-Blanc; Oregon produces two wines suitable for this dish, Pinot Gris and Chardonnay. *Baked.* Dry, medium to full white—Chardonnay, dry Chenin Blanc; from Washington, try a Chardonnay or the drier Rieslings.

*Scallops.* Dry to slightly sweet, fruity, medium-bodied white—Chenin Blanc, Vouvray, Chardonnay, Soave, medium-sweet Riesling; the fruity character of Washington wines, especially the Chenin Blanc, Riesling, and Chardonnay, match up perfectly.

*Shrimps and Prawns.* Dry to delicately sweet, fruity, light to medium white—Riesling, dry Muscat, Chenin Blanc, Mosel; the delicate Oregon Rieslings or western Washington Chenin Blancs.

*Sole.* Dry, medium-bodied white—Chardonnay, Mâcon-Blanc, Pinot Blanc, Riesling; try a Washington Chardonnay or dry Riesling.

*Trout.* Dry, light to medium white—Muscadet, Riesling, Chardonnay, Pinot Blanc, Oregon Riesling when dry.

## MEAT

Use these suggestions as a general guide only, realizing that meat can be prepared in many ways.

### BEEF

*Steak.* Dry, medium- to full-bodied red—Medoc, Bordeaux, Burgundy, Oregon Pinot Noir, Washington Cabernet Sauvignon or Merlot.

*Roast.* Dry, full-flavored reds—Cabernet Sauvignon, Médoc, Pinot Noir, Côtes de Nuits, Châteauneuf-du-Pape, Washington Cabernet Sauvignon or Merlot, Oregon Pinot Noir.

*Stew.* Dry, medium to full red—Cabernet Sauvignon, Bordeaux, Côtes du Rhône, Zinfandel, Washington Merlot. If wine is used in preparing the stew, serve the same wine with your meal.

*Stroganoff.* Dry, medium to full red—Pinot Noir, Savigny-les-Beaune, Barbaresco, Zinfandel, Moulin-à-Vent, Gamay, Oregon Pinot Noir. As with stew, if you've used wine in preparing the food, use that same wine to accompany the meal.

*Hamburger.* Dry, medium-bodied, slightly fruity red— Zinfandel, Gamay, Beaujolais, Barbera, Grignolino, California Burgundy, Oregon Pinot Meunier.

*Liver.* Dry, medium-bodied, spicy red—Zinfandel, Bordeaux Superieur, Cabernet Sauvignon, Beaujolais, Washington Grenache.

*Corned beef.* Dry, medium-bodied, spicy red—Zinfandel, Grignolino, Pinot Noir, Valpolicella, Nouveau Beaujolais, Oregon Pinot Noir.

### LAMB

*Roast.* Dry, medium- to full-bodied red; Zinfandel, Hermitage, Petite Sirah, Saint-Émilion, Cabernet Sauvignon, Barólo, Washington Merlot.

*Chops.* Dry, light to medium red—Zinfandel, Gamay, Beaujolais, Côtes du Rhône, Barbera, Washington Grenache.

*Moussaka.* Dry, medium to full red with character— Barbaresco, Beaujolais, Zinfandel, Côtes du Rhône, Egri Bikaver.

### PORK ROAST

Dry, medium-bodied red or white—Cabernet Sauvignon, Washington Chardonnay and Sauvignon Blanc.

### VEAL

Dry, medium to full white or medium red—Chardonnay, Fumé Blanc, Cabernet Sauvignon, Washington Sauvignon Blanc.

## GAME AND POULTRY

### CHICKEN

Dry, light to medium white or red—Mácon-Blanc, Soave, Pinot Blanc, Washington Sauvignon Blanc, Oregon Chardonnay.

*Coq au Vin.* Dry, medium red—Oregon Pinot Noir.

*Liver.* Dry, medium-bodied white or light red—Chardonnay, Graves, Beaujolais, Zinfandel, Bardolino, Washington Sauvignon Blanc.

*Curry.* Dry, medium-bodied, fruity white or light red; Mosel, Valpolicella, Zinfandel; Washington Gewürztraminer is perfect.

### DUCK

Dry, full-bodied white or red; Chardonnay, Saint-Émilion, Côte-de-Nuits, Barólo, Washington Chardonnay and Oregon Pinot Noir.

GOOSE

Dry, full-flavored white or full red—Hermitage, Cabernet Sauvignon, Washington Chardonnay and Riesling, Oregon Pinot Noir.

RABBIT

Dry, medium-bodied red—Valpolicella, Zinfandel, Pommard, Barbaresco, Oregon Pinot Noir.

TURKEY

Dry, medium-bodied to full white or red—Cabernet Sauvignon, Médoc, Saint-Émilion; Washington Gewürztraminer, Riesling, Chardonnay, and Merlot; Oregon Chardonnay.

CHEESES

SOFT-RIPENED

Brie, Camembert, Boursault
Dry, medium- to full-bodied reds or tawny port—Cabernet Sauvignon, Bordeaux, Burgundy, Zinfandel, Oregon Pinot Noir.

HARD-PRESSED

*Semisoft.* Jarlsberg, Creamy Havarti, Turunmaa, Tilsit.
Dry, medium to full white or medium red—Pinot Noir, Zinfandel, Barbera, Petite Sirah, Côtes du Rhône, Oregon Pinot Noir.
*Hard.* Gruyère, Kasseri, cheddar, Emmenthal.
Dry, medium to full red or tawny port—Rubesco, Barbaresco, Pomerol, Cabernet Sauvignon, Washington Cabernet Sauvignon or Merlot.

BLUE-MOLD

Roquefort, Stilton, Gorgonzola
Tawny or vintage port, California cream sherry, California port.

WINES SERVED ALONE

Sauternes, port, sherry, the sweeter Rieslings from California or Germany, Coteaux du Layon; the Northwest produces some beautiful, sweet, late-harvest Rieslings and Gewürztraminers.

WINES TO DRINK WHEN YOU ARE HOME ALONE

The unqualified favorite here is port.

# MARKET
# SPECIALTY SHOPS

In the Pike Place Market, it is possible to find just about any ingredient called for in any recipe in any cookbook—whether it be a book on Cajun cooking or a cookbook of curries.

Many of the farmers and high-stallers have the more exotic oriental greens and vegetables, such as boktoy, patula, bitter melon, and Japanese eggplant. They have fresh, pungent basil for pesto and fresh fennel and horseradish. The fish markets have, in season, fresh catfish, talapia, and gaspergoo. And at the meat markets, you will find meat prepared for such dishes as sukiyaki and rouladen.

There are specialty groceries that carry the foods, herbs, and spices native to just about every country in the world. There are delicatessens, bakeries, and wine merchants. There is everything in the Market that you will need for a complete meal, from the appetizers to the zabaglioni.

The following list of Market specialty shops should help you find what you are looking for. Fish, meat, poultry, and cheese counters are listed at the end.

*Asian Pastry, Triangle Building (682-6780)*

Sweets, meat-filled pastries, and other oriental bakery specialties.

*Barb's Delicatessen, Main Arcade (622-2975)*

Smoked meats, cheeses, salads, imported beers, pickles, olives, and relishes.

*Bavarian Meats, Soames-Dunn Building (682-0942)*

The city's center for German food. All kinds of wursts, meat for rouladen, imported herring, smoked meats, cheeses, imported chocolates, bakery goods, bulk sauerkraut, mustards, and imported grocery specialties. Sausage casings available on one-day notice.

**Bayview Bread,** *Triangle Building (no phone)*
Breads and cinnamon rolls baked while you wait.

**Brehm's Delicatessen,** *Main Arcade (622-9172)*
Smoked meats, cheeses, bulk peanut butter, fruit-cake supplies, salads, pickles, relishes, and olives.

**Bulk Commodities Exchange,** *Western Avenue (447-9516)*
For food-buying clubs and co-ops, the place to call for fresh, local produce in bulk.

**The Creamery,** *Triangle Building (622-5029)*
Raw milk and cream, goat's milk, butter, eggs, yogurt and kefir, and tofu.

**De Laurenti's,** *Economy Market (622-0141)*
A delicatessen, wine shop, and international grocery, with emphasis on Mediterranean specialties: pasta, dried beans, fruit-cake supplies, filo.

**English "T" Crumpet Shop,** *Corner Market Building (682-1598)*
English crumpets baked in the shop. Maple syrup, domestic and imported jams, jellies, and preserves.

**The Juicery,** *Triangle Building (623-2500)*
Freshly squeezed vegetable and fruit juices; canned juices and ciders.

**La Coppa Pan,** *Triangle Building (623-8166)*
Fresh pasta; pasta sauces, patés, salads, and antipasto.

**La Mexicana,** *on Pike Place (682-2822)*
Mexican groceries, tortilla presses, fresh flour and corn tortillas, chorizo, and frozen prepared tamales.

**Liberty Malt,** *mezzanine level, Main Market (622-1880)*
Beer- and wine-making supplies; crocks and jars and recipes.

**Market Whole Foods,** *mezzanine level, Main Market (223-9582)*
Bulk grains, pasta, nuts, dried fruit, bulk mineral water and olive and safflower oils; Italian grocery items and imported beers.

**Oriental Mart,** *Corner Market Building (622-8488)*
Philippine, Japanese, Chinese, Korean, Thai, Cambodian, and Vietnamese grocery items.

**Pike and Western Wine Merchants,** on Pike Place (623-1307)
Domestic and imported wines; imported beers.

**Pike Place Natural Foods,** -1 level (first level under Main Arcade), Main Market (623-2231)
Complete health-food store.

**Pike Place Nuts,** Economy Market arcade (682-NUTS)
Bulk nuts and seeds; nut butters.

**Rex's Market Delicatessen,** on Pike Place (624-5738)
Patés, salads, croissants, preserves, pastries, imported grocery items, and pasta.

**Roos' and Roos',** Triangle Building (624-2945)
Day-old breads and rolls.

**Rotary Grocery,** Main Arcade (622-5829)
The Market's mini-supermarket.

**The Souk,** Soames-Dunn Building (623-1166)
Middle-Eastern, Indian, and Pakistani grocery items; Turkish coffee, bulk grains, spices, tahini, and falafel.

**Specialty Spice,** Main Arcade (622-6340)
Home of Market Spice Tea; other teas and coffees—and all the spices, herbs, and seasonings you can think of.

**Starbuck's,** Soames-Dunn Building (622-8762)
Beans or freshly ground coffees; teas, spices, chocolates, jams, and jellies.

**Three Girls Bakery,** Sanitary Market (622-1045)
Bagels, breads, and pastries.

**Tolmich Bakery,** Main Arcade (622-3191)
Breads, pastries, and cookies baked in ovens two floors below.

### Fish Markets

City Fish, Main Arcade, north (682-9329)
Pike Place Fish, Main Arcade, south (682-7181)
Pure Food Fish, Main Arcade, middle (622-5765)

### Poultry and Meat Markets

Chicken Valley, Main Arcade, middle (624-2774)
Exclusively poultry, game, and rabbit.
Crystal Meats, Sanitary Market (622-5499)
Don and Joe's, Main Arcade, south (682-7670)

*Loback's, Main Arcade, north (622-7450)*
*Pure Food Meats, Main Arcade, middle (622-2975)*

**Cheese Shops** *(in addition to listed delicatessens)*

*The Cheese People, Sanitary Market (624-3771)*
*Pike Place Cheese, Main Arcade, north (622-3055)*

# INDEX OF RECIPES